WHERE THE EARTH ENDS

Stone Age People Tell Their Story

by Alice Gibbons

Copyright © 2009 by Alice Gibbons

Where the Earth Ends
by Alice Gibbons

Printed in the United States of America

ISBN 978-1-60791-571-3

All rights reserved solely by the author. The author guarantees all contents are original and do not infringe upon the legal rights of any other person or work. No part of this book may be reproduced in any form without the permission of the author. The views expressed in this book are not necessarily those of the publisher.

All Scripture quotations in this publication, unless marked otherwise, are taken from the Good News Translation (Today's English Version, Second Edition) Copyright © 1992 American Bible Society. All rights reserved. Bible text from the Good News Translation (GNT) is not to be reproduced in copies or otherwise by any means except as permitted in writing by American Bible Society, 1865 Broadway, New York, NY 10023 (www.americanbible.org).

Scripture quotations marked (NIV) are taken from the HOLY BIBLE, NEW INTERNATIONAL VERSION®. NIV®. Copyright © 1973, 1978, 1984 by International Bible Society. Used by permission of Zondervan. All rights reserved.

All photos were taken by the author

www.xulonpress.com

ACKNOWLEDGMENTS

I give repeated thanks to Barbara Larsen and Jan Hasak
who helped turn my rough manuscript into a finished piece

I'm grateful to Mary Braz for using her talents to produce the maps

I appreciate Dr. James Dobson and Focus on the Family who
when I returned to the US, helped me understand moral issues
in the current American culture and reorient my Christian witness to it

I extend my admiration to the Damals and Danis whose stories are written here
and to the thousands of others they represent

I give thanks to the Lord for the privilege of spending my life in Papua
and to all those who supported Don and me there with prayer and finances

I give honor to my husband Don, for without the joining of our lives for 57 years
this story would not be told—and I give honor to our missionary colleagues

Above all I acknowledge the grace of God, His love and mercy actively involved
in the lives of the six people who share these stories

**I give unending praise to our sovereign God who brought these people,
one of earth's last tribes, languages and races who will one day sing:
"To him who sits on the throne and to the Lamb,
be praise and honor, glory and might,
forever and ever!"**

WHAT READERS ARE SAYING

Where the Earth Ends is a riveting account of how the message of Christ transformed a people and culture. In their own words, Papuan believers tell how they were freed from their fear of evil spirits, how their passion for war and revenge was taken away, and how their lives were filled with a joy and hope they had never known.

This book is a compelling and moving narrative that accurately records what I personally witnessed in numerous visits to Papua. Thanks to Alice Gibbons, these stories can now be told in every church that has supported the effort to send the Gospel to the ends of the earth. Read *Where the Earth Ends* and be prepared to see your personal passion explode for the completion of the Great Commission.

Peter N. Nanfelt—*former President of The Christian and Missionary Alliance, Vice President for International Missions and missionary*

The stories in *Where the Earth Ends* are life-changing. Families, home-school groups, adult small groups, as well as Christian school Bible classes will learn about the culture of the vanishing Stone Age people. More importantly however, are the Bible passages and *Issues to Consider* at the end of each chapter. These will encourage discussion and challenge readers to see how God, who created all people of every culture, also has a purpose and plan for all individuals who surrender their lives to Him, no matter how vastly different our stories may be.

Mary Dallenbach—*Teacher and co-leader of the chapel worship at Vacaville Christian School, California*

This is a fresh and uncommon journey into a world at the uttermost part of the earth—a book in whose pages you will read the unbelievable life stories of five remarkable Stone Age people of Papua, told in their own words. The miraculous power of the Gospel brought to them by missionaries transformed them from uncivilized, uneducated people, who could neither read nor write, into giants of the faith. How this faith sustained and upheld them through unimaginable trials and dangers will thrill you over and over again as you read these accounts of His amazing grace.

Author Alice Gibbons, with her husband Don, was one of the Papua missionaries. She ends the book with her own story, telling us how her call from the Lord led her to that land on the other side of the world where she and Don ministered for over forty years.

Barbara Larsen—*Christian writer, poet, and writing coach/editor*

Can you imagine Stone Age people still living in the 20th century? *Where the Earth Ends* is an amazing story told by tribal people as their lives merge with the modern world brought to them by missionaries. This is a unique must-read book, that you will find hard to put down and bears repeat reading.
Kathleen Carey—a lifetime avid reader of missionary books.

A thought provoking, inspiring and insightful view of a community little seen by western eyes. This book allows the reader to venture into the minds of a Stone Age civilization transformed by the saving grace of Jesus Christ. It also reveals how humble servants of the Lord can be used in mighty ways to further His kingdom. Don and Alice Gibbons are true heroes of the faith!
Charles Dorsey—Bible study teacher/leader for 20 years and member of the Christian and Missionary Alliance Church in Paradise, California.

I find this missionary book a wonderful story of the Lord's work and providence in caring for His people who are called to spread the gospel in uncharted areas. One very unique facet to this story is that it is told largely from the perspective and in the words of the indigenous Christians who were ministered to and who still continue that ministry to this day.
Larry Gentry—Church Missions Team Leader, Vancouver, Washington

CONTENTS

PRELUDE 1
GENERAL MAP OF THE AREA 4
COME WITH ME TO PAPUA 5

SIX STORIES

I THE COMING OF *HAI* 9
    1   The Spirit-Man 10
    2   Why Did He Come? 15
    3   Chief Den Makes a Decision 19
    4   Learning to Walk the Jesus Path 24
    5   To Beoga with the Message of *Hai* 29
    6   Teamwork in Telling the Gospel 34
    7   Surprise Visitors 41

II BORN TO BE A CHIEF 51
    1   War in Two Worlds 54
    2   Death, Peace and War Again 57
    3   New Life in Sinak 62
    4   Seven Years of School 66
    5   The Big City 71
    6   Still Trusting God 76
    7   The Unexpected Tragedy 81
    8   The Wise Dani Chief 84

III OUT OF THE STONE AGE 93
    1 Everyday Life 94
    2 Paths of Right and Wrong 100
    3 Enter—Missionaries 105
    4 Faithful in Every Season 111
    5 Always he said, "I'll Go" 116

IV LUKAS AND THE REBELS 124
    1 Born to Live—Not Die 126
    2 Peeking Through the Crack 130
    3 Reading Wide-Leaves 134
    4 Lukas Meets Two Pretty Girls 137
    5 The Preacher Boy 141
    6 Manna on a Jungle Vine 145
    7 A Bride for Lukas 148
    8 Rebels and the Magic Key 152
    9 Let's Kill Lukas 156
   10 God Sends His Angels 160
   11 God's Miracle, Not Man's Magic 164
   12 The Rebels' Final Strike 168
   13 Forgiving One by One 172

V THE JULIANA STORY 179
    1 To Be a Missionary 180
    2 The Roaring River 185
    3 Captured by the Rebels 189
    4 Miraculous Escape 193

VI ONLY ONE LIFE 198
    1 God's Call to Alice 199
    2 Three More Questions Answered "Yes" 205
    3 Pushed Out to Fly on My Own 212
    4 Called to the East 217
    5 Disappointments and Danger 224
    6 Math, Music and Becoming a Missionary 232
    7 Teaching Damals to Read a Talking-Leaf 239
    8 Five Special Daughters 246
    9 Go and Make Disciples 253
   10 The First and the Last 259
   11 Epilogue 265

PRELUDE

On an October day in 1953 a 26-year-old man and a 22-year-old woman, Don and Alice Gibbons with their baby daughter Kathy, walked up the gangplank to board a freighter docked in the Port of Seattle. This was not a ship carrying passengers for pleasure but a cargo ship carrying wheat across the ocean. However, for a few passengers the freighter offered the least expensive way to cross the Pacific.

Don and Alice were missionaries headed for Netherlands New Guinea—a place *Where the Earth Ends.* Don was to become an explorer hiking native trails for weeks at a time to discover people who were unknown to anyone in the outside world. As they boarded the freighter, their commitment to their God and to their sending mission, The Christian and Missionary Alliance, was to serve for a lifetime in Netherlands New Guinea which later became Papua, a province of Indonesia.

Don held in his hand a spool wound with ribbons. As he climbed the gang plank, the ribbons unwound. The other ends of the ribbons were held in the hands of a small crowd of people on the dock. These people included the couple's parents and siblings, friends and a number of students from Simpson Bible Institute, the school from which Don and Alice had graduated two years earlier.

The ship began to move ever so slowly, the ribbons grew taut and then broke. All the ties the couple had to family and to life as they knew it were broken. On shore the crowd waved and called out, "Goodbye, goodbye, God go with you." A few tears were shed at both ends of the ribbons, yet within the heart of each person was the assurance that this separation was God's perfect plan. On the boat Don and Alice waved and called back as the boat turned into Puget Sound. Everything from their familiar world passed out of sight.

Don was always ready for anything—impassioned, impetuous and fearing nothing. Alice balanced his gifts with her caution, organizational ability and attention to detail. Don led the way and Alice was always by his side. The two shared a strong love for the Lord and a common goal or call to bring the good news of Jesus Christ to people who had never heard. This three-week trip across the Pacific began their journey into the unknown.

Had they known of the trials and hardships, the loneliness and discouragement, the separations and life-threatening dangers, the languages to be learned, and on occasion, the lack of even the basic necessities of living, would they have turned back?

No! They would not have turned back! They did not turn back! For over 40 years the Gibbons family lived and worked among the Damal tribe as these people began their journey into the world of the 20th century. The Damals and their neighbors, the Danis, lived in the high mountains in the central part of the island of New Guinea and didn't even know that other human beings lived on the earth outside of their mountain fortress. They were people forgotten by time, people still living in the Stone Age.

Each of the following short stories was told to Alice by an individual. She retells them in English—keeping the details and conversation true to tribal culture. The storytellers are real life heroes yet they live in a culture unknown to the modern world.

After Alice wrote the stories, she realized they were filled with incidents that could apply to the life of anyone who reads the book. Without changing the story she added a closing segment to each chapter. These include a Bible lesson and two or three issues to consider.

This book is ideal for adults as well as for use in home and Christian school curriculum. Families with children may choose to read the book together at the story hour. As a devotional, adults may enjoy reading one chapter each day. Others may find reading the first chapter to be like eating one nut from a dish of nuts. Who can stop with eating only one nut? Who can stop with reading only one chapter?

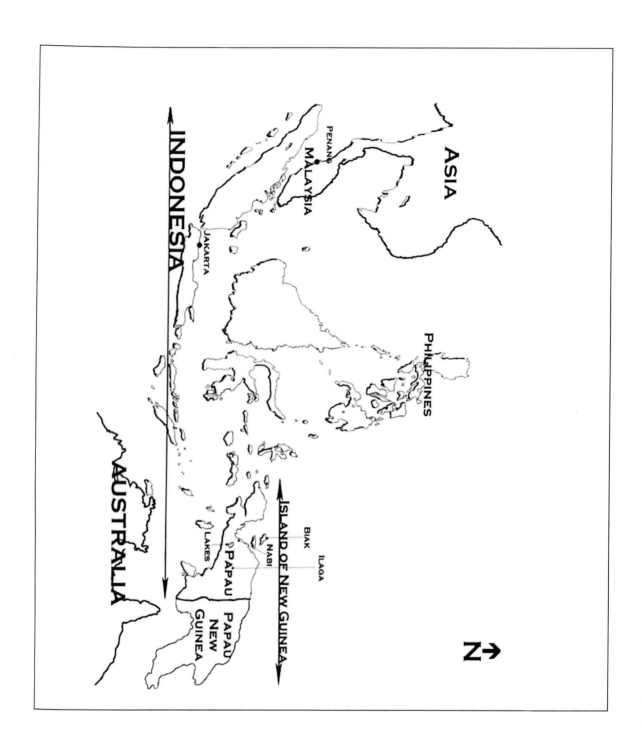

COME WITH ME TO PAPUA

The island of New Guinea is the second largest island in the world. When the Gibbons arrived on the island's shores in 1953, the western half of New Guinea was governed by the Dutch and called Netherlands New Guinea. Ten years later, this half of the island became part of Indonesia—its eastern-most province. For many years it was known as Irian Jaya. In an effort to pacify the people of Irian Jaya the government changed the name of the province to Papua. The tribal people chose this name because some years earlier the indigenous people who lived in the eastern half of this large island had received their independence from Australia. They took the name Papua New Guinea. In 2002 yielding to the express wish of the people, the western half of the island became Papua. The similar names give a feeling of unity to all the indigenous people of the island. However, to the rest of the world the similar names—Papua, (a province of Indonesia) and Papua New Guinea—are somewhat confusing. [See Map in front of book]

Foreign names and places in a story can be hard to pronounce and harder to remember. In these stories some names have been shortened or a name even changed to an English word to make it easier for the reader to follow the story.

Growing up, Alice Gibbons read and understood the King James Version (KJV) of the Bible. It was always her choice. She memorized from this version and it was the text used in the Bible School she attended. Years later a missionary coworker and Bible translator introduced Today's English Version (TEV) to her. The coworker used the English and Indonesian language versions of TEV for his work of translating the Damal New Testament. With some reluctance Alice tried reading from this new version. To her surprise the TEV made the Scripture come alive in a new way. Soon it became her choice for devotional reading, as it continues to be today.

Today's English Version is written in clear, conversational English—the everyday language used in newspapers. It is not written in formal English or in the contemporary language of youth. Often it uses shorter sentences and is easily understood by people of all ages including a person who speaks English as his second language.

An illustration of the differences in translations is found in Psalm 95:1b. King James Version says: "Let us make a joyful noise to the rock of our salvation." New

International Version reads: "Let us shout aloud to the Rock of our salvation." Today's English Version writes: "Let us sing for joy to God, who protects us."

In this book all Scripture quotations are taken from Today's English Version unless otherwise marked.

The maps in this book are important. They help the reader understand the setting of the story more quickly.

When considering the distance to be traveled from one point to another or looking at a map most people immediately think in terms of miles. However, in the mountains of Papua distance is measured by the number of days it takes to walk between points. If there is an airstrip at each place, distance may be measured in minutes of flying time. When the pilot figures his flying time he also considers how many feet in elevation he must climb. Sometimes he may circle to get over a mountain or fly the longer route around by following the river valley.

The Damal people do not reckon direction by north, south, east and west, but rather think of elevation change—whether one must climb or descend to reach his destination. In most instances this would be upriver or downriver because rivers and streams are everywhere. To the Westerner's way of thinking, measuring distance by walking-days and reckoning direction by up or down the river is not very precise. But for both the expatriate and native who travel by foot in these rugged mountains, it really makes sense.

On the pages of this book five individuals who are emerging from the Stone Age have an opportunity to tell their own story. In the sixth story the author tells of her life as it intertwined with the lives of the Damal people. The reader will find the world of each storyteller to be very different from his own. Yet, in heart and mind both face similar decisions and challenges throughout life. Indeed, each one is created by God and in His image.

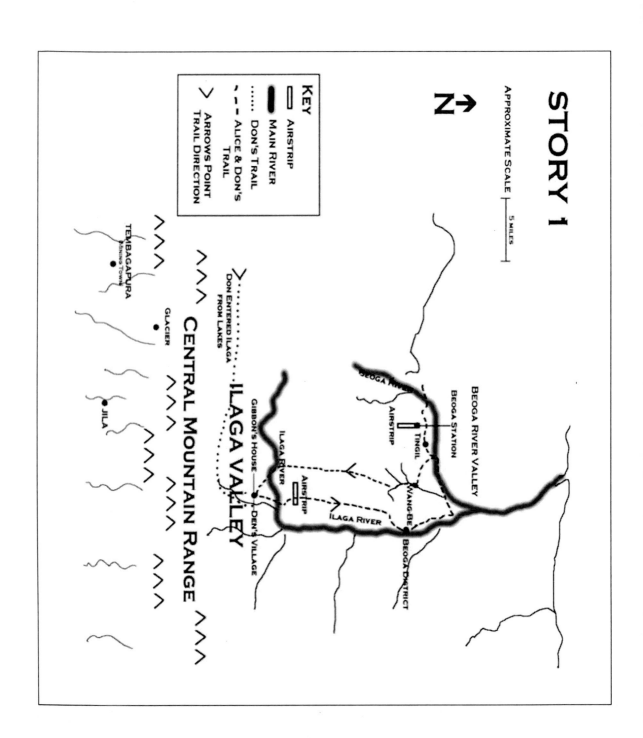

STORY ONE
THE COMING OF *HAI*

Introduction

THE COMING OF *HAI* is a true story. The story is told in the words of Pengame who was a teenage boy when the story begins. I have given him the nickname Peddy in this story because his Damal [Da-MALL] name is hard to remember and difficult to pronounce.

Hai [Hi] is a Damal word. The closest word in English for *hai* is paradise. *Hai* was thought to be a good place **after** death, but how to get to paradise the Damal people did not know.

Chapter 1

The Spirit-Man

Peddy begins his story:

I live in the high mountains of Papua [formerly known as Irian Jaya] in a valley called Ilaga. [ee-LA-gah] The day I'm going to tell you about is one I will never forget.

Early that morning, I hiked up the mountain with my father and uncle—way up to the edge of the forest. The project of the day was to work on our new family garden. For several days my father and uncle had cut trees and cleared out brush on this ground which had never before been used as a garden. Today, the men worked cleaning out rocks and roots and breaking up the black soil with long, wooden digging sticks. I had a job too. With my hands I crumbled the clods of dirt, making the ground smooth and ready for planting.

Mid-morning, my father took his fire-making stick out of his net-bag. He placed the partially split stick on the ground and held it in place with the toes of one foot. From his net-bag he took a little bundle of dry leaves and placed them under the split end of his fire-making stick. Also from his bag he took a piece of rattan vine and slipped it into the stick's groove next to the leaves. Holding each end of the vine with his hands he straightened up and began a seesaw motion rubbing the vine back and forth on the stick. Faster and faster he worked the vine back and forth until a thin column of smoke began to rise from the dry leaves he had placed under the stick. Putting the stick aside he blew on the leaves, coaxing a little flame to appear in the smoking leaves. Carefully he added small sticks until he had a full fire going.

All day we threw roots and sticks on the fire as we cleaned up the hillside. Its heat felt so good on my bare skin. I kept coming back to the fire even without anything in my hands.

After awhile I went exploring in the forest and soon discovered a new crop of wild mushrooms tucked away under the fallen logs. I popped each mushroom into my net-bag thinking how good they would taste when they were cooked.

In the afternoon my father suddenly announced, "Come on, Peddy. We're going home."

The Spirit-Man

I called back, "I'm not ready to go yet. I'm going to gather a few more mushrooms before I come." What I didn't say was that I was going to cook and eat the mushrooms before I started for home.

"Let the boy have his fun," my uncle said. "The sun is still shining. There will be light enough for him to get down the mountain a little later."

After they left I went back to the forest. Every time I spied one plump mushroom, it seemed I saw two more under the next log.

"I'd better cook these mushrooms and head down to the village," I said to myself. "I don't want to go home alone in the dark."

I put the mushrooms, one by one, on the hot coals left from our fire and then popped them into my mouth. They sure tasted good!

With so many mushrooms still in my net-bag, I decided to take some home with me to share with my father and the other men who slept in the hut. In the evening I liked to sit around the fire in the men's hut. The men told stories, including ones passed down by their fathers. The stories were about my people, the Damal people, and our neighbors, the Dani people. I learned that we had always lived just as we were now living. We, and our neighbors, were the only *key meh,* real people with flesh and blood, in the whole world. At least that is what the men said.

Sometimes as they talked, I heard the word "*hai.*" Someday *hai* would come. A messenger would come to show us *key meh*, real people, the way to *hai*. What was *hai* anyway? Usually when the men began to talk about *hai,* I curled up and went to sleep.

Now I had eaten enough. It was time to go home. I stood up and slipped the band of my net-bag over my shoulder.

Suddenly I heard voices. I looked up and couldn't believe what I saw. Out of the forest came a long line of tribesmen bent down under the packs they carried. Leading the string of men was a tall, white being, a spirit-man. Here I was, all alone, and this spirit-world-being was coming straight toward me. I wanted to run, but there was no place to hide.

One of the men carrying a pack must have seen the fear on my face, for he called out, "He's not an evil spirit. He won't hurt you."

"*Amolo! Amolo!* Hello! Hello!" this giant said, coming closer. "Come on. Let's go down the trail together."

"No! No!" I blurted out. "I'm afraid."

The Coming of Hai

"Come on!" he insisted, and shoved his red, water canteen in my hand. "Carry it for me!"

Without thinking, I obeyed. I slipped the carrying strap of the canteen over my shoulder next to the strap of my own net-bag and went with him down the trail.

Soon I wasn't afraid anymore. I was almost proud as I walked at the head of the single file procession going down to the valley.

People began to appear as we walked along. "What is it?" they were saying.

"It's a spirit-being."

"It's an evil spirit."

"Look! Isn't that Peddy walking with him?" Several men and boys, and even a daring girl or two, stepped into our line winding down the hillside.

Everyone stopped when we reached the first village. This spirit-being, or man, or whatever he was, said something. He spoke in the Moni [MOW-nee] language and one of the men who carried his packs translated his words into our Damal language. What was he telling us?

"I'm going to talk to my friends," he said. "My friends are two weeks walk away from here. They will talk back to me through this little box." He pointed to this thing, this box, sitting on the ground. In his hand he had a roll of something like rattan vine but it was shiny. He fastened one end of the shiny vine to the box. Pointing to a tree he spoke to a man who had carried one of his packs. The man climbed up the tree and tied the other end of the shiny vine to a tree branch.

People all around me were saying, "This is spirit-magic."

Suddenly there was a loud crackling noise and it sounded almost like a human voice coming out of the box. Men's voices all around were saying, "*Bau-a! Bau-a!* Amazing! Amazing! Truly this is spirit-magic." Then the box was silent.

The carrier translated for the man. "I have come to your valley to live among you. This talking box tells me that tomorrow, after one sleep, the flying-boat will come to the Ilaga. It will come over there, across the valley," He pointed to an area on the other side of the valley. "The *hol-koma,* the flying-boat, will come close to the ground, and it will drop something."

"What is a flying-boat?" people were asking.

"What does all this mean?"

"Who is this spirit-being?"

Above all the shouting and confusion I heard one word again and again. "*Hai, Hai, HAI*!"

The crier of our village went into action. "*Hai oletak-o-o-o!*" the crier shouted out. "*Hai* has come, *Hai* has come."

"*Hai oletak-o-o-o-o!* Paradise magic has come!"

As twilight quickly turned to darkness the message was relayed from village to village across the valley. Men in the next village heard the words and asked, "What does this mean?" Without knowing the answer, another village crier stepped out into the darkness and called out, "*Hai oletak-o-o-o! Hai* has come! *Hai* has come!"

BIBLE LESSON

> A Samaritan woman came to draw some water, and Jesus said to her, "Give me a drink of water." . . .
>
> The woman answered, "You are a Jew, and I am a Samaritan—so how can you ask me for a drink?" (Jews will have nothing to do with Samaritans.)
>
> Jesus answered, "If you only knew what God gives and who it is that is asking you for a drink, you would ask him, and he would give you life-giving water." . . .
>
> Jesus [said], "Whoever drinks this [well] water will get thirsty again, but whoever drinks the water that I will give him will never be thirsty again. The water that I will give him will become in him a spring which will provide him with life-giving water and give him eternal life." John 4: 7, 9-10, 13-14

The date on the outside world's calendar was September 22, 1956. On this day Peddy was the first person, of the 10,000 Damals and Danis [DON-EE] living in the Ilaga Valley, to meet the missionary Don Gibbons.

The Damals were bewildered by the appearance of this strange spirit-being and what he might have to do with *hai*. And the missionary, knowing nothing of their language, had no idea of what the Damals were saying with their words, "*Hai oletako! Hai* has come!"

The Coming of Hai

For untold generations the Damals had been looking for *hai*—this place vaguely described as paradise, a good place without death. The definition of *hai* varied from person to person, but all agreed on one point. No one knew the way to *hai*.

From the Bible we learned that for generations the Samaritans had been separated from the Jews in their religious practices. The Samaritan woman did not know the way to eternal life. When Jesus walked into her life and asked for a drink of water she was startled, for Jews do not ask such from Samaritans. As they talked she was unsure of what Jesus meant when he offered her not just drinking water but life-giving water.

So it was with the Damals. They sensed that something extraordinary was about to happen. But what it was they did not know.

ISSUES TO CONSIDER

1. Reflect on what this story told by Peddy and the story of the Samaritan woman have in common.
2. Why do you think the Damals' definition of *hai* was somewhat vague and varied among individuals? Today in our culture does the definition of moral values vary among some individuals? If so, why?
3. Since they had no previous contact with the outside world, how could it be that the Damals even had this concept of paradise?

Chapter 2
Why Did He Come?

Peddy continues his story:

The next morning my father and I were on our way across the valley to see the promised flying-boat. People were coming from all over the valley.

We were almost there when we heard a faint buzzing noise. The noise got louder as this thing in the sky got closer. It swooped down like a bird—making a thundering roar. Bundles dropped from the stomach of this big bird and landed on the ground. Three times it swooped down, each time dropping something. Then, up, up, up it went higher into the sky and disappeared behind the clouds.

My father kept saying, "*Bau-a! Bau-a*! Amazing! Unbelievable!"

An old man was saying, "*Hai-e-yeh!* It's *hai*! It's *hai*!"

We were even more amazed when we learned what was inside those bundles—axes made of steel. We Damals had only axes made of stone.

The spirit-man made an announcement, "Together we are going to make a resting place for the flying-boat. I will mark off sections on the airstrip site. A man can contract to clean off the mud and level the ground in his section. When the job is finished, I will pay him a steel axe."

My father took a contract. The steel axe he earned completely changed the work of my father and uncle. It took days of hard work to cut a tree using stone tools. It took only an hour to cut the same size tree with a steel axe. This metal tool changed our lives.

The big chief in our village, Chief Den, had a son who was several years older than I but not old enough to be called a man or be married. The son had walked the two-weeks out to the big lake where he learned to speak Indonesian. Just before the spirit-man appeared, he returned. These two, the chief's son and the spirit-man, could talk to each other in the Indonesian language.

Using his son to translate, Chief Den said to the spirit-man, "Let's be friends and trading partners. You can build your house in my village." The spirit-man agreed and chose a little hill overlooking our village where he would build his house.

The Coming of Hai

More and more the spirit-man was learning to speak our language. Living with us as he did, eating our food, sleeping in our houses and learning to speak our language, we began to change our thinking about who this being really was. He was different from us, no doubt about it. Yet, he must be some kind of a man.

One day when a crowd of people had gathered, the man held up his two hands and said, "Look at my hands." He counted to six, putting down a finger for each number, just like we did when we counted. "One, two, three, four, five, six," he counted. "Each finger represents a day." What was he talking about? We sometimes counted men or pigs with our fingers but never days. He counted again. With the six fingers down he held up his two hands and said, "For six days you should work on the airstrip and work in your gardens." Holding on to his seventh finger, he continued, "This day is the Creator's day, Sunday. On this day you should all gather in the village yard of Chief Den. After people gather, I will teach you about the Creator."

Word got around. On the seventh day people came from nearby villages. While they waited for everyone to get there, people danced and sang. As the weeks went by, more and more people came. The men and women decorated their faces with red and black markings. Some men added bright feathers to their arm band or head covering. Every woman wore her long, colorful net-bag hanging down her back—not the everyday net-bag she used in her daily work. Gathering on the seventh day, Sunday, became almost like the celebration on a feast day—but without food.

The man told us stories—stories about a man of long ago named Jesus. "Jesus was the Son of the Creator," he said. To tell a story in our language was hard for the man, so he spoke in Indonesian and the chief's son translated sentence by sentence.

Our old men were saying this spirit-man must have the message of *hai.* Surely he knows the path to paradise. Even at first when it was hard to understand his words, we listened carefully. Every Damal wanted to know what the man was saying.

Months were passing. People brought poles and bark slabs from the forest, and the man built a house for himself. All the time crowds of people worked across the valley building the landing field for the flying-boat.

Always the man listened to his talking box. Then one day after talking to the box, he was so excited he could hardly speak. "Tomorrow, yes tomorrow after one more sleep, my wife and my two little girls will come to the Ilaga in the flying-boat!"

The next day I was at the airstrip along with crowds of people from all over the valley. I'd never seen so many people in one place before. Up and down the airstrip groups of people marched, singing and dancing. Would it really come? We waited.

Why did He Come?

Then someone called out, "*Hol koma motak-o-o-o!* The flying-boat is coming. I hear it. It's coming! It's coming! Get off the airstrip! Get off the airstrip!"

The plane sat down at the bottom of the airstrip and moved slowly to the top where we waited. Out of the airplane stepped a tall, thin being, a woman taller than any of our men. She didn't look like a woman. She wore clothes similar to the man's, not a grass skirt like Damal women wear. Everyone pressed to see the two little girls. The girls just looked back at us in silence. By pushing some got close enough to touch them. Would the white of their skin rub off? It didn't.

The family started on the long walk across the valley. They were headed for my village and the bark house the man had built. I pushed through the crowds of people so I could walk closer to them.

Shortly, the man recognized me and said, "Peddy, we need some help in our house now that my family has come. Would you like to help us? We need you to chop firewood and carry water from the river."

"Yes!" I said. I wasn't afraid of these foreigners anymore. They were people not spirit-beings. Besides, it was fun to be up close and see everything that was happening.

BIBLE LESSON

> Jesus is the one of whom the scripture says. . . "Salvation is to be found through him alone. In all the world there is no one else whom God has given who can save us." Acts 4:11-12

> As the scripture says, "Everyone who calls out to the Lord for help will be saved." But how can they call to him for help if they have not believed? And how can they believe if they have not heard the message? And how can they hear if the message is not proclaimed? Romans 10:13-14

The Damals had lived for hundreds of years without knowing there was a good and loving God. All they knew were spirit-beings whom they feared. Because they feared the power of evil they had over their lives, the Damals tried very hard to please these evil spirits. However, the spirits never rewarded them with anything good.

Even deeper in their hearts the Damals clung to a hope, a God-given hope, that someday a messenger would come bringing the words of *hai,* words of eternal life and

The Coming of Hai

the way to paradise. This concept of *hai* had been passed down from generation to generation. The Holy Spirit used this faint hope in the hearts of the Damals to draw them to the message of Jesus.

Mission organizations around the world use various approaches to bring the gospel to a new group of people. Some begin with education, often building schools for the children. Providing a better standard of living and medical help is the avenue some pursue. Others use translation of the Bible and teaching people to read as their approach. Still others begin their teaching with the story of creation and other Old Testament stories.

The initial approach used with the Damals was none of these. Rather, it was telling the stories of Jesus in the language the people spoke.

ISSUES TO CONSIDER

1. Compare the initial approach used to convert the Damals to the verses above from Acts and Romans.

2. From the viewpoint of a Damal, who is emerging from the Stone Age, what do you think was the most amazing new thing to him in this chapter?

Chapter 3
Chief Den Makes a Decision

Peddy continues his story:

I went in and out of the missionary's house all day long, bringing in fire wood for the kitchen stove and buckets of water for washing and cooking. Before long I was peeling vegetables and I learned how to wash dishes. From the family's kitchen I watched and listened to everything that was going on.

The man was speaking Damal more clearly all the time, and he understood us better. His wife was also learning. They each carried a pencil and paper everywhere they went. When they heard a word new to them, they wrote it on the paper. This helped they said, to remember the word and use it. I watched Kathy, the older daughter. She had a pencil and paper too. I don't think she was really writing like her mother did. However, that didn't stop her from learning. The girls just talked with their friends. Joyce, the younger one, didn't even speak the language of her parents. Her only words were Damal words. Unlike their parents though, the girls spoke our language without an accent.

Sometimes people who were sick or had a sick baby came to the man. "Pray for my baby," they said. "He's very sick. We've already done spirit appeasement and it didn't help."

"I'll pray for your baby," he answered, "but you must stop calling on the spirits for help. God will not hear our prayers if you are still trusting in your charms." The parents agreed and the baby got well. Surely this God was powerful, more powerful than the spirits.

After the woman and children had come to our valley, the crowd of people that gathered on Sunday got even bigger. More and more people were walking from distant villages. All these months the man would stand to speak but the chief's son who put his words into our language remained seated. He was not old enough to stand and speak in public. People who sat on the edge of the crowd could not hear.

Then one Sunday the man stood up to speak and did not use the chief's son to translate for him. He spoke loudly so everyone could hear. When the words of his sentence were not quite right, one of the older men corrected him. The man listened. Then he repeated in good Damal what he had been trying to say.

The Coming of Hai

One Sunday the man spoke with unusually strong feelings. "You must make a choice. Which path will you follow? The path of Jesus leads to heaven, to *hai* and eternal life. The path of Satan and spirit appeasement, which you Damals have always followed, leads to death and hell. You cannot walk on both paths at the same time, for they lead in opposite directions. Every person must make this choice."

The next day I saw the man go off into the tall grass with Chief Den and other village leaders. I knew they had gone to a place where their important talk would not be overheard by women and children. After each meeting in the tall grass the village men, secluded in their houses at night, repeated and discussed what the man had said. I overheard the men's talk but always acted as though I had no interest in their talk.

"We asked the man," one man said, "If we destroy our sacred objects and follow this new path to *hai*, who will protect us in war if our enemies attack us?"

"The Creator will," he answered. "God is stronger than your charms." The man told them a story from his Book. "Long ago, God protected his people from their enemies; the people who trusted in God were delivered."

We asked him, "Who will help us in sickness?"

"God's Book tells us to pray to him about everything," the man said. "He can even heal sick people."

"What will happen to our gardens? We will be hungry if we don't have garden charms."

"No," the man answered. "Your gardens will grow more food than before if you trust in Jesus. Remember, if you choose the Jesus path you must destroy all your charms. You cannot walk on two paths at the same time."

Another day Chief Den had asked, "How shall we destroy our charms? Will the flying-boat take our sacred charms away? If it did, they'd really be gone."

"I don't think that's a good idea," the man answered. "The charms belong to you. They are from your forefathers. You yourselves must destroy them."

Someone suggested throwing them in the Ilaga River. Another man said, "No, that wouldn't work. The Danis might fish them out somewhere down stream."

The man opened his Book and told them. "Long ago followers of Jesus who lived in a place called Ephesus decided to destroy their sacred books of magic. They burned all their books." [Acts 19:19] "Burn your sacred objects."

Chief Den Makes a Decision

As a teen-ager, I was not supposed to know about the sacred objects. Only the old men knew the secrets about these things which had been passed down from generation to generation. I did know they were an assortment of pig tails, little sea shells like we used for money, and stone tools. Each object had been dedicated to an evil spirit. That is what gave it special power. All the pig tails were from pigs that had been killed in spirit appeasement or a war ceremony. In all past generations we Damals had depended on them to appease the evil spirits. They were our only help in sickness, in war and to keep us from hunger.

The decision was made! News spread over the valley like wildfire. Chief Den was going to lead his people in burning their sacred charms.

On Sunday people came into the village marching and singing. Chief Den brought boards from his hut—boards that made a rack on the wall to hold his sacred objects. In the center of the yard he laid these boards with other firewood in crisscross fashion building a large structure. The bonfire was laid and ready to light.

Several men came across the fence and into the village carrying long, smoke-blackened bundles. These were more sacred charms. Women had never seen these sacred objects.

The Damal men danced in the village courtyard each carrying his bows and arrows. Among the dancers were some men who carried long spears. These were Danis. They had come to protest the fetish burning. They shouted out their warnings. "Don't burn your fetishes. Sickness, war and hunger will come to all of us if you do. When tragedy strikes, we Danis will go to war against you who have defied the spirits."

The time came for everyone to be seated. The men sat on one side; the women and children sat on the other side and around the edge. In all this mass of black bodies there was one spot of color in the women's section: seated with their mother was Kathy wearing her red cowboy hat and Joyce wearing her white sunbonnet. The Danis, standing with their spears as if ready for action, ringed the outside.

The man spoke first. He explained again the decision the people were called to make. Every person who would decide to walk the Jesus path should stand and move near to the stack of firewood.

Before anyone moved Chief Den stood up and spoke with all the eloquence of a big chief. He exhorted the crowd. "Don't stand unless you have only one mind to follow Jesus. If you plan to keep back part of your charms, don't move at all."

Slowly, older men stood and moved to the center. Along with them a few women were standing, and younger men too, all moving to the center to sit down around the

The Coming of Hai

carefully laid wood. More men kept coming until the group was very large. Finally, no one else moved.

Chief Den ran to his hut, got a fire brand and lit the bonfire. Men began to run and shout as they threw their large bundles of charms into the blazing fire. Women tore charms from their arms and from around their necks, tossing them into the fire. Black smoke rose as the fire burned.

Some thought the spirits would surely show their anger; perhaps flashes of fire would come from the sky, but nothing happened. The blazing fire turned to glowing coals and then to gray ashes.

Our charms and fetishes were all gone.

BIBLE LESSON

"Now then," Joshua continued, "honor the Lord and serve him sincerely and faithfully. Get rid of the gods which your ancestors used to worship in Mesopotamia and in Egypt, and serve only the Lord. If you are not willing to serve him, decide today whom you will serve, the gods your ancestors worshipped in Mesopotamia or the gods of the Amorites, in whose land you are now living. As for me and my family, we will serve the Lord."

The people then said to Joshua, "We will serve the Lord our God. We will obey his commands." Joshua 24:14, 15, 24.

On this day of May 27, 1957, as we walked down the hill to the village, Don and I really did not know what was about to happen. We were young and inexperienced missionaries. Don had only been in the valley eight months, and I for three. We watched in amazement as 220 stepped forward from the crowd of 700. With this action they broke from many centuries of the past to follow this new way to *hai*.

God knew exactly what was happening. This was all in His plan from before the creation of the world. He placed in the hearts of all the Damal people a longing for *hai*, and he chose Chief Den to lead his people in the burning of their sacred charms and fetishes.

Den's father had also been a chief. Shortly before he died, the old man repeated to his son the expectation passed to him from his father that someday, perhaps in Den's lifetime, the way to *hai* would be made known to the Damal people. A being would come from the outside who knew the way to *hai*.

Chief Den Makes a Decision

Chief Den thought Don was this expected being. Without knowing their expectation Don was faithful, even in his faltering Damal language, to tell the Damals the story of Jesus.

Den led in the fetish burning as chief of the area. He had earned this position of influence. Den was a strong leader, a good business man, a political chief and a generous person who sponsored large feasts. He also controlled many of the sacred charms in his clan, but he was not a war chief.

It is important to point out one thing about Damal culture that made it possible for Chief Den to lead his people in group action to defy the spirits and burn their ancestral charms. The Damals did everything in life as a group. When a garden was planted, a house built, a marriage planned, or a war fought, every person in the group took part. This same group decision process held true in turning from spirit appeasement to following Christ. The decision by the group made it easy for each individual to affirm his personal determination to walk the Jesus path.

God used this event in the Ilaga to initiate a major turning to Christ. Almost like a row of falling dominoes, the tribal people who lived in the high mountains across the island also made this same choice to walk the Jesus path.

To God be the glory great things He has done!

ISSUES TO CONSIDER

1. Reflect on this story and how it was all a part of God's eternal plan.
2. Joshua said, "As for me and my family, we will serve the Lord." How did that pattern work with Chief Den? Can this be said in your family today?
3. Has the decision of another person influenced you in spiritual matters? Vice-versa, do your spiritual decisions influence others?

Chapter 4

Learning to Walk the Jesus Path

Peddy continues his story:

Hundreds of people were still singing and dancing around the smoldering fire after the burning of their ancestral charms.

"Hear me!" the missionary called out. "I have one more thing to say. After two sleeps everyone must gather before you go to your gardens." Pointing to the ashes he said, "All your evil spirit appeasement things are gone. Now come, and I will teach you of your new life and how to walk on the Jesus path."

On Tuesday I looked down, from my vantage point in the missionary's kitchen window, and saw the men and women gather for the first class. Everyone who came had decided to walk the Jesus path. I was also one of them, but my time of learning came later in the men's house. In the evenings instead of talking about war maneuvers or how to appease the spirits, the men repeated the things they had learned about walking this new path.

I heard that women were also repeating the same things in their houses. Some of the old men who had controlled spirit appeasement rites felt uneasy about the women doing this. It had been taboo for a woman to know anything about their sacred charms. To break this law of the spirits meant sickness or even death to the woman. Hearing of this confusion, the missionary assured the old men that Jesus-talk was for everyone, including women.

We all learned together. One man recited what he had learned and the rest of us repeated it after him, line by line. "Jesus was God's Son. His mother was Mary. She was a virgin and had never slept with a man. God's power came upon Mary and she became pregnant. Joseph was only the man who lived like a father to Jesus in their home. Jesus was human and lived on earth like a man but he never once sinned." If someone didn't say it quite right, someone else corrected him and we all repeated it again.

Learning to Walk the Jesus Path

I had watched the missionary family bow their heads and close their eyes when they sat down at the table. The man, or sometimes the children, prayed before they ate. Now, we all learned that every person walking the Jesus path could pray. God would hear our prayers too. We memorized a prayer to pray before eating. It began with "God, our heavenly Father," and ended with, "In Jesus name we pray. Amen." From then on I bowed my head, closed my eyes and prayed to the Creator before I ate my sweet potatoes.

Once we learned about prayer, people began to pray about other things too, not just before eating. After three months a leading man stood up in church on Sunday and prayed. Prayer was becoming a part of all of our lives.

We Damals had no more charms to ward off sickness. Whoever was sick came asking for prayer. When someone was too sick to walk, the missionary went to his village and prayed for him there. Again the men were saying, "*Bau-a*! It's amazing! It's a miracle!" This time people were saying this not about the airplane but about the sick people who were getting well.

I heard a woman say, "God made my uncle well." Someone else said, "God heard our prayers for my niece and she is healed."

Many were saying, "God is much stronger than the charms for sickness that we used to believe in." Not only Damals were saying this, but our Dani neighbors were saying the same thing.

The missionary had a vegetable garden planted near his house. Sometimes it was my job to weed the garden. We all watched and wondered what sort of a vegetable would appear from those strange-looking plants.

One plant had little green fruit which got bigger and then turned bright red. Another with feathery leaves had a long, orange root under ground. A tall plant had fruit with rows of yellow kernels wrapped in green leaves. But the one that everybody talked about most grew on a vine on the ground. We watched the green fruit grow bigger and Bigger and BIGGER. It was huge and then turned bright orange. The day the missionary picked the three biggest ones, it took a husky man to carry them, one by one, from the garden to the house. The missionary cut them up and passed out the many pieces. Everybody wanted a piece to take home. It was steamed in the family's cooking pit with greens and sweet potatoes. When the pit was opened each person got a taste of this new vegetable.

The missionary passed out vegetable seeds to lots of people for these same plants. (At the time we Damals had never seen vegetables like these and had no names for them.

The Coming of Hai

Later we used the Indonesian word for the tomatoes and built descriptive Damal words for the corn, carrots and pumpkins.) We planted the seeds right between the sweet potato vines in our gardens. Everything grew! The old men said, "We've never seen our gardens grow like this before. *Bau-a!* It's amazing! God is causing our gardens to prosper." We gave thanks to God for the abundance in our gardens, and we thanked Him for these new vegetables.

One night the men were talking about the Danis. [DON-ee] "We Damals are allied with the Danis in war only because we all live in the same valley. We didn't start the Great War, the Danis did. Now, we're fighting people from our own Damal [da-MALL] tribe who live in the Beoga [BAY-o-gah] because the Ilaga Danis, with whom we are allied, are fighting all who live in the Beoga."

One man said "The Great War has been going on for years. Just before we burned our war charms the Beoga Damals, with their Sinak [SEE-nock] Dani allies, came to the Ilaga in that surprise attack. They got only as far as the airstrip because the Ilaga Danis, who live across the valley, were quick to fight back. The Ilaga warriors must have killed ten or more of the enemy. Some died on the airstrip. Others were wounded and got as far as the forest before they died." The man concluded, "One of these days there's going to be another surprise attack by the enemy trying to even the score."

"Yes, I agree," his friend commented, "Next time the Beoga Damals come, there will be many more Sinak Dani warriors with them, and they will be the victors. Any day this could happen and we have no war fetishes to protect us."

"That's true," said a younger man. "But look how long it's been and no attack has come.

Could it be that God is even stronger and can protect us better than our war charms?"

BIBLE LESSON:

Jehoshaphat was king of Judah. . . Early in the morning the people [of Judah] went out to the wild country near Tekoa [to fight against the many enemy soldiers who were attacking them.] As they were starting out, Jehoshaphat addressed them with these words: "Men of Judah and Jerusalem! Put your trust in the Lord your God, and you will stand your ground. Believe what his prophets tell you, and you will succeed."

The king ordered some musicians to march ahead of the army, singing: "Praise the Lord! His love is eternal!" When they began to sing, the Lord threw

Learning to Walk the Jesus Path

the invading armies into a panic, [and the invading armies destroyed themselves.] Condensed from 2 Chronicles 20: 20-24, 31

    Jesus performed many other miracles. . . But these have been written in order that you may believe that Jesus is the Messiah, the Son of God, and that through your faith in him you may have life. John 20: 30-31

Never again was there a battle in the Great War! Both the Damals and the Danis saw clearly it was God who brought peace. In time past no war ever came to an end without payments being made and the traditional war settlement ceremony with spirit appeasement. Without any of this the Great War was over.

For two years, in the Damal villages where the people were trusting God, not one adult died even though the missionaries at that time had no significant medical help to offer. This was truly a miracle, displaying God's power not only to the new believers but to all their unbelieving Dani neighbors.

The gardens of the Christians produced an abundance of food. God demonstrated to everyone, to the heathen and Christians alike, that He was good, more powerful than any evil spirit or the charms they and their forefathers had trusted.

The Damals felt compelled to share this Good News with the rest of their tribe. They traveled over the mountain ranges to the north and to the south—even when their lives were sometimes in danger because of the boundaries drawn by the Great War.

Eighteen months after Chief Den led his people in destroying all ties to spirit appeasement, the Danis in the Ilaga began to burn their sacred charms. Den's father-in-law, a Dani chief, was the first and then fetish burnings spread like popcorn all over the valley. With no travel restrictions due to war the Danis were free to travel with their story. They walked to the east, to Dani-speaking people, even to some valleys so distant the travelers had only heard the place names through the tales of old men. The new believers traveled telling all the wonders God had done in the Ilaga.

Consider the miracles of Jesus. These had more than one purpose. A chief one demonstrated that Jesus was truly the Son of God. Another led many who observed the miracles to a life-giving faith. (John 20:30-31)

For the new Damal believers God showed His power through wonders which stood out in clear contrast to the results of their former spirit appeasement. Wonders blessed the lives of the new Christians, and beyond that, God's power was demonstrated

The Coming of **Hai**

to tens of thousands of tribal people across the mountain ranges. Soon these people from a half-dozen different tribes and languages also believed. Within seven years 100,000 Stone Age tribesmen burned their ancestral charms and began to walk the Jesus path.

ISSUES TO CONSIDER

1. Why is there an apparent difference in the way God showed his power to the new Damal Christians and the way He answers the prayers of Christians in America today?

2. With John 20:30-31 in mind, what do you think one important reason should be for us to ask the Lord to perform a miracle in our life or the life of another?

3. How important was it for the Damals who burned their charms to begin learning the doctrines of the faith? What about people in our culture who make a decision to follow Christ?

Chapter 5
To Beoga with the Message of *Hai*

Introduction

Sometimes old words in our language take a new meaning. This was certainly happening for the Damals with the word "*hai*." Once the word meant an unending perfect life and that life included having many pigs—paradise. Now, *hai* was being used with the Bible definition of heaven. *Hai* joined with the Damal word "*kal*," words or talk, became "*hai-kal*"—heaven-talk, the gospel, the good news of Jesus.

Peddy continues his story:

Working in the missionaries' house I had an inside track in knowing what was happening. The missionary man had just gotten home from his first trip to Beoga when he announced, "I want to go back to Beoga. The hearts of the Beoga people are wide open to receive Jesus and the message of *hai*. On my trip I only went to the top part of the valley. This time I want to travel the full length of the valley." [See story 1 map]

His wife responded, "Then, I want to go with you!"

"What about Kathy and Joyce?" the man asked. "The trail is much too rugged for us to take them along."

"Oh," she said, catching her breath, "that means I'd have to leave them here in the Ilaga. I've never been away from my girls even for one night." After thinking for a time she raised her head and said, "My Kathy and Joyce will be all right staying with the new missionary couple. I'm going to Beoga with you!" With that decision everyone in the little cabin was focused on preparing for the trip.

The missionary piled things for the trip in one corner. There was a tent, two sleeping bags and two air mattresses. "No, we can't take the mattresses. They're too heavy." he said. "We'll have to pile grass under the tent floor and sleep on that." Extra clothing and a bar of soap was added. From the kitchen he brought oatmeal and powdered milk, cans of corned beef, some soup mix packets, salt and cooking oil. "Beyond that we'll eat what the people bring us."

The Coming of Hai

"Don't forget the camp cooking kit and canteens for boiled water," his wife said, "and two flashlights."

"Two of the loads will be the two-way radio and the 12 volt car battery to operate it. The field director says we can't go without the radio. That makes eight loads."

The next Sunday the missionary announced in church, "We're going to Beoga. We need eight men to carry loads for us. I'll pay you well."

No one wanted to go. Everyone was afraid because the Beoga people were our enemies in the Great War. For years no one had traveled between the two valleys except in war. On the trip a month earlier the missionary traveled with only one man for a guide. The guide had relatives in the first village they entered. They traveled light, no tent, no radio; they slept in the people's houses and ate their food. Even this man who made the first trip was afraid to enter the Beoga by another trail. [See story 1 map]

Finally, five men and one woman (the wife of one of the men) signed up to carry loads. All had relatives in the first villages on the trail we were taking.

The missionary said, "I'll carry a load. That leaves one more."

The farthest I had ever been from my village was to the edge of the forest where I met the missionary. I had no relatives in the Beoga. Then I heard myself saying, "I'll go too."

The next day [December 2, 1957] we set off across the valley and into the forest beyond the airstrip. The trail was new to all of us except for one of the carriers. He was our all-important guide. After two hours of easy hiking we came to the rock cliffs that were visible clear across the valley from our village. The trail led right up the face of the cliff. The missionary woman had a hard time pulling herself up, grabbing branches and roots, sticking her toe into the cracks. She was handicapped, I thought, because she wore shoes. Bare feet are better for climbing like this. [The face of the cliff was a 60 to 65 degree grade, even 85 degrees at one short place.] I was glad we were climbing up, not down, and I guessed the missionary woman felt the same. When we finally got to the top it began to hail.

In the afternoon we came to a meadow with eight large jungle huts. The missionary set up his tent; we carriers were going to sleep in one of the huts. The Beoga warriors slept in these huts just a few months earlier when they were on their way to attack the Ilaga. That night the carriers talked about the Beoga men who built the huts. Many of these men were killed when they got to the Ilaga. Now, we were going to the Beoga. Would they kill us?

To Beoga with the Message of Hai

Shortly after dawn the next morning we set out walking through a marsh. With each step we took, our feet sank into the mud sometimes to our knees. Every step required a plan of attack, trying to avoid the knee-deep holes. I watched the missionary woman probe the mud at the side of the path with her walking stick, always hoping to find a shallow spot before taking the next step.

In the forest again, still climbing higher, our steps were over a log, climbing around the roots of a big tree, walking up the top of a fallen log or sinking into a mud hole. The missionary woman never raised her eyes from the path because each step must be carefully chosen without slowing the pace.

The next section of the trail was really steep as we worked our way toward the top of the mountain. We had no view of where we had been or where we were going because we were hiking through heavy forest. When we came to a stream, we knew we had crossed over the top. Then we began to really go downhill.

The trail followed the stream bed as the water plummeted down hill. Huge boulders, taller than I am, littered the narrow stream bed. On both sides the mountains rose straight up. All the way down in steep descent we were stepping into the cold water, and then climbing up and over another huge rock. Carrying my pack wasn't easy. It was good there was no rain right at that time. In a downpour the stream could turn into a torrent in no time at all and there was no way to escape.

Then we were back in the forest again, this time walking along the side of a steep mountain. We walked for hour after hour, clinging to the roots and branches that were there. Our pace was slow because the missionary woman was slowing down. The mountainside was so steep there wasn't even a place where we could sit down to rest even for a minute. One wrong step would have meant falling to one's death in the canyon below.

Suddenly we were out of the forest. We could see the steep sides of mountains ahead. Smoke was rising from houses across the river. Night was fast approaching as we walked the last way down the stream bed toward the first village. At this point the missionaries walked in front and I walked close behind them.

Here I was, Peddy, carrying a load for the man as he entered a new valley—a valley of people who had never seen a spirit-man. It seemed so long ago—that afternoon when I was cooking mushrooms and the spirit-man stepped out of the forest. But really the time was short [14 months]. The time was shorter yet [eight months] since warriors, on their way to kill anyone who lived in the Ilaga, had left the village we were about to enter.

The Coming of Hai

A village man looked up and was startled to see a line of people, led by two spirit-beings, coming into his village. In a glance he knew we had come in peace, for no one in our party carried bows and arrows. The man called to his fellow villagers, "The spirit-people have come from the Ilaga. Come and see. The foreigners are here in our village!"

Men, women and children popped out of their houses. Without hesitation their shouts of greeting filled the air. "*Amolo! Amolo!* Greetings in love! Greetings in love!" Everyone was snapping fingers with everyone else, which is the way we shake hands.

The tension in our group relaxed. We were being received as friends. The day had been a long one, traveling slower than usual because the woman could go no faster. We started before the sun was up and now it was dark. The words of the villagers to us who carried loads were so good to hear. "Come, you are welcome to sleep in my house tonight." We knew this meant they would feed us too and we were starved.

The missionary woman remained sitting on a carrying tin all hunched over. She refused the soup the man had made for her. "I'm too exhausted to eat anything." she said. "I just want to lie down."

I watched her as she slowly took off her muddy, hobnail boots and then the long, heavy socks. She had blisters on her feet. I was tired too but my bare feet had no blisters.

Word of the missionary's earlier trip to the upper Beoga had reached this village. Now, the village headman stepped into the dark to start a chain of calls from one village to the next. "The foreign man, the speaker of *hai*, is here! He's in our village. Everyone gather tomorrow!"

BIBLE LESSON

How wonderful it is to see a messenger coming across the mountains, bringing good news, the news of peace! Isaiah 53:7 [A practical, modern paraphrase]

How beautiful on the mountains are the feet of those who bring good news, who proclaim salvation. Isaiah 53:7 NIV [A more literal poetic translation]

"My [work]," Jesus said, "is to obey the will of the one who sent me and to finish the work he gave me to do. . . . Take a good look at the fields; the crops are now ripe and ready to be harvested! The man who reaps the harvest is being paid and gathers the crops for eternal life; so the man who plants and the man who reaps will be glad together. John 4: 34-36

This was my first trip to take the gospel to people who had never heard. Many times my husband, Don, had hiked trails like this one, or trails even more rugged, in exploration and laying the ground work for later moves, but this was my first time. What a privilege!

Today, places like the Beoga Valley with people who have never heard are virtually nonexistent. Most unreached people live in big cities. The physical difficulty in reaching the city people is not as great, but it is much harder work because most often the people are not as eager to hear as the Damals were.

The verses in John 4:34-36 speak of those who go and of those who stay and provide support. Both groups are of equal importance in the harvest. Neither one can do his work without the other. The reward will be the same for the many who pray and give as it will be for the few who go. Each is doing the will and work of the Father in reaching people with the gospel. The need is for young people as well as older folks to be on one of the two teams for their whole lives—the "sender's team" or the "goer's team." Both will receive their reward.

Without the large group who stayed at home and gave their support, we could not have taken this trip. To our "sender's team" I want to say—thank you!

ISSUES TO CONSIDER

1. Consider the concept of a "goer's team" and a "sender's team" for missions in your church. Who is on each team and how are they functioning?
2. I faced many physical challenges in reaching villages to spread the gospel. Do you face obstacles in your mission work, whether on the "sender's" team or "goer's" team?

Chapter 6

Teamwork in Telling the Gospel

Peddy continues his story:

The next morning the missionary woman was up and ready to go again. The tent was packed and all the loads were put together, but the carriers had not come to pick them up. Instead they came to the missionary saying, "We brought you this far but we want to go home now. If we go any further, someone might kill us."

"Okay, I understand," the missionary said. "I'll get men from Beoga to carry the rest of the way. Just take us a little further today to the main village." They agreed.

"Peddy, how about you? Will you stay with us all the way? I hope so."

I thought about it. Maybe it would be safer to go home, but then again, the missionary needs me. Everywhere the missionary goes God takes care of him. I think God will take care of me, too. "Sure," I said, "I'll keep going with you."

The trail that morning led us across a very steep mountainside like the one we'd walked the day before, but this one was planted with sweet potato gardens. There were no trees or bushes to grab hold of. Even though the missionary woman used her walking stick like a third leg she could hardly keep from sliding down the mountain.

After a couple of hours we came to the main village. The crowd of people already there was almost as large as the ones that gathered in the Ilaga on Sundays. The missionary asked them all to sit down and he began talking. They listened intently as he told them about Jesus, the Creator's Son.

Then he said, "Before I speak again my wife will give injections of penicillin to all who are sick with yaws. Anyone who has this disease should go over to the side and sit down." Immediately from all over the crowd people got up and went to where the missionary woman was standing.

I had never seen anything like this skin disease of yaws; no one in the Ilaga had it. Huge sores were eating away at the bodies of people who stood up. Some had missing fingers and toes. One man's nose and part of his face were gone. Others were carried over on a stretcher. The missionary told the people, "With one shot of penicillin suspended in an oil base your sores will be gone in ten days."

Teamwork in Telling the Gospel

After teaching another lesson, a greens feast with sweet potatoes was served to everyone. More shots were given, and then we all listened to the final teaching-talk before the sun began its descent. At the first session, with the help of the Ilaga carriers, the missionary taught the crowd to sing the two Christian chant-songs we sang in the Ilaga. Now the Beoga people sang these with a passion.

All night long in the men's house near the missionaries' tent the men never stopped singing. Over and over they sang the two songs from the Ilaga and composed new chant-songs about the missionaries coming. They sang of their joy in hearing of the way to *hai.* They sang of their desire to follow this new path to eternal life. At intervals one man recited a Bible verse, line by line, he had learned that day. Soon everyone in the house could say it. No one got much sleep that night but it didn't seem to matter.

The next morning the missionary man said "We must move on." The woman countered, "Can't we stay here one more day? These people are so eager to hear—even more so than the Ilaga people. They must learn more so they can truly believe."

"I wish we could" the man said, "but this is just the first area of the Beoga. If we're going to get home by Christmas, we must go on."

"Well," she said, "at least tell them that in the future our family will build our house in the Beoga and live here with them." He told the people and they were glad.

The missionary passed out the loads to the eight new carriers he had recruited from the crowd. This time the missionary and I had no load to carry; all we carried were the water canteens. Up the mountain we started. A large group of people went with us, singing and dancing all the way up the first mountain. Finally they turned back.

We hiked on, up and down the mountainsides through a stretch of dense jungle and across a small landslide. The new carriers composed songs and sang as they walked. One they sang over and over. This chant-song gave the missionaries new names, Damal names. From then on all of us Damals called them by these names. They sang:

We love Damal-Neme [da-MALL-eh-meh] (Friend-of-the-Damals—the man)

We love Damal-In [da-MALL-een] (Damal-woman—the woman)

Let's all pray

Let's all learn the gospel

No more war

No more serving Satan

We love all the Damal people

The Coming of Hai

By afternoon we reached the next village and set up camp. Again the people were very excited to see the missionaries. The next day they listened with full attention while Damal-Neme preached his three sermons. Damal-In continued to give penicillin shots.

As we moved up the Beoga River, things began to fall into a routine. One day we hiked; the next day Damal-Neme taught the people. My job was to help set up the tent and then boil water for drinking. Each morning I was to cook their oatmeal over a camp fire trying not to burn it. I decided cooking sweet potatoes in the ashes was much easier and tastes better than oatmeal.

Damal-In kept telling me, "Peddy, you're such a big help. And look how the people are receiving the words of *hai*. They were just waiting to hear the words of Jesus. What if we hadn't come?"

On our sixth day in Beoga the trail led us down the side of the mountain to the roaring Beoga River, a river twice the size of the Ilaga River. At the river crossing was a very long [125 ft.] swinging bridge made of rattan vines. It was suspended high above the rapids below. The bridge was constructed like a "V" with hand rails at the top and a narrow walkway, the width of a person's foot, at the point. Only one person at a time could be on the bridge. Also, it was in poor repair; many of the smaller vines were broken and blowing in the wind.

I watched Damal-In climb up the roots of the tree to the bridge and begin crossing very slowly. Carefully she put one booted foot in front of the other. Almost to the middle I saw she was struggling because one boot was caught in the narrow walkway. Finally she freed her foot and moved on. We were all glad when Damal-In got safely across and I think she was glad too.

In the afternoon our guide surprised us all. He told Damal-Neme we'd have to cross the Beoga River again. The trail was now close to the river and I was walking behind Damal-In. Suddenly she pointed to the river and said, "Look, Peddy! There are three logs lashed together bouncing down the rapids. I've never seen anything like this before in the river water. What could it be?"

In a few more minutes we came to the bridge site, but there was no bridge. Those logs we saw had been part of a temporary bridge the men were building.

Damal-In took one look at the men working on both sides of the river and said to her husband, "The bridge is gone. I CANNOT cross the river here!"

Damal-Neme went to talk to the Damals who lived in the area. He came back saying, "We must cross here; we have no choice. We can't go back the way we came and

Teamwork in Telling the Gospel

the Ilaga is on the other side of this river. If we are going to get home in time for Christmas, we have to cross this river today." [See story 2 Map]

Damal-In sat down on the river bank to watch the men work and I sat down beside her. On the opposite side near the edge there was a huge dead tree which had been washed down the river. It was lodged on boulders under the water. To build a walkway, men had positioned three poles from the bank to the tree branches out in the river. Other men were building from the dead tree to the side where we sat. They were placing long poles from the tree branches to the bank on our side of the river. The poles we had seen in the river must have been in this same position from the dead tree to our side of the river.

Would I be able to cross this bridge? I wondered what Damal-In was thinking. We both knew that anyone who fell into the river would not survive. No Damal woman would be brave enough to cross on a make-shift bridge like this one. Damal-In had a hard time crossing the rattan swinging bridge earlier this morning. That bridge had vines for handrails. This one had none.

Soon the men had three poles across the river to our side. Working out over the water they were lashing these crooked poles together with vine. They seemed no more afraid than if they were working over a mud hole.

When the crew finished tying the last vine, two strong young men came across the bridge, grasped Damal-In's arms and led her to the water's edge. They started across, one man ahead and one man behind holding her very tightly. With their weight the poles bent to within a foot of the black boiling water. Damal-In took little hesitant steps always feeling for a place to put her boot on those uneven poles. The two men holding her arms had no trouble; they had an advantage with their bare feet. Finally she reached the opposite bank and fell to the ground in a heap. Everyone who was watching let out a sigh of relief; Damal-In was across the river!

On the last day of our time in Beoga, Damal-Neme had finished his third teaching session when a woman came to Damal-In and asked her to pray for her. The woman had a huge goiter hanging from her throat. She could hardly breathe or even eat. [See picture]

Damal-In did pray. Then she said to the woman, "In heaven there are no goiters. Yours will be gone in heaven."

Later, the woman's husband brought the woman with the goiter back to Damal-In. "Give her a shot like you do for other people," he said. "She can't live much longer like this."

The Coming of Hai

Damal-In replied. "I'm so sorry, but I have no medicine and no shot to help a goiter. My shots only help people with yaws."

Then the woman turned to her husband and spoke with conviction, "In heaven my goiter will be gone!" I saw tears come to Damal-In's eyes. We were all very sorry for we knew she would soon die.

"Peddy," Damal-In said walking away, "If nothing else happened on this trip, it would be worth the whole trip just to know that today this woman heard the true message of *hai* and she will be in heaven."

The next morning at dawn, while the others were still packing up the camping gear, Damal-In and I started hiking up the mountain headed for the Ilaga. This trail was easier than the one we had come on, even though the crossing was higher and very cold. As we climbed higher it was hard to breathe. At noon we reached the top. Trees didn't even grow this high up. [11,400 ft.] By afternoon we came to an open area and set up camp for the night. This time crossing the high mountains Damal-In wasn't totally exhausted. [See story 2 map]

The next day, before leaving the forest, Damal-Neme picked out a short evergreen tree.

"Peddy, cut this tree," he said, "and carry it back home for me."

"What is it for?" I asked. "You can't burn the wood of this little tree."

"It's five sleeps until Christmas," he said. "You'll see what we do with it."

It was mid-afternoon when we crossed the last fence and reached the cabin where the missionaries lived. I watched as Kathy and Joyce ran into their mother's arms. Everyone was talking and hugging and laughing. We were all safely back home.

Kathy knew what the tree was for and talked about it excitedly in her own language. Later Damal-Neme stood the tree up in the corner of their house. That evening they all decorated it with shiny balls.

I was kept extra busy building and watching the fire in the cook stove. Damal-In made cookies and candy and I always got a taste. The girls helped their mother make cookie men. When the cookies came out of the oven they painted them with bright colors. The family listened to their kind of music on a wind-up phonograph. Each morning there were more packages under the tree. When the evening came to open the packages there was a rubber ball for me and two big dolls for Kathy and Joyce.

Every one was excited with our return, but no more excited than the Damals of the Beoga had been, when Damal-Neme and Damal-In walked into their village.

Teamwork in Telling the Gospel

BIBLE LESSON

For the body itself is not made up of only one part, but of many parts. If the whole body were just an eye, how could it hear? And if it were only an ear, how could it smell? As it is, however, God put every different part in the body just as he wanted it to be. So then, the eye cannot say to the hand, "I don't need you!" Nor can the head say to the feet, "Well, I don't need you!" On the contrary, we cannot do without the parts of the body that seem to be weaker.   1 Corinthians 12:14, 17, 18, 22, 23.

Be ye doers of the word and not hearers only. James 1:22 KJV

Whatever you do . . . do it all for God's glory. 1 Corinthians 10:31

Listen, Jesus said . . . I will bring my rewards with me, to give to each one according to what he has done. Revelation 22:12

Who took the story of Jesus to the Beoga Damals? The missionary man taught them from the Bible, the missionary woman gave shots and prayed for them and the missionary children, Kathy and Joyce, stayed at home so their parents could go. Peddy's help, first as a carrier and then in cooking and boiling drinking water, was essential to life on the trail. Each person had a different role and all were dependent on other team members to accomplish the purpose of taking the gospel to the Beoga people.

Every team member was a "doer," personally active in the project, not just a "hearer" who was content to let someone else "carry the ball." Each was doing his part for the glory of God. For years Don had been working tirelessly toward this trip, first by leaving his home country, then by exploring to find where the Damals lived and learning their language. Alice was following right behind her husband. The girls did their part by adjusting to each new challenge. Peddy, a teenager not yet fully grown, had left the carefree life of his peers to be the only person in all of the Ilaga brave enough to make the full trip.

Don't we all need to apply these same principles right where we live? For each of us there is an active role to play, not just being a person who says "God bless you," while

The Coming of Hai

watching someone else do the work. Each person has his place in God's work whether at home, at church, at school or at work. Jesus promises a reward to every Christian according to what he has done.

ISSUES TO CONSIDER

1. Do you think these totally unreached Damals could understand the brief message given to them? What were some of the clues that they did understand?

2. Do you think the woman with the goiter is in heaven?

3. It's easy to hear the word and nod in approval. The challenge is to be a doer of the word in the world in which we live.

Chapter 7
Surprise Visitors

Peddy tells another story:

I want to tell you one more story of adventure I shared with our missionaries. Many years had passed. I still lived in the same village but now I had a wife and family. I was just an ordinary village man. I'd never been to school or learned to read. I slept in the men's house just like my father had done. I wore only the attire of Damal men of generations past, not the new clothing of the foreigner like many wore.

Over the years several missionaries had come and gone from our village. None lived here now. Chief Den, who had led all of us Damals in burning our charms, was now a very old man—but a man who still walked the Jesus' path. My oldest daughter was married. The missionary's daughters Kathy and Joyce were also married and living in America. Damal-Neme and Damal-In lived in the Beoga Valley.

Four times a year our missionaries returned to the Ilaga and stayed with us for a week. They came to teach and give help to church leaders. The little cabin on the hill, where the missionaries first lived, was gone. In its place stood a bigger house. On their visits Damal-Neme and Damal-In stayed in this big, empty house. I helped Damal-In in the kitchen—building the fire, cooking vegetables and washing dishes—just like I used to do when I was a teenager.

Damal-In thanked me, in the same way she used to. "Peddy, you're such a help to me! What would I do without you? I guess we just wouldn't eat, because I'm busy all day long helping the Damals."

It was true. All day long the yard was crowded with Damals and Danis. Some had walked a day or even two to buy a Bible. Others hoped to pass their final literacy exam and get their reader's card so they could buy their first Bible. Damal-In had trained a group of men and women who worked year-round in their local church area giving tests and advancing students from one literacy book to the next. All this was done in the process of learning to read. Today they all worked together. Selling a Bible to someone who had just passed his final literacy test was the high point of all the activity of the day.

The Coming of Hai

Damal-Neme was busy down in the village. Two hundred church leaders and their wives were gathered in the church for the Bible seminar lessons. Before he began to teach, he counseled the delegates about a current issue facing everyone in the Ilaga.

"I hear the rebels are in the area again and tempting you to join their cause," he said. "All of you know the Bible teaches us that we should live in peace with all men. The rebels want to take up arms and fight to overthrow the Indonesian government.

"Open your Bibles to Romans 13. It says that whoever opposes the government, which has been put there by God, will bring judgment on himself. My dear brothers, do not line up with the rebels; to do so will only bring hardship and suffering to you and gain nothing in the end. These rebels may be your brothers by blood but they are not your brothers in the Lord."

On this day [May 9, 1978] I had come back to the missionary house after dark to wash the supper dishes. The missionaries were still sitting at the table talking and drinking tea. I went to the kitchen, sat in the dark and waited for them to finish.

"I've hardly seen you all day," Damal-In said to her husband.

"True," Damal Neme said as he adjusted the flame in the kerosene lantern. "And I'm tired! After I finished teaching the last seminar lesson several pastors came and wanted to talk."

A knock at the door interrupted their conversation.

"Who could that be?" Damal-In asked. "Nobody goes anywhere in the black of night."

"It's probably another pastor wanting to talk." Without getting up Damal-Neme called out, "Come in!"

In walked a man in a uniform carrying a rifle. Behind him came five other men each carrying a jungle knife or bow and arrows.

"Only police have guns." Damal-In said in a whisper. "What are the police doing here this time of night and two hours walk from their post?"

"They are not police," Damal-Neme answered. "And they are not friends. A friend would never bring a jungle knife or bow and arrows into our house. These men are carrying weapons, not garden tools and hunting gear. They are rebels!"

The man with the gun took charge. He seated the missionaries so they faced him. He told a helper to stand at his side holding the gun. Rearranging the chairs he seated the four other men behind him so they faced the missionaries.

Surprise Visitors

"Why are you teaching the Damals to remain loyal to the government?" the leader asked. "Don't you know that we rebels will soon take over the whole country? If you want to stay in this land you'd better be on our side when we take over. Don't just sit there. Answer me!" he demanded.

"I've only been teaching from the Bible." Damal-Neme answered. "I must stand for what I believe."

"I'm a Dani, born right here in the Ilaga," the man responded. "You and all the Damals must join us in fighting the government."

For over an hour this Dani, turned rebel, continued to threaten the missionaries. "I'm ready to fight and die for my cause. We rebels are taking full control. We've punished others like you." He gestured to the gun. "If you don't cooperate your lives won't be worth much of anything.

"Give me writing paper," the man demanded. "I need paper for our cause."

(I knew there was a pile of blank paper in the cupboard right behind them.) "No," Damal-Neme responded. "I will not give you paper because I do not support your cause."

At that point Damal-In began to shake violently.

The men with the long, jungle knives seated behind the leader were rebels by choice, but they were also Damals by birth. They saw Damal-In shaking in fear. They came from a distant valley and had never seen Damal-In in person, but they knew who she was. One man and then another raised his hand and motioned in Damal sign language, "My mother, don't be afraid. *Amolo!* We care for you. Don't be afraid."

Finally the rebels all left. As the commander went out the door he said, "Don't you dare tell anyone about our visit tonight, not the Damals or the police. If you do, you'll be sorry."

They were gone.

"Peddy," the missionary said, "I guess you can come out and wash the dishes now."

The missionary paused and said, "Do you think the leader will come back in the middle of the night—alone?" No one ventured to answer that question, neither the speaker nor the two listeners.

Damal-In spoke, "I really think the leader would be willing to die for what he believes. He must have risked his life to take that gun from an Indonesian military man—or even killed the man in the process."

The Coming of Hai

"There is nothing we can do but trust in God," Damal-Neme answered. "Let's read the Bible like we were about to do before they came. The reading for tonight is Isaiah 7.

BIBLE LESSON:

When King Ahaz ruled Judah, war broke out. Word reached the king of Judah [that] the armies of Syria were already in the territory of Israel. King Ahaz and all his people were so terrified that they trembled like trees shaking in the wind.

The Lord said to Isaiah, "Tell King Ahaz to keep alert, to stay calm, and not to be frightened or disturbed. The anger of the Syrians is no more dangerous than the smoke from two smoldering sticks of wood. Syria, together with Israel, has made a plot. They intend to invade Judah and terrify the people into joining their side.

"But I, the Lord declare that this will never happen." Condensed from Isaiah 7:1-7

All of you are Christ's body, and each one is a part of it. In the church God has put all in place: in the first place apostles, in the second place prophets, and in the third place teachers; then those who perform the power to heal or to help others or to direct them [in administration] or to speak in strange tongues. 1 Corinthians 12:27-28

When I was in Bible school, I began following the daily Bible reading calendar arranged by Robert Murray M'Cheyne. (I still read my Bible today following this calendar.) The reading listed for that evening of May 7, the day the rebels came, was Isaiah 7. It told of the message the Lord gave to Ahaz, the king of Judah. It seemed it was also God's message specifically for me.

I knew all too well that the rebels had kidnapped foreigners, marched them deep into the jungle and held them for weeks. Nothing was beyond what they might do to anyone who stood in the way of their passion for revolution.

During our nearly two hours of intense interrogation, it was a comfort to me to know that Peddy was in the kitchen, although I knew he could do nothing.

Certainly the Damals in the village would protect us, even at the risk of their lives, but they knew nothing of this nighttime visit.

I couldn't stop shaking even after the rebels left. But my shaking did stop when I applied Isaiah's words to our present plight. I heard an inner voice: "Stay calm and don't be afraid. The anger of the rebels isn't any more dangerous than a smoking stick of wood. They want to terrify you and the Damals into joining their side. But they will never take over the government." I took this as God's word to me. That night I went to bed and slept.

When Don and I returned to the Ilaga for a visit in 2004, Peddy and his wife were among the small group who met us at the airplane. Peddy is a man, now with gray hair in his beard, who has never accomplished anything notable in his life—or so his peers might say. We would say, Peddy was always there when we needed him.

In 1 Corinthians 12: 27-28 Paul gives a list of gifts which are active in the church—all seem to be dramatic gifts or involve leadership, except for one: the gift "to help others" (translated "helps" in KJV). This gift of helping others is illustrated by Peddy's actions. Peddy was always ready to serve and aid others.

ISSUES TO CONSIDER

1. The God-given gift of helping others is easily overlooked. What are your thoughts about this gift? In your circle of life do you recognize this gift in operation?
2. The question is sometimes asked, what does a missionary do? Did the story, THE COMING OF *HAI,* give you any new insights into missionary work?

Don, Peddy's wife, Peddy, Alice 2004

Chief Den made first decision to burn fetishes 1957

Alice preparing to give penicillin in oil shot for yaws

Crowd at first fetish burning – White hats of Kathy & Joyce seen on left

Man carriers a load across a rattan swinging bridge

Woman with double goiter (Later, women didn't develop goiters when we gave an iodine treatment)

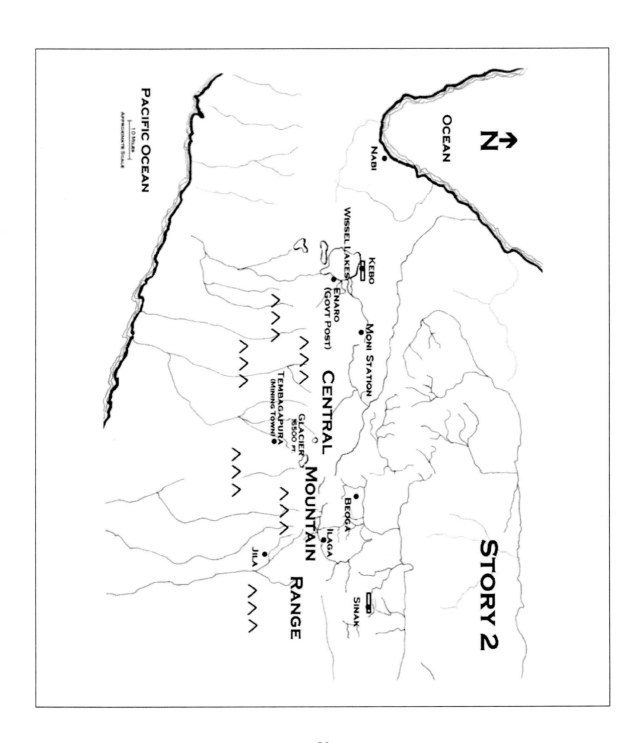

STORY TWO
BORN TO BE A CHIEF

Introduction

This is the story of a boy born to a Dani tribal chieftain. Everyone knew the boy's father, Amon, [AH-moan] was a chief of high rank because he had five wives. To have five wives meant he was a man of great business ability and wealth because a large payment of pigs and cowry shells had been made for each wife. This baby was the first born child of Amon's fifth wife. In this story we will call him Zakarias, [Zack-a-REE-us] the name he took when he was older.

The child was born on the island of New Guinea. The western half, where he was born, belonged to the Dutch and was one of the many Pacific islands known as Netherlands East Indies. Although the island was the largest in the archipelago chain, Netherlands New Guinea was the least important to the Dutch.

Yet, by the early years of the twentieth century the Dutch had built a number of towns around the island shores. All were accessible by ship. In the towns were shops and schools, government offices and police stations.

A wide band of swampland around the island kept the native coastal people from traveling even to the foot of the towering mountains that encompassed the interior. Since its discovery almost 500 years ago, most outsiders only knew of the people living on the coast. (In 1909 the Dutch had their first contact with people living in the mountains.) However, most of Western civilization still considered the vast interior with its endless waves of rugged mountains to be hostile and uninhabited wasteland. [See map at beginning of book]

This understanding was to change not long before World War II. A pilot working for a Dutch oil company made a detour from his regular route of flying around the island's edge. The day was unusually clear and he could see the mountain peaks. He flew up and over the mountain ranges. There, hidden in the high mountains, he discovered three lakes—a large one and two smaller ones close by. These lakes were not charted on

Born to be a Chief

any map. The Dutch named them the Wissel Lakes after the pilot who discovered them. Wissel discovered more than lakes for on the large lake he spotted canoes scattered across the lake and gardens all around its edge. Canoes and gardens meant there were people.

People lived in these rugged interior mountains!

In 1937 as a result of this discovery, the Dutch sent an overland patrol from the coast and opened a government post among the Mee [MEH] tribal people living around the large lake. A year later, following the same route, missionaries of The Christian and Missionary Alliance hiked into the interior to open a mission station. However that same year, because of the outbreak of war in Europe, they were evacuated.

Far to the east in the center of the island lived the Dani people—people not even known to the Mee tribesmen who lived around the Wissel Lakes. For uncounted generations the Dani people had lived hidden away in the highest rugged mountains of the island. This was the home of Amon the war-chief.

Everyone heard the exciting news—Chief Amon had a son. The baby's Dani name was Wilakom, but in fact he had no name at all for many months. If he had no name, the spirits would not notice him—or so his parents thought. And if he were unnoticed the spirits would not bring sickness or death to their beautiful baby boy.

Each of Chief Amon's wives had born him children. Amon's children, like all the children in the village, were weakened by malnutrition and hunger and often died with the slightest illness. When his son who we call Zakarias was born, the chief had only two living children and they were both girls.

This child was a boy child, prized much more highly than a girl child. A girl child would soon be married into another family and leave her father's domain. Not so for a boy child. Amon had plans for his son to grow up and be one of his followers. His son would become a brave warrior, even a war-chief like his father.

The year Zakarias was born was, perhaps, 1941. I say "perhaps" because Amon had not the slightest idea of measuring time. He knew nothing of years or months and very little of counting at all. He counted no more than the pigs he owned.

In the same year, 1941, the United States entered World War II. Soon the Japanese in their conquest across the Pacific took this tropical empire away from the Dutch. As the War progressed, the US military pressed across the Pacific taking back island after island from the Japanese. Fierce battles were fought in the beautiful coral waters around the island of New Guinea. Ships sank. Men fought and died. In time the island was turned back to the Dutch, and the US military moved on across the Pacific.

During all of this fighting much of the world still assumed that no people lived in the rugged mountain interior. The 500,000 tribal people who lived hidden away in these mountains had no idea that a war was going on—somewhere in another world. They did not even know there were people, real flesh and blood people, not spirit-beings, living beyond their mountain fortress. Two worlds of men existed side by side. One world lived on the island shores—and beyond. The other world lived in the unending mountain ranges of the interior of the island. Each knew nothing of the other, yet they had one thing in common—their lives were filled with fighting and war.

The story of Zakarias is the true story of a man still living today. The tale that follows is written in the words of Zakarias just as he told it to me. In the telling we conversed using the Indonesian language because neither of us spoke another common language. He was a Dani speaker and I spoke Damal. The two languages are as different from each other as English is from Greek. Dani was the language used by Bill and Beverly Steiglitz, the missionaries who first brought the gospel to Zakarias and the people of Sinak. [SEE-nock]

It is my hope you will get to know and appreciate Zakarias as I do.

Chapter 1
War in Two Worlds

Zakarias begins to tell his story:

My very first memories are of war, of running from our village and hiding in the forest because enemy warriors were coming. I remember being hungry, hungry all the time. And I was afraid. I knew if an enemy warrior caught me, he would kill me.

That war did come to an end, and there was peace for a time. My mother gave birth to a baby girl. Three years later she gave birth to a boy and I had a brother! My brother had not yet been named when a new war broke out. Fighting began when a man from my father's clan stole the wife of a man from another clan. In anger the offended husband killed the offending man. Immediately the men under my father rallied to fight. A man in our own family line had been killed. On the first raid into enemy territory my father, with his warriors, killed two men from the clan who had killed one man in our clan. War had been declared and the enemy lines were drawn.

Fighting continued for many months. A surprise attack was always a danger. During war the men didn't have time to dig new sweet potato plots. The women, afraid to leave the village and go to the gardens, left them untended. Often they dared not go even long enough to dig a few potatoes for the day. We were always hungry. Perhaps this explains why I am so short. During my growing up years many times there was nothing to eat.

One day my father took me aside. My son, he said, "You are growing up. It is time for you to leave your mother's hut and sleep in my hut where only men sleep. It's time for you to learn the ways of men."

That night I waited until it was almost dark before I went to my father's hut. Outside it was shivery cold but inside so very warm. In the firelight I could see the men seated around the fire—maybe eight or ten of them. I took my place next to my father. I'd been in this house many times before, but tonight was different. Tonight I would sleep with the men of the village.

"Son," my father said, pointing with his nose, "Bring me those sweet potatoes over there."

He took the potatoes from me and began to toast them at the edge of the fire's flame. I knew very well that each must be toasted just enough to make the skin crisp but not enough to burn the potato itself. Without a crispy skin of protection, the sweet potato would have tasted like ashes after it was baked.

"Now you finish the job," he said.

I picked up a stick and dug in the hot ashes to make a place so I could bury each potato. In an hour it was time to dig in the ashes again and find the steamy hot potatoes. Each of the men took one, dusted the ashes off and began to eat. They peeled the potato as they ate. And I ate my potato in exactly the same way.

The men talked about the day's activities. One man spoke of repairing a garden fence. Another told of the trouble he had chasing a stray pig out of his garden. After awhile a man moved to the low doorway and put the boards in place across the opening to secure the hut for the night. Now, all the women and children were shut out from the world of men. Tonight I was on the inside.

The conversation changed. The men began to talk of things known only to men. They spoke of the enemy, of fighting and of killing. After a long time I lay down and slept but only fitfully.

The next night, and the next, and the next were all the same. The men boasted of their bravery in war. My father led in every story that was told, for he was the war-chief. They talked of how they destroyed the enemy's sweet potato gardens and how they were able to steal a pig. They recounted the events of each killing—the killing of ten people. Two of the ten were a woman and a child. They boasted that the number who died on their side was smaller than the number on the other side.

Anger rose in their voices and they plotted how they might ambush the enemy and kill more—more of our Dani neighbors who lived just down the valley. Until this war began those Danis had been our friends and trading partners. Marriages were arranged between members of their clan and ours. Now they were all enemies to be killed.

Sitting there each evening I understood I was in training to become a warrior. Yet somewhere deep down inside of me I knew I did not want to follow in my father's footsteps. I did not want to become a warrior and kill people in fighting and war.

One afternoon when I found my father alone in the yard I gathered all of my courage. I was ready with my little speech. "*Lavok noba*," I began. "Father, my dear father, I have something to say to you. I will not sleep in your hut again. I'll go back to

Born to be a Chief

my mother's hut and sleep there." That night I did not go to my father's hut or sleep with the men.

Immediately, all the men and boys in the village began making fun of me. "*Tigabut, tigabut*" they taunted: "Sissy, sissy! You sleep in the women's hut with the women. You should wear a skirt. You are not male enough to sleep in the men's house."

But I had made my decision and I stuck to it.

BIBLE LESSON

Even before the world was made, God had already chosen us to be his through our union with Christ. . . [He] had already decided that through Jesus Christ he would make us his sons—this was his pleasure and purpose. Ephesians 1:4-5

Do not conform yourselves to the standards of this world, but let God transform you inwardly by a complete change of your mind. Romans 12:2

Let's reflect on the place where Zakarias was born, a very remote and unknown place at the end of the earth. Does God have a plan and purpose for people even before they are born? Ephesians 1:4-5 says He does. How would God work in the life of this one little boy? For God to do this took a very complicated arrangement of people and circumstances. It also took decisions, the right decisions, made by Zakarias himself. The first right decision he made was to go against Dani tribal culture and refuse to follow his father's plans. He said, "No, I do not want to grow up to be a warrior and kill people. I will not even take the first step toward that end."

At any age the right choice will sometimes include standing up against the culture of our world and the pressure of our friends and peers—not doing what everyone else is doing.

ISSUES TO CONSIDER

America was plunged into World War II in 1941, the same year Zakarias was born. Compare the similarities and differences of wars in our world and in the world of Zakarias.

Chapter 2
Death, Peace and War Again

Zakarias continues his story:

My little brother was growing up. He was my very best friend, and we were always together. I used to take him along with me on my big-boy adventures. We had so much fun sharing the world together. But one day when he was about four, he got very sick. He was hot with a fever and could hardly breathe. He didn't want the sweet potatoes I brought to him. He just lay there by the fire in my mother's hut. All I knew to do was to sit beside him and talk to him.

We Danis knew nothing about medicine, and we did not know about prayer to God. We did not even know there was a God. When someone was sick we only knew that the evil spirits who we believed in were angry and were punishing us. Spirits were causing my brother to be so very sick—at least that is what we thought. My parents knew they must give a sacrifice so the spirits would be pacified. Then they would go away and leave my brother alone. When a child was sick, usually one pig was killed and given as an offering. My father killed three pigs. But even three pigs did not help. My little brother died! A loud cry of grief rose from my mother's hut. The death wail announced the news to everyone in the village.

My world came to an end. My brother was dead. All the villagers were crying and wailing and smearing themselves with mud. Some cut themselves with a bamboo knife so blood ran down on their faces. Others cut off a finger. All this was a continued effort to appease the spirits. We had no hope!

After two days they cremated my brother's body in a large fire built in the center of the village. My uncle took a bamboo knife and sliced off a piece of my ear and threw it in the funeral pyre. I understood he did this to show the evil spirits our deep sorrow over the death of my brother. My ear hurt and it bled, but that was nothing compared to the emptiness of my life without my little brother.

Eventually a time of peace came to our community. Bows and arrows were used again for something besides killing people. My father and his men were planning a hunting trip to the high forest country. He said I could go with them. I needed my own bow and arrows so my father made me a set. Then he taught me how to shoot. I practiced shooting a lot and set up a target near the village. Sometimes I had a moving target when a little lizard dared to come near. Learning these skills of a man was great. I wanted to be a good hunter.

On this trip the men planned to hunt a small jungle animal that lived in the trees. Animals of any kind were very hard to find in the forest around our village. However, knowing this didn't dampen the enthusiasm of the men to be off on a hunt, and I was right with them. I didn't actually get a shot at an animal or even see a live one, but my uncle did. He shot one and shared the meat with all of us. The meat was roasted in the camp fire and it tasted so good.

That night sitting around the camp fire, the men told story after story, very exciting stories, about hunting and being in the forest. There was no talk of killing the enemy. On this trip I really liked being with the men. They even treated me like I was one of them.

I began to admire my father more and looked up to him as he led the other men. He was a good hunter and I wanted to be a good hunter too. He knew how to survive in the jungle and find food. He was skilled in all the ways of Dani men—ways of life passed down from our ancestors. I wanted to be a man like my father.

The season came to harvest the pandanus palm nut clusters that grew in the forest. [These nuts ripen every 18-20 months.] During a time of war the precious nuts were left to fall and rot on the jungle floor or be eaten by rodents and insects. It was too dangerous to go nut hunting during war, for the enemy would surely find your camp site. Why was this true? No one can survive in the cold, rainy forest without a fire. Where there is fire, there is smoke. The enemy would soon spot the smoke and it would lead them right to where we were. For this reason no one made a camping trip into the forest during a time of war.

This nut-season there was peace. A party from our village set out on a two-week camping trip to hunt jungle nuts. For the first time in my life I was going nut hunting. We got to our base camp that evening. The next morning we fanned out in groups of two or three looking for a palm tree with nuts. I found my first cluster. There it was high up in the tree almost covered by drooping palm fronds. I let out a hoot and my buddy came to help me cut the large, nut cluster. Then we had to lug the heavy nut cluster through the dense undergrowth, up the steep mountain side and back to camp.

At the end of the day I learned how to roast the large cluster in the fire, break off chunks and then crack the small nut kernels open with my teeth. The rule of the game was to eat all you could hold and then wrap the rest in palm leaf packages ready to carry home. When there were no more nut palms to be found, we all set off for home. I carried a heavy bundle of nuts to share with my family who had stayed in the village.

My next adventure was a fishing trip, or I should say a shrimp gathering trip. In the mountains there are no fish in any of the rivers. The water is just too swift for fish. I had never even seen a fish nor had any of the men in my village.

My father and I, and three other village men, set out for the lake. Each of us carried his bow and arrows, for a man never went anywhere unarmed. He might come across a jungle animal or meet an old enemy. For two days we hiked higher and higher into the mountains, so high no more trees grew at this elevation. Then I saw the shimmering waters of a little lake—our destination.

At the lake it was really cold even in the day time. One morning I discovered a white crust on a puddle by our camp site. This was something I'd never seen before—ice. I'd heard men say it was too cold to grow sweet potatoes in the meadows by the lake or for people to live there. Now I believed them.

However, the little shrimp seemed to thrive in the cold water. My father taught me how to trap the shrimp. It was hard, cold work standing in the shallow water, but at the same time it was fun to catch those little wiggly creatures. When I got too cold, I'd go back to the campfire and warm up. For two days I helped gather shrimp. Both nights I roasted and ate my fill of this special food.

On the third morning we started down the long trail for home. How proud I was to carry this big bundle of live shrimp. As I came into the village, people were greeting me, "*Lavok, lavok,* hello, hello! Welcome back!"

My mother came out of her hut and saw me coming toward her with the bundle on my shoulder, "My son, my dear son, have you brought these for me? I'm so hungry to eat shrimp!"

"Mother, my dear mother, Yes, I brought them just for you!"

A sudden end came to our hunting and gathering trips when another war exploded into our lives. Men from our Sinak Valley had made a trading trip to the Ilaga Valley two days walk to the west. In a dispute over their trade, an angry Sinak man shot an Ilaga man with an arrow. When the Ilaga man died several days later, fighting began. The war lines were drawn. Revenge must be taken. Every man from the Ilaga Valley was duty bound to kill men, any men, from the Sinak Valley. On each side men must be killed until the

Born to be a Chief

score is even or until all men have had their fill of fighting. So began the Great War. [See Story 1 map]

The Ilaga people were Danis like we were. They were from the same tribe and spoke the same language. We even had relatives who lived there. These relatives were now our enemies. With new war lines being drawn the people from the Sinak villages who had been our enemies in all the smaller wars of my lifetime were now our allies in fighting the Ilaga people.

No one knew when and where the next surprise attack would take place. Sporadic fighting continued for months which then turned into years. Many people were killed on both sides—just how many our warriors did not know. As anger grew over more deaths, hatred and the desire to kill in revenge also grew. More clans of people aligned themselves to fight on each side. Damal tribal people who lived in the Ilaga Valley joined the side of their Dani neighbors. Together they declared war against the Damals of the Beoga Valley. Thus the Beoga Damals became allied with us, the Sinak Danis. This was *the* Great War of all time as defined in the living memory of our old men. According to their war councils, it was only to get bigger.

One day I heard a strange sound that grew louder and louder. Everybody heard it. Suddenly the valley erupted with the calls and hoots of men, the call of alarm that warriors give to announce an attack from the enemy. But this was not an attack from our Ilaga enemies. The sound grew still louder—louder than the hooting of every man in the valley. Then I saw it—a roaring bird. Closer and closer it came. It swooped low several times and then flew away just as suddenly as it had appeared. What could this be? It wasn't a bird, at least not a bird from our world. Perhaps it came from the spirit world.

This time I wanted to hear the talk of the old men, as they sat around the fire at night. They kept all knowledge of the spirit world. What was this strange thing that had appeared? The men would surely know.

Some declared it was from the spirit world. Others said they had heard of strange foreign beings that had come to the Ilaga. These beings must be the source of the roaring bird. No one dared to walk the two days to the Ilaga Valley to find out, because they would surely be killed. Rumors continued to circulate as fast as the roaring bird had flown.

BIBLE LESSON

Our brothers, we want you to know the truth about those who have died, so that you will not be sad, as are those who have no hope. We believe that Jesus died and rose again, and so we believe that God will take back with Jesus those who have died believing in him.

1 Thessalonians 4: 13-14

Everyone who calls out to the Lord for help will be saved. But how can they call to him for help if they have not believed? And how can they believe if they have not heard the message? And how can they hear if the message is not proclaimed? And how can the message be proclaimed if the messengers are not sent out? Romans 10:13-15

Anthropologists who oppose the message of the Bible argue that primitive tribal people like the Danis should be left untouched by missionaries. They say outsiders should not destroy their beautiful culture. True, the hunting and gathering trips that Zakarias enjoyed with his father were beautiful. In things like this the missionary should not and did not interfere. However, their wars were anything but beautiful. There was no hope for the family who lost their little son in death. The Bible message does bring change; it brings peace in place of war. It brings hope to grieving families.

The roaring bird that flew into the Sinak Valley was flown by a man who in World War II had flown from a US aircraft carrier in the Pacific. Now he flew a missionary over the Sinak to look for a place where an airstrip could be built. This was another step, arranged by God, to bring good news into the life of Zakarias.

ISSUES TO CONSIDER

1. Do you agree with the anthropologist who says the missionary should leave primitive people as they are? If not, why not?
2. Reflect on a family's hope when a member who is a believer dies. Compare this to when the little brother of Zakarias died?

Chapter 3

New Life in Sinak

Zakarias continues his story:

One day, quite some time after the roaring-bird had appeared, a lone white man [Bill Stieglitz] walked into our valley and pitched his tent in an open area where no one lived. There he stayed. He spoke in broken Dani, and offered to pay wages to anyone who would work for him in clearing the field where he camped. He told us the Danis in the Ilaga had cleared a field and on that spot the roaring bird sat down. If we would clear this area the roaring bird would also sit down in our valley.

Everyone was talking about this strange being and what he was saying. Was he a man like we were? Rumor from the Ilaga had it that he was a man but different from us. Most said whatever he was didn't matter. He was giving out cowry shells. This little seashell was our currency. He also gave beautiful blue beads and everybody wanted these. The shells and beads were for daily wages to anyone who worked on clearing the field. Also he gave a steel axe to men who contracted to clear a larger section of the rocky field. Man or spirit being, it mattered not. We wanted the things he gave to anyone who worked for him.

I went up to this field with a lot of other teenage boys to see what was going on. I was small for my age so I pushed to the front of the crowd to get a good look at this strange-looking person. All of a sudden the man handed me his Dani net-bag saying, "Carry this for me." Inside the bag were tokens he was giving out to people working on the airstrip. Later he redeemed the tokens for cowry shells or blue beads.

He motioned that I should follow him, and I did. For a couple of hours I stayed right with him as he crisscrossed the field talking to men who were working. Later we arrived at his tent. He took two cookies out of his things and gave them to me. At first I was afraid. Was this something to eat? Then I took a bite. This flat little thing didn't taste much like a sweet potato, but it was good. From then on, I was the missionary's helper.

New Life in Sinak

The missionary began to build a cabin. Men brought in poles, rough boards and bark and he paid them well. However, he did not ask for rattan vine to use to tie it all together like we did in building a house. He had metal nails and used these to hold the boards in place.

When the cabin was finished someone else came walking into our valley. It was the missionary's wife [Beverly Stieglitz] with her baby daughter. I now became the family helper, splitting fire wood and building the fire for cooking. They had dishes, something I'd never seen before. I learned to wash dishes. Sometimes it was my job to watch the little girl so no harm would come to her.

Every day hundreds of Danis worked on the airstrip. The work took a long time to move the dirt and all those rocks because we Danis had only wooden digging sticks and our bare hands to do the work. It seemed the missionary never stopped saying, "We must make this area smoother," or "It's not long enough. We must prepare a new section at the bottom."

At last, one early morning we again heard that strange roaring sound. It grew louder and louder. Again our valley echoed with the war calls of men, announcing not the arrival of the enemy but the arrival of the roaring bird. The little airplane circled and this time sat down on the airstrip. Out of the roaring bird stepped a man—how amazing! There was singing and dancing on the airstrip that day. The roaring bird had come to our valley.

Two years went by. During this time the missionary was learning to speak our language better. One day he said, "Zakarias, come and sit down with me. I want to tell you about a man named Jesus." The missionary held a paper in his hand, and he read John 3:16 in Dani. He had me repeat the words until I could say them myself. Then he explained that God loved all people so much that he sent his son Jesus to earth. He died for our sins. I needed to believe on Jesus myself so that I might have everlasting life. That day I opened my heart and life to Jesus and something happened. I had a peaceful feeling inside of me for the very first time. I know now that it was the Holy Spirit who came into my life. I was a new person.

From then on when the missionary went to a village to tell people about Jesus, he took me with him. You see, the missionary spoke our Dani language, but most people still had trouble understanding what he was saying. In the village, after the people gathered, the missionary talked to them. He spoke one sentence at a time and I repeated it after him, changing his words into better spoken Dani. Even though it wasn't proper for a teenage boy to speak to adult men about things of the spirit world, they listened as I spoke the words in clear Dani. The men began to understand. Something else was happening, although I didn't realize it at the time. I was learning how to tell others about Jesus.

My family lived in a village across the big river from the airstrip. Sometimes I crossed the river on the long and very old bridge to visit them. How I wished the missionary would go with me, for I had a deep desire in my heart to have my father and my mother come to know Jesus too. But the missionary never came because of the bridge. He said to me, "Zakarias, you can tell them of Jesus without me."

I did begin telling my parents and all the people of my village about Jesus. I knew they understood what I was saying. Soon the villagers began to make fun of me like they did when I was a boy and refused to sleep in the men's house. This time they became so upset they threw me out of the village. Even though this happened more than once, I still kept going back.

First my mother asked Jesus to come into her heart. What a happy day that was for me. It was harder for my father, I think, because he was an important war-chief and leader in all the spirit appeasement rituals in Dani life. Later, he did make that decision and put away all the trappings of the past. I look forward to one day being with both my father and my mother in heaven.

BIBLE LESSON

So then faith comes from hearing the message, and the message comes through preaching Christ. Romans 10:17

The next day John [the Baptist] was standing there again with two of his disciples, when he saw Jesus walking by. "There is the Lamb of God!" he said.

The two disciples heard him say this and went with Jesus. . . and spent the rest of that day with him.

One of them was Andrew. . . At once he found his brother Simon [Peter] and told him, "We have found the Messiah.". . .

The next day Jesus . . . found Philip and said to him, "Come with me!" Philip found Nathanael and told him, "We have found the one whom Moses wrote about in the book of the Law." Condensed from John 1:35-43

New Life in Sinak

It's truly amazing—that a boy, born to a Stone Age Dani war-chief in a valley high in the mountains on the island of New Guinea, born in a tribe and place completely unknown to the outside world, heard the message of Jesus and was born again. Before this took place in 1961, there was a vast network of God's people, working over many years, to make it possible for this missionary family to walk into the Sinak Valley at this precise time.

Zakarias learned how to explain the message of salvation because he was a language helper to the missionary. Then, with his strong love for his family, he went across the river and shared his faith with his own mother and father.

God has a perfect plan, a very intricate plan for the life of every one of us. What a privilege it is to follow that plan and then be involved in sharing our faith with others.

ISSUES TO CONSIDER

1. From the point of view of the missionary, note the things that had to take place before Zakarias could hear and receive Christ.

2. From the point of view of Zakarias, note what took place before he made his decision for Christ.

3. In John 1:35-43 it's interesting to observe the number of men who came to Christ and how they were connected to one another. This same natural chain of conversions happened in the life of Zakarias and spontaneously all over the mountains of Papua. Reflect on a similar chain of conversions that you may have observed.

Chapter 4
Seven Years of School

Zakarias continues his story:

I was the first Dani in the Sinak Valley to receive Jesus. I was also the first one to be baptized. Not long after I gave my life to God, others in the valley made this same decision. After a time the missionary planned a baptismal service. Remember that none of us had ever seen such a service. Also at that time there were hundreds of people, including my father, who strongly opposed our decision. When Sunday came, I was the only one who stepped into the pool of water prepared for baptism. None of the others were brave enough to take this public step of testimony. The other candidates came to the service, watched and cried the whole time, knowing they too should be baptized. One week later God gave them courage and they were baptized.

Soon after this, whole villages in the Sinak began to turn from the spirit appeasement practice of their ancestors and follow the Lord. A missionary linguist who lived in the Ilaga had written an alphabet for the Dani language and translated the Book of Mark into Dani. With reading primers sent from the Ilaga our missionary taught me how to read. Then it was my turn to help others in learning to read. All the new Christians wanted to learn, because they wanted to read God's Word.

Again the missionary invited me to sit with him for a special talk. "Zakarias," he said, "I can see that God has something special for you to do with your life. I believe he is calling you to teach your own people. I have explained to you the way of Jesus; I taught you many of the stories in the Bible and I taught you how to read. But there is much more in the Bible that I cannot teach you. So far, there are only a couple books from the Bible translated into your Dani language. You need to study the whole Bible in the Indonesian language. Then you will be able to teach your people the complete Word of God. But first, before you attend an Indonesian Bible School, you must learn the Indonesian language. There is a new school just for that, and I think you should go. It is in the Ilaga Valley and . . ." [See story 2 map]

After the words, "Ilaga Valley," I heard no more. True, it was said the Great War was over. But the Ilaga meant only one thing to me—fear of being killed. This was the place where our enemies lived. In war the aim was to kill more on the enemy's side than

Seven Years of School

were killed on our side. If the enemy was unable to kill warriors, then killing any unprotected person was just as good. To kill was all that mattered.

My mind flashed back to war when I was a child. I had to run and hide in the forest. Hiding there for days I had nothing to eat. I was so afraid I couldn't sleep. All this came back to me.

Then God quieted my heart. I was learning to trust God to take care of me even when I was afraid.

So I did walk the two days to the Ilaga Valley and began to attend the school. First I learned some everyday phrases in Indonesian, and then I learned to read and write. For three years I attended the "Prep School," as they called it, taught by a man from the Mee Tribe. I got a copy of the Indonesian Bible and I was learning to read it.

Most of the students in the school were from the Ilaga, so their families supplied their food. My family, who lived far away in Sinak, could not bring me food. And there were no stores to buy food in Dani country. Yet all the time I attended the Prep School I had enough to eat. Guess where my sweet potatoes came from? I ate the potatoes and lived in the house of my distant relatives—a family who had been our bitter enemies during the Great War. They, like most of the others in the Ilaga, were now Christians. God had taken the desire to kill right out of their hearts.

After finishing the Prep School I was ready for the next step in my life, the Indonesian Bible School. It was located in a village more than two week's walk to the west—so far that, in Sinak Dani history, no one had ever walked there. To get there I had to fly in an airplane—one just like the roaring bird that first flew into our valley. [See story 2 map]

I was excited and a bit scared on the day I climbed into the airplane. For almost an hour we flew over mountains and valleys, over rivers and more mountains. All my life I had lived in these mountains, hiked the trails up and over one mountain just to go down the other side. Now I was flying, with no effort at all, over mountains that were unending—as far as I could see.

When we landed on the dirt airstrip, mountains still surrounded us, but their peaks were at some distance. The airstrip was near a large lake. This lake was huge compared to the little lake where I had hiked with my father to catch shrimp. Shrimp lived in this lake too, but these were much larger.

The Mee people who lived here had dugout canoes. In their canoes the women went out on the lake at night to fish for shrimp. Some nights I could see dots of light all over the lake. Each dot was a little fire in a canoe. The fire helped keep the woman warm as she worked with her net to catch shrimp. In these same canoes in daylight hours, the men paddled back and forth across the lake to carry on their business deals. The village people spoke a language I could not understand, yet they were still mountain people who planted sweet potato gardens for their food. Their traditional attire was the same as ours, and their houses were similar to our Dani houses.

The Bible School was quite different from the Ilaga bush school. Here the students all wore western clothes. Most of the classes were taught by a missionary and his wife, John and Janine Schultz. What wonderful people they were to me. They taught me much about God in the classroom, during the chapel hour and in every contact I had with them.

One student had a wristwatch. He rang the bell to signal the time for all of the student activities. We got up with the bell; we went to school with the bell; we changed classes every hour with the bell; and again after dark we went back to school to study with the ringing of the bell. At night we didn't study with light from a fire but with light from a kerosene pressure lamp which hung in the center of the room. How different this was from my childhood days when the only regulation to our day was the rising and setting of the sun.

I spent four years at this Bible school, studying every part of the Bible. New subjects to me were church history and world religions. We also had classes on how to develop and preach a sermon and how to serve as the pastor of a congregation.

In some ways though, these were long and lonely years for me because no one else at the school spoke my Dani language. At times I longed to have a wife like some of the other students. Yet it was a time to keep-on-keeping-on, a time to finish the course set before me.

When I got back home after graduation, I found my family had chosen a young Christian woman to be my wife. In our Dani culture the groom's family always chooses his bride. Another part of the marriage arrangement was payment of the bride-price. The groom's family paid this to the family of the bride. All this was done for me just like the marriages of my ancestors. I had no money to add to the payment, but that didn't matter. My turn would come in the future to help with a payment when other young men in my family were to be married. As in generations past, pigs were the main part of the bridal payment. There was one change though. Now, instead of using cowry shells in the payment, Indonesian money was given. I was glad I was to be married. I liked the young woman my family had chosen for me.

The next years were some of the best years of my life. Five children were born into our family. I felt very happy to be the pastor of a large and growing church and to see my Dani people come to know and serve the Lord.

BIBLE LESSON

>Fear of man will prove to be a snare, but whoever trusts in the LORD is kept safe. Proverbs 29:25 NIV

>Add to your faith goodness; and to goodness, knowledge; and to knowledge, self-control; and to self-control, perseverance; and to perseverance, godliness. 2 Peter 1:5-6 NIV

>Let us run with perseverance [determination] the race marked out for us. Hebrews 12:1 NIV

Zakarias overcame his lifelong fear of being killed by "the enemy" by placing his trust in the Lord. He went to the Ilaga where God turned this threat into a blessing. Those former enemies now provided him with food and housing for the three years he was in Prep School.

Using terms of today's world, we might compare the war experience of Zakarias to child abuse. Whatever fear we might have because of negative treatment, there is real deliverance from that fear through trust in the Lord.

God's call to Zakarias was to become a pastor of his own people. To do the best job in this calling required seven years of school, all away from home. These years were not easy for a young man who had never been far from his small village or ever attended a school of any kind. (Read again 2 Peter 1:5-6.) Beginning with faith in Christ, Zakarias added knowledge through study of the Bible. He learned self-control, which brought perseverance. These disciplines, taken step-by-step, brought him to a life of godliness. Zakarias passed the tests of these years; however bigger tests were yet to come.

ISSUES TO CONSIDER

1. Fears! We all have them. Since we can't always eliminate the cause, how should we deal with them?

2. We're never too young or too old to learn. Learning doesn't have to take place in a formal school setting, although it often does. Learning does need to be in a place, or in a way, where you gain knowledge that fits your life and gifts. What skill, course of study or new book might interest you?

Chapter 5

The Big City

Zakarias continues his story:

Life was good. I was serving as the senior pastor of a large and growing church. My wife had just given birth to our fifth child. I now had three sons and two daughters. Everything was going very well for me.

Then one day, the missionary asked me to come to his house. This missionary was new to our valley, and I was not close to him like I'd been to the first missionary. Seated in his living room the missionary said, "Zakarias, a new Bible school is going to be opened soon. This school is an advanced Bible school taught in the Indonesian language. I think you should go."

My first question was, "Where is this school?" I'd gone from Sinak to the Ilaga—where our enemies lived—for my first years of school. Then I'd gone to the Indonesian language school where the Mee people live—for four more years. "Is it in the mountains?" I asked.

"No, it's in Nabi. You've heard of Nabi, I'm sure. It's an Indonesian town on the coast where MAF (Mission Aviation Fellowship) airplanes are based." After a pause he added, "Nabi is really a *kota,* it's a city. In the city people don't plant sweet potato gardens, and they don't live in Dani style huts. But don't worry. You'd live in the Bible school dormitory." [See story 2 Map]

"But I have a wife and five children," I said.

"Yes, I know. You'd have to go alone at first, and later they could join you."

"Thank you," I said, and left.

As I walked the long trail home from the missionary's house, my heart was pounding. Did God want me to go to Nabi? Did I want to go? I had no money. Sunday offerings given to me as pastor were given in sweet potatoes, not in rupiahs. The two other times I'd gone to school I was single. This time I had a family. The missionary had said I'd have to leave my wife and children in Sinak.

Born to be a Chief

In a week I knew what my answer would be. I decided to trust God and go. I went right to the missionary's house. Standing in his doorway I said, "Please arrange a flight for me. I'm going to school in Nabi."

"Great, I'm glad you made that decision," he said. "I'll radio the pilot with your flight request. After they read the flight schedule next Thursday, I'll let you know when the flight will be made. One seat from here to Nabi costs 36,000 rupiahs. Will you have the money by then?"

I nodded my head and left. I didn't tell the missionary, but I had no idea where the money would come from.

All my friends and relatives heard my story, but no one offered any money—no one that is except my uncle. He gave me 15,000 rupiahs.

The morning came for my flight. I said goodbye to my wife and children. Still trusting God to get me to Nabi, I headed up the long trail to the airstrip. I was almost there when I heard the faint buzz of the airplane and once again shouts erupted around the valley. Everyone was running to the top of the airstrip. When I got there, the missionary asked for the money for my ticket. "I have to give 36,000 rupiahs to the pilot," he said.

"Here's my 15,000 rupiahs. This is all I have."

The missionary shook his head in disapproval, took it and said, raising his voice, "That's not enough!"

Right then the plane was at the top of the airstrip. Everyone was talking and running around the plane in total confusion. No one paid any attention to me. I knew God wanted me to attend the new Bible School in Nabi, so I decided to climb into the one empty seat and buckle my seat belt. This I knew how to do because I had flown before. Just before the pilot closed my door he checked my seat belt and handed me back the same 15,000 rupiah bills I'd given the missionary. Someone had paid for my ticket I knew, but to this day I don't know who that was.

We landed in the big city. At the plane the missionary from the Bible school met me. "We're sorry Zakarias," he said, "but we have no place for you to stay. The new school complex is not completed yet. I'm sure you can find some fellow Danis and stay with them." The missionary knew, and so did I, that any Dani, though he be a complete stranger, is always welcome in the home of another Dani. I would be welcome in any Dani house.

"Thank you," I said, and he was gone.

The Big City

I walked away from the air field and stood in the shade of a building. This was no Dani village. This was a *kota*. I had seen airplanes, and always men rode in them, but I'd never seen an airplane without wings, or one that ran on the ground and didn't take off. Then I remembered the Indonesian word, *oto,* from a story I had read about a city. These must be *otos*, I thought. There were lots of them going every which way and honking their horns.

Darting in and out between the autos was something else. These things each had a man sitting on a seat supported by only two wheels. The noise these things made was almost as loud as the sound of an airplane. I shook my head in amazement. And how strange-looking the people were who rode in the cars and on the motor bikes. They didn't look like people from the mountains or like missionaries. They were Indonesians. Watching all of this I knew there were no Dani people in those cars. Even if there were some Danis in this city, I had no idea how to find them.

I saw a path along the side of the street. Picking up my bundle of clothing, I started walking. After some time I came to a very large building with a sign saying, "Government Representative Building." I went inside this government office building and asked if there was a place I could stay. The man I asked happened to be the head official of the area, but this I did not know. He looked me over and after what seemed a very long time he said, "If you will sweep the courtyard, you can sleep tonight in that large empty room at the back." Pointing toward the back he handed me a broom.

Sitting on the cement floor in this large meeting room I was very lonely and VERY hungry. Looking through a window I spotted a single banana tree with a small stalk of ripe bananas on it. Bats always eat bananas left on the tree to ripen, but no bat had even nibbled on these bananas. The more I looked, the hungrier I got. I wondered, would that be stealing if I ate those bananas? I remembered the story of Jesus, and how He ate corn from someone's field when He was hungry. So that night I ate bananas, used banana leaves for a blanket and slept alone on the cement floor.

The next morning I found my way to the church where classes of the new Bible School would meet until a building for the school was completed. In that first class there were 19 men from the Mee Tribe and me. The first tuition payment, 15,000 rupiahs, was due that day. That's exactly what I had, the same worn rupiah bills my uncle had given me.

After school I was wondering how I could earn some money to buy food. God had provided bananas for my first day, but I couldn't expect that to happen again. Walking down the street I came upon a coastal man splitting fire wood. I figured out he was a man from the coast, because his skin color was just a bit lighter than mine, and his hair was kinky, like mine, not straight like an Indonesian's hair. Splitting wood was something I learned to do when I was a teenager, so I asked him, "May I help you split your wood?" The man agreed, and handed me his axe.

Near evening, the owner of the large house where we were working, came out and talked to me. Mohammad was his name, and he asked my name. Calling me by name he said, "Zakarias, I see you are a hard worker. Would you like to work for me as a yard-boy? You can sleep at the back of my house and eat with my servants."

"Yes sir, I would like that very much," I replied.

This was a new world for me. Two days earlier I had said goodbye to my wife and five children. I had been the pastor of the largest church in the Sinak valley. Now I was to live with the servants of a prominent Muslim man from another island of Indonesia, earning my keep as his yard-boy. All of my life my food had been sweet potatoes; now it was to be rice. Yet I was thankful, for God was providing everything I needed.

One day walking on the street, I spotted a man who looked like a Dani. He turned out to be a Dani from the Ilaga where I had first gone to the bush school to learn Indonesian.

It was so good to hear someone speak my own language. "There is quite a group of Dani men here in Nabi," he told me. "We live in Dani style huts at the edge of town."

I was thinking, God has provided a much better place for me to live than huts way out of town. I was living right in town and my food was provided in the deal.

I said to the man, "Is there a Dani church group meeting here in Nabi?"

"No," he replied, "And most of us don't go to church because we don't understand the Indonesian spoken in the churches here."

My quick response was, "I can be your preacher, but where can we meet?" Then I thought of the large empty room in the government building where I had slept my first night. I went to the official and asked him. He gave his permission to use that room on Sunday. So it was, I began preaching every Sunday morning to my new Dani congregation in a room that belonged to the Indonesian government.

The Big City

BIBLE LESSON

Those who trust in the Lord are protected by his constant love. Psalms 32:10

Keep your lives free from the love of money, and be satisfied with what you have. For God has said, "I will never leave you; I will never abandon you." Let us be bold, then, and say, "The Lord is my helper, I will not be afraid." Hebrews 13:5-6

An ordinary man from the mountains would never have had the audacity to enter a prestigious government building in the city and ask for a place to sleep. But Zakarias was both the son of a Dani chief and the son of his heavenly Father. He spoke with the dignity of a chieftain and the humility of a Christian who was trusting God to supply his immediate need.

Zakarias landed all alone in an unfamiliar world, yet he was surrounded by God's loving care. His Heavenly Father provided his "daily bread" not in the familiar sweet potato but first in the form of bananas and after that, rice. His money was just enough to pay his first school bill.

We may need to trust God in something involving money, or perhaps we need a job. Maybe it's getting along better with another person, or adjusting to a new situation or to new food. With each step of faith that Zakarias took God provided his immediate need. All the while his steps of faith were preparing him for greater tests to come. And this same pattern is true in each of our lives.

ISSUES TO CONSIDER

1. In the life of Zakarias what character trait do you admire?

2. Has God provided some things in your life in an unusual way, as he did for Zakarias?

Chapter 6

Still Trusting God

Zakarias continues telling his story:

One evening two weeks after I'd come to Nabi, I was sitting with the other servants in the room behind the big house. The talk of the men was of no interest to me. My thoughts turned to the day I came to Nabi. One thought led to another—like climbing up the branches of a tree.

In the plane the day I flew to Nabi, I was glued to the window all the way. After the endless jumble of mountains I had seen this dark mass in the distance. Was it more mountains? As we got closer I knew it must be water—maybe that was the ocean. On descent, the plane circled several times over Nabi. Each time around I had caught another glimpse of the ocean. There it was sparkling in the sunlight. After the plane landed and I was on the ground, I looked down the airstrip to see the ocean again, right at the end of the runway.

All this was forgotten until this evening. I'd been in Nabi for two weeks and still hadn't seen the ocean water up close. Right then I determined I'd go the very next day and see it.

After classes were over the next afternoon, I set out walking, headed toward the water. I took my Bible with me thinking I could read it in silence, away from the talk of the other servants. The walk was long and the afternoon hot. I longed for the cool of the mountains and for my family. I kept walking and finally came to a barrier of brush and trash. I pushed through it and there before me was the ocean!

The water shimmered in the sunlight, and tiny waves broke along the shore. I could see no end to the water; no mountain peaks marked the far edge. The beach stretched in both directions until in the distance the land curved. No human was in sight.

I spotted a clump of trees down the beach and started walking in that direction. Under the shade of a tree I sat down, not to read at first, but just to look at the water. I thought, I'm seeing what God did in the story of creation when He said, "Let the water under the sky be gathered in one place, and let dry ground appear." Until today, looking at the ocean, I could not imagine what this meant.

Then I saw a lone figure walking down the beach coming in my direction. As he got closer I saw it was a man with black kinky hair like mine, a tall man, taller than any man from the mountains. He must be a coastal person, I thought. Closer he came. He was huge, bigger than any man I'd ever seen. He saw me sitting under the tree and turned—walking toward me. A pang of fear struck me. Maybe I shouldn't be here.

"*Selamat sore*," he said.

I stood and returned his greeting, "Good afternoon."

This giant of a man looked at my Bible and then he looked right at me and said, "Where are you from?"

"The mountains," I answered.

He persisted, "Where in the mountains?"

"I come from a valley called Sinak, far back in the mountains."

His next question: "What are you doing here in Nabi?"

"I'm attending the new Bible school which meets in Bethel church" He asked more questions, and I told him my name was Zakarias Tabuni. "Before coming here I served as pastor of a large church."

"Are you married?" he asked.

"Yes," I told him. "I left my wife and five children back in Sinak because I have no place for them to stay."

The man paused, looking me over again. "My name is Goliath Bariyat," he said.

I thought to myself, I can see why he has the name of Goliath. He really is the size of a giant.

The man went on, "I'm a school teacher and I attend the GKI protestant church. I want to help you in Bible school, Zakarias. At the beginning of each month, after I get my pay check, I want to give you a tithe of what I earn."

Goliath must have sensed my disbelief. He took a scrap of paper from his pocket and wrote on it. Handing it to me he said, "Here! This is my name and address."

Born to be a Chief

Goliath turned and walked away. What kind of a joke is this? I thought. No one would ever do such a thing. He thinks I'm naïve—like a child; it would be fun to tease me. I stuck the paper in my Bible and began to read.

Then one day, just as our classes were finishing at the Bethel church, a man appeared and asked for Zakarias Tabuni.

The missionary pointed to me and said, "That's Zakarias right over there."

It was the first day of the new month, payday for government workers. My heart skipped a beat. Could this be something to do with Goliath and his promise?

The man said, "My friend, Goliath, asked me to come here. He wants you to come to his house. I'll take you there on my motorbike."

"Okay," I said. "But, but—I've never ridden on a motorbike."

"You'll be all right; just sit behind me."

I held my breath and we started off. This scared me more than flying in an airplane. Now I was one of those people who was darting about between the cars, and just balancing on two wheels.

In no time at all we arrived at the little house where Goliath lived. After we exchanged greetings Goliath explained, "I want to help you attend Bible school by giving you the tithe from my wages. I will deliver it to the missionary each month, to pay your school expenses."

Goliath Bariyat did just that. At the first of every month for the next three years, Goliath made a payment for my tuition and books at the Bible school.

When I look back over my life, I think I've learned a lesson about money. I had no money to attend the school in Nabi, but I knew God wanted me there. I went and God supplied just what I needed every time. I learned never to hold back because of money. Go and do what God is calling you to do; He will supply your needs.

I wrote a letter to my wife back in Sinak and told her of the miracle God was doing for me. All my school expenses were being paid by Goliath. I told her the school buildings still were not ready. I hoped, as soon as they were finished, she could come to Nabi. When I wrote that letter, I had no idea what was just around the corner.

Still Trusting God

BIBLE LESSON

They put their trust in God and prayed to him for help, and God answered their prayers.

1 Chronicles 5:20

Honor the Lord with your wealth, with the firstfruits of all your crops. Proverbs 3:9 NIV

"Bring the whole tithe into the storehouse," . . . says the Lord Almighty, "and see if I will not throw open the floodgates of heaven and pour out so much blessing that you will not have room enough for it." Malachi 3:10 NIV

Zakarias continued to trust God even in this world of the big city. Who would have dreamed of Zakarias meeting Goliath and the outcome it brought? How often God answers our prayers, not exactly in the way we asked. And then sometimes He answers in a way that is far beyond anything we had imagined.

Even as I wrote the paragraph above, my carefully put-together plan to meet a financial need of someone close to me was rejected by a person in authority. Though it did not actually affect my own bank account, the need was still a very emotional matter to me. During the night hours when I should have been sleeping, this whole thing was churning in my mind. Then I remembered the verses I'd just written on this page. "They put their trust in God and prayed to him for help, and God answered their prayers."

God reminded me of the times, too many to count, when He had supplied my financial need, and the times when He allowed *me* to supply the need of another person. I'll let you know how this one comes out. Well, not really. I already know the outcome. God is faithful. He will supply the need and do it in His way, not in mine.

Even though Zakarias never told me, I know Goliath was blessed by God—blessed to overflowing because he faithfully returned to God his tithe. How do I know? God's Word says so. Anyone who gives his whole tithe will be abundantly blessed.

I too can testify of God's abundant blessing. I began to tithe with my first earnings as a young teen. With my husband we have given a tithe and more to God's work all our life. Perhaps God has adjusted our thinking to be modest in what we desire and given us some wisdom in managing what we have, but always we have more than enough.

Born to be a Chief

ISSUES TO CONSIDER

1. Do you think the practice of giving a tithe of one's income is important to a follower of Jesus?

2. Put the story together that must have been in the background of Goliath. Do you think he was already tithing before he met Zakarias? How did it happen that Goliath was walking on that beach at that time so he could make the promise to help Zakarias?

Chapter 7

The Unexpected Tragedy

Zakarias continues his story:

Three months after I arrived in Nabi, the missionary called me aside saying he wanted to talk to me. He said, "I've just received a message from Sinak on the short wave radio. It's very bad news, Zakarias. I wish I didn't have to tell you this. Your wife died yesterday."

What was he saying? My mind was totally confused. I didn't even know my wife was sick.

The missionary added, "She had a high fever—and then died, very suddenly."

My wife, who I had said goodbye to three months ago, was gone. The mother of my five children was gone. I had promised to bring her to Nabi soon and now she would never come. My life went blank before me.

The next morning at daylight I was on a plane flying back to Sinak—to bury my wife. Now I must be both mother and father to my five children. My sorrow was overwhelming, but with it was a quiet peace and hope. My wife was in heaven and I would see her again some day.

Stepping out of the plane in Sinak, I saw my baby boy. A woman carried him. His first two teeth had just appeared. Someone must nurse him, or he too would die. First one woman who had a baby of her own shared her breast milk. Then another woman nursed my baby, but this could not be a long term arrangement.

I took my son to my mother. She began to suckle the baby at her breast. At first, this was like giving him a pacifier, but after a time her body began to produce a little milk and then a little more. God did a miracle in causing my old mother to have breast milk. The missionary lady also gave my mother a baby bottle and powdered milk. She taught her how to mix the milk powder with water and feed my little son.

I left the baby with my mother. In time my baby grew. Most babies at his age had only their mother's milk. My mother learned how to give my son other foods like bananas and cooked sweet potatoes. She also gave him food that did not even exist in

Born to be a Chief

Sinak when I was born—chicken eggs and peanuts. The peanuts were boiled and then mashed. My baby boy grew and even thrived without his mother.

I gave my three-year-old daughter to another relative who would care for her and become her step-mother.

In our Dani tribe the family is a large unit of people and very tightly knit. It was this extended family that arranged my marriage and made the large bride price payment. Now it was natural for all the children to be raised by my extended family. I knew that only a woman could care for the two smaller children.

I wanted to keep the other children with me. It was not our Dani culture for me, as a single father, to raise my three older children without a wife. However, within the week my three children and I were in the little airplane flying back to Nabi and school.

The Bible school complex was still not ready. For almost a year my children and I lived with the servants at the back of the big house of Mohammad. I enrolled them in an elementary school. There was no government school in my Sinak village, so they had never been in school and they did not speak Indonesian. All three were put in the same first grade class. I think being able to start off together in the same classroom helped them adjust to this new world. Their age mates in Sinak did not have the opportunity of going to school but my children did!

Life was complicated for me keeping up in the Bible school and at the same time being both mother and father to my children. Through all this time God was faithful in supplying our every need. Each month Goliath paid my school bills. My ability in the Indonesian language really improved, for Indonesian was the only language I could use in school and in town. I learned to know and appreciate people from all parts of Indonesia—even the man I worked for, a Muslim from another island and from a very different culture.

In three years I graduated with my class, this very first class to enter the Nabi Bible School.

BIBLE LESSON

Jesus said, "Do not let your hearts be troubled. Trust in God; trust also in me. In my Father's house are many rooms. . . I am going there to prepare a place for you. And if I go and prepare a place for you, I will come back and take you to be with me that you also may be where I am." John 14:1-3 NIV

The Unexpected Tragedy

Good people suffer many troubles, but the Lord saves them from them all. Psalms 34:10

My friends, consider yourselves fortunate when all kinds of trials come your way, for you know that when your faith succeeds in facing such trials, the result is the ability to endure. James 1:2-3

Tears almost came to my eyes as I put this part of Zakarias's story on paper. He experienced the ultimate trial of losing his wife and the mother of his children. God never left Zakarias and Zakarias never turned away from God. When I compare my life to his, the life I live today seems rather mundane. Yet I know as I put my faith and trust in God, God will see me through my challenges and trials. He will do the same for you.

John 14:1-3 was a comfort to Zakarias as it has been to millions of others since the time of Jesus. The words of Jesus are not only an encouragement in life, but a comfort in death.

ISSUES TO CONSIDER

There are some ways a person may be prepared to face the death of a loved one and in other ways in which no one is ever prepared. What are your thoughts concerning this statement?

Chapter 8
The Wise Dani Chief

Introduction

I met Zakarias in the mid 1980's when my husband and I were expanding our ministry with the Damal people to include visits to the Danis who live in the Sinak. I came to know this man as a gentle giant who refused to become a war-chief like his father and instead became the Christian chief of the entire Sinak Valley.

In 1996, two years after we had retired, Don and I returned to Papua (formerly called Irian Jaya) for a visit. Our schedule was set up to minister in the five church districts where we had formerly served. On this visit while we were in Sinak, I pressed Zakarias to tell me his life's story. The story he told me I have written for you. With further encouragement he also told the three stories that close this chapter—episodes that were happening right at the time of our visit.

Zakarias continues telling his story:

At long last, after our years in Nabi, my three children and I were flying home to Sinak. In the plane we could not talk to each other because of the loud roar of the engine. This created a time for my thoughts. Three years of Bible school and three years of being a single father were coming to an end. I wanted to marry again. This was a good thought to me and it came often. I'd lived too long without a wife.

Then my mind jumped back to the first time the roaring bird flew into Sinak. Before this event the world of my childhood was filled with fighting and was ruled by war-chiefs. After the roaring bird came the missionary. The missionary chose me to be his helper, and I learned to know Jesus myself. I was one of the first to make this decision but soon many others made this same choice. Now in the Sinak Valley most of the Danis attend one of the almost 50 churches located throughout the valley.

The Wise Dani Chief

The plane circled over the airstrip, came around again and landed. People who were standing on the sides of the airstrip swarmed out to surround the airplane. They had heard we were coming. My family and many others were there with hugs and tears to welcome us.

For a second time my extended family made the bride price arrangements so that I could marry. God gave me a good Christian woman to be my wife, and in time He blessed our union with two children.

The annual meeting of the Sinak district pastors came around not long after I returned. These pastors, over a hundred in all, had been trained in one of the Bible schools. This was the year to elect a new district superintendent, the man who leads the pastors and the church of Sinak. I was chosen to serve in this office as their leader. To be given this place of leadership was truly an honor. This made me, in some ways, the Christian chief over the entire Sinak Valley.

As the years went by the Indonesian government became well established in the valley. Government operations included a civil post as well as police and military posts. The civil government officials oversaw endless paperwork, the elementary schools and a clinic. But the real power of government in the entire valley was in the hands of the men who carried the guns, the police and the military. Power rested on their personal discretion or their whims as the case might be. Most police and military men came from other islands of Indonesia. On their tour of duty in Sinak they made no attempt to learn our Dani language or understand our customs, which are very different from theirs.

In 1996 our adopted missionaries (Don and Alice Gibbons) were returning for a visit. Letters had gone back and forth to America with the planned date of their coming. All the church leaders had been invited to come for a seminar and on the weekend there was to be another seminar for the youth. The mission residence which they had given to the church was cleaned and ready for their use once again.

I walked down the steep trail from the airstrip with the lady missionary. She said, "You know, since we are retired, we no longer have a permanent visa which allowed us to teach in your church. My husband cannot speak at the planned seminars unless the chief of police gives his approval and signs our visitor's permit."

Sensing her concern I turned to her and said in a quiet voice, "Don't worry, my mother. The chief of police is a Muslim, but he is also my friend. He will sign your permit." And he did.

Born to be a Chief

In the afternoons of that ten-day visit I told my life story to the lady missionary. When she pressed me for a more current story, I told her about the chief of police and why I was confident he would sign their travel and speaking permits.

This is the story I told her:

Two years ago this new chief of police was appointed to the Sinak District. Madae was his name. He was young, inexperienced and a Muslim from another island. Very soon all the people of Sinak feared this man. Sometimes Madae struck a Dani man for no apparent reason. Worse than that, he personally killed pigs in his style of maintaining law and order.

Being new he did not know that pigs were more important in our Dani economy than rupiahs, the Indonesian currency. To kill a man's pig would be like taking a large part of everything he owned—and to do this for a minor offense was unthinkable.

One day, Madae with two of his officers came across the river to my village. He came to settle a dispute in which a villager had stolen the pig of a lower-ranking policeman. Most of the village people were afraid of the police and had run away and hidden. The villagers could not even talk to the police party, because they did not speak the government language. Since I could speak Indonesian, I stayed in the village with the thief. On entering the village the police chief put handcuffs on the man who stole the pig.

I stepped forward. Madae recognized me as the church leader of all the Sinak. I said politely but firmly, "Sir, open those handcuffs and I'll arrange this." I realized that if this police chief pushed the Danis too far, they might rise up as a group and retaliate.

Madae turned to me saying, "Stand aside or I'll shoot you."

I responded, "Sir, I will report you to your superiors in Nabi if you go too far. You don't know how to handle this dispute."

Immediately, Madae stepped back. He was suddenly quiet and afraid. "Take the handcuffs off," he quickly said. "He must pay five pigs."

"No," I said, "He should pay one big pig for the small one he stole. The penalty should fit the crime."

The next day the thief and I arrived at the police post with a big pig. After the pig was given to the offended man I went to the police chief's office. Madae invited me in. I said to him, "I want to help you. What you are doing is wrong and you must change. Things will go well with you if you and your men don't go about striking people, or killing their pigs, or bothering their women. I'm afraid the Danis may rise up against you if no change is made." God worked in Madae's heart and he accepted what I said.

Two days later I was back in his office. Our friendship had begun. He became "my son" and I became "his father." Madae speaks openly to others about our relationship. He has asked my advice on many cases that come to him. When we are alone, I talk to him about God. Although he is a Muslim, he allows me to pray for him. He often says, "Zakarias, you are my father and God blesses me because of you."

Another story told by Zakarias:

A month ago a group of rebels came to the Sinak. In their party were three big-name rebel leaders and ten other supporting men.

As I began this story, Alice Gibbons interrupted me. I sensed fear in her voice as she said, "Rebels? They were right here just a month ago?"

We both knew the rebels are a small group of tribal men pledged to the violent overthrow of the Indonesian government and takeover of the country. They are ready to fight and die for their cause. Anyone who opposes their plan is their enemy, and that includes the missionaries.

The rebel party was demanding food and lodging from the people as they worked the area recruiting supporters. This put all of us in a difficult position, both with the rebels and the government. Anyone who denied the request of a rebel for food and lodging might receive brutal treatment. Any village that received the rebels, giving food and lodging, could be punished very harshly by the military for supporting the rebels.

I told all the people to receive these men with full Dani hospitality, as they would receive any traveler. Give them food, listen politely to their talk, but don't follow them! Fortunately for the rebels and for me, they kept their exact whereabouts a secret.

Then I went to the heads of the police and military and told them what was going on. I advised them not to go out shooting, or trying to kill a rebel leader and not to punish the village people who fed them. The rebel leaders would be long gone before the military got there. They would only harm innocent people. Both the military and the Dani people took my advice, peace was maintained and the rebels left our valley.

When the rebel leaders left Sinak they went to the Ilaga. The next scheduled stop for the missionaries was also the Ilaga. After hearing this story the missionaries called the Ilaga by two-way shortwave radio, spoke to the district superintendent and asked about any rebel activity in the area. The reply came back, much to everyone's disappointment, the rebels were working in the Ilaga. The church leader felt the rebels might come in the night and harm the missionaries. The trip had to be cancelled.

Born to be a Chief

A third story told by Zakarias:

The newest church to open in the Sinak has an interesting story behind it. For years Nilome, a chief from a near-by village, had called himself a Christian. Sometimes he attended church but that was all. He had three wives and had always promoted local wars.

Chief Nilome decided he wanted to see the world, so he bought a plane ticket and flew to Nabi. From there he got on a large passenger ship that was going to the capitol city of the province. Nilome did not speak Indonesian, and he did not know his ticket restricted him to the fourth class area deep inside the ship. He began exploring, going through doors and passageways and finally found himself with the first class passengers on the open deck of the ship.

He was overwhelmed! He could see nothing but unending water in every direction. This frightened him. And the people—they spoke to him with anger. He didn't understand a word of what they were saying. They pushed and shoved him like he might treat his dog. Nilome had no idea how to get back to where he had come from. In desperation he squatted on the deck in Dani fashion and was almost crying. At last, a man in uniform came to him. Nilome thought he was the captain. In kindness the man led him back to his place inside the ship.

Through this experience the Lord spoke to Nilome. He was lost and would never find his way to heaven unless he would carefully follow the teaching of the Bible. Nilome returned home and began to follow the Lord fully. He spearheaded the opening of a daughter church which soon grew to 100 in attendance. In the year that followed the congregation collected money and built a church building that will seat 200 people. Whenever this seasoned war-chief tells the story of how the Lord got hold of him, tears come to his eyes. He was lost and now he is found.

This story of Nilome the chief is the last story Zakarias told me.

I don't know if Madae, the chief of police, ever made a Christian profession but certainly he witnessed a clear Christian testimony. I do know that Zakarias was able to help his Dani people through a very difficult time. The Dani Christians had often prayed the Lord's Prayer, ". . . deliver us from evil." God used Zakarias to literally deliver them from government oppression. His leadership as a Christian chief brought peace to all the Dani people of the Sinak Valley.

The Wise Dani *Chief*

Eight years had passed. It was 2004 and Don and I had returned to Sinak for another visit. Once again Zakarias met us on the Sinak airstrip and welcomed us with love and hospitality. We were ten years into retirement. Zakarias was also retired from his position of leadership as district superintendent. A much younger man now served in that position as church leader. This man was from a new generation, a generation with changed values and approaches to ministry from those held by Zakarias. Yet Zakarias showed every respect to the younger man who had taken his place. Any question we asked about ministry was deferred to the new man. Zakarias had stepped down gracefully in his retirement. All the while we saw that the people still honored him for his wisdom and spiritual leadership.

Zakarias remains a chief!

BIBLE LESSON

Jesus told the parable of the Prodigal Son.

There was once a man who had two sons. . . . The father said . . . For this son of mine was dead, but now he is alive; he was lost, but now he has been found. And so the feasting began. Luke 15:11, 24

The wisdom from above is pure first of all; it is also peaceful, gentle, and friendly; it is full of compassion and produces a harvest of good deeds. James 3:17

Your life in Christ makes you strong. Be humble toward one another, always considering others better than yourselves. [Christ] was humble and walked the path of obedience all the way to death—his death on the cross. Philippians 2: 1a, 3b, 8

Years ago I wrote in my notebook that Zakarias expresses agreement with you when he first hears your idea. Then he goes on to express any disagreement he may have but states it in a positive way. When you suggest to him a plan of action, if he thinks it isn't quite right, he will tell you politely but firmly why he disagrees. He is a wise man.

The Dani political chiefs of yesteryear—and even of today—expressed themselves in a loud, opinionated way. However, Zakarias, though fully a chief and leader of his people, is a humble man. He expresses himself using strength and gentleness, honesty and love. These are the characteristics of a wise man who is following Christ. Throughout his youth and retiring years, Zakarias continues to be a worthy role-model, a hero to each of us wherever we are in life.

ISSUES TO CONSIDER

1. Notice the ways Zakarias spoke to other people setting an example and challenge for each of us to follow.
2. Note how the background of Chief Nilome made it possible for God to speak to his heart when he was lost on the ship.
3. What characteristics in the life of Zakarias make him truly an example and hero to all of us?

Zakarias behind father, chief Amon. Pig carried on pole for the feast.

Zakarias 2004

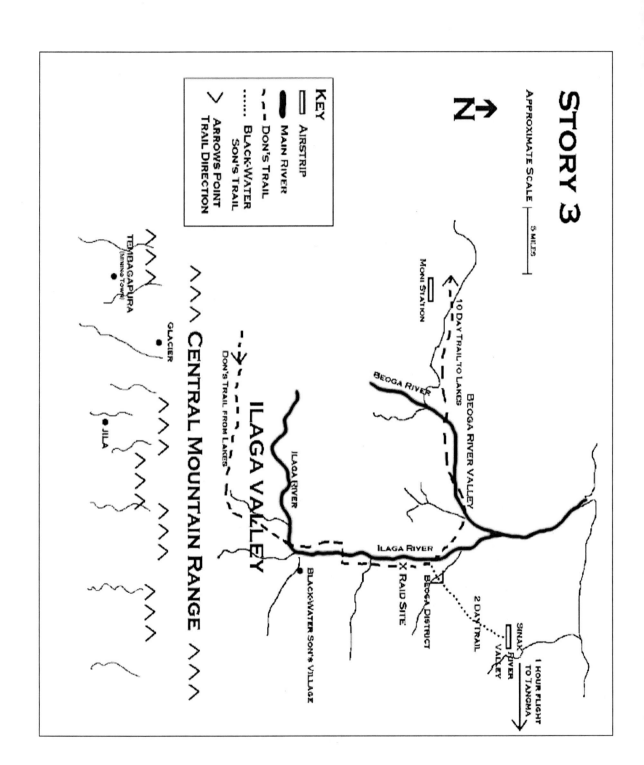

STORY THREE
OUT OF THE STONE AGE

Introduction

This is the story of a Damal man, Black-Water-Son, who was born and grew to adulthood still living in a Stone Age world. The year of our hero's birth was perhaps 1918. In our world the First World War ended in 1918. Of course, that event in history has nothing to do with Black-Water-Son. It only helps to place the date of his birth in our thinking.

Scientists who believe in the theory of evolution teach that mankind evolved over millions of years. Passing through the Stone Age was in relatively recent time, they say. In this theoretical process they depict Stone Age men living in caves and having only fire and stone tools to aid in their survival. Their theory of the process of evolution is not viable because it is not true. On the sixth day of creation God created man in His own image.

However, some men created by God did live in the Stone Age rather like the evolutionist depicted them. It is fascinating to us who live in the Twenty-first Century to flash back in time and be in touch with men, still living today, who lived in a truly Stone Age world.

Several times in the telling of this story Black-Water-Son's name was changed. Each time, his name change is significant to the story. However, we will continue to call him Black-Water-Son throughout these pages.

In sequence of time OUT OF THE STONE AGE would be the first story in the tales of men who live *Where the Earth Ends.* In our book we give it third place. Enjoy the story as Black-Water-Son takes you with him first into the world of Stone Age men and then as he and thousands of others around him heard of God's Son and believed.

Chapter 1

Everyday Life

Black-Water-Son begins telling his story:

O-Duk-Al (Black-Water-Son) was the Damal name my father gave me when I was born. Damal names have a meaning—usually the name reflects some happening or emotion in the life of the parents at the time of birth. For me, I was born near the Black-Water River; thus Black-Water-Son was my name. This is what people called me for the first part of my life.

My parents lived in a small village in the lower end of the Ilaga Valley. Down river from our village I could see where the rugged mountains that ringed the main valley met and joined together. At that point the only divide in the steep mountains was the Ilaga River cutting a deep gorge through those mountains as it flowed on its journey to join the Beoga River. I had heard stories about the rugged terrain and the trail that followed the river down through the gorge to where the two rivers met. Only a few from my village had ever hiked this trail and even less had gone beyond the meeting of the two rivers. [See story 3 map]

My father was a Damal and this made me a member of the Damal tribe. My mother's tribe was Dani. Both of my parents were fluent in speaking the language of the other. So I grew up speaking both Damal and Dani—two very different languages. In our village half of the people were Damal and half Dani. People tolerated and even appreciated the tribal customs that were unique to each tribe, even though each person was tagged as belonging to his father's tribe.

Every person in the village helped all the others with any needed project to maintain life. If a man was planning to dig ground for a new garden, each of the neighbors brought his own wooden digging tool and helped to dig the garden. And in turn all helped the next man when he had a garden to be dug. If a man needed split boards to build a house, all the men worked together making the boards. If a man was planning to marry a wife, all his relatives helped to make the bride price payment. If a man got into a fight, his clansmen stood up immediately to defend him in the conflict. Always we stuck together in caring for one another. No man could survive alone.

No one ever ventured very far from home. It was possible to walk to the top of our valley in one very long day, but not one person in my village had ever done that. The frequent wars or the possibility of a revenge killing, even after a peace settlement, kept us from traveling any distance. Anyway, there was no need to travel far.

Our food was sweet potatoes three times a day and greens every afternoon. The greens we ate were leaves from sweet potato vines and other spinach-like plants. These we steamed in a small pit which was lined with grass and leaves. Heat came from rocks that we heated in the fire and then buried in the greens. Potatoes were often steamed with the greens but mostly they were baked in the ashes around the fire. One special food we sometimes enjoyed was the taro root grown only by the men. We also raised pigs and occasionally feasted on pork. The pigs foraged for their food during the day and in the evening were fed sweet potatoes. Since the sweet potato was our main food and there were never enough of them, we had few potatoes left to feed to pigs. Thus our pigs were few in number and highly prized in value.

Death was always near in our lives—death either from sickness or from war.

Everyone knew hunger. If we weren't hungry because of a war which made it too dangerous to go to the garden, then we were hungry because a wild pig had gotten into our garden. The pig always seemed to find the weak point in the fence. One pig, having the run of a garden overnight, could destroy much of a families' food supply for six months. Even though the pig didn't eat very many of the potatoes, it rooted around and tore up most of the plants. We were often hungry.

Weather in the Ilaga was cold and rainy—raining almost every night and sometimes during the day. We never left home without our rain cape. The women made these by sewing palm leaves together. At night our rain cape doubled as a sleeping mat. Often we were cold during the day but never at night. A fire burning all night and a good roof kept us dry and cozy.

Our huts were built using rough split boards. A double row of boards was thrust into the ground in a circle and then tied together with rattan vine. To keep the wind out, grass and moss were stuffed between the double rows of boards. The house was finished with a cone-shaped roof covered with slabs of bark and topped with grass thatching.

Although our environment offered few raw materials to use in making body coverings, we had a very strict code of modesty in our attire. The women fashioned skirts

Out of the Stone Age

using grass and bark. They also made string from the bark of a certain small tree. Using this string and their fingers they "crocheted" a long net-bag. One of these net-bags hung down the back of every woman; this was part of her covering. Other net-bags were used to carry sweet potatoes home from the garden. Some net-bags served as a cradle to carry the baby. Finally, strings of beads made from dried berries or tiny yellow reeds added a tough of color to the women's attire.

Men used a dried gourd to cover their private parts. It was held in place with a string around the waist. Every adult man wrapped his head with a net-bag. He was never seen in public without this turban. When it was worn people never knew when he began to bald. Older men who could afford it wore a neck band woven from bark string and accented with tiny sea shells or a highly polished pig tusk. With these coverings in place everyone felt properly dressed.

Each village cultivated a few gourd vines which were trained to grow up on a rack. As the gourds grew they hung down from the rack. Some gourds were hollowed out and dried to become drinking gourds, our only container for liquids. Another variety which produced long slender gourds was used by the men to fashion their only covering. Any gourd not of a usable size or shape went into the evening vegetable stew of steamed greens and potatoes.

Every man had his own bow and arrows; he went nowhere without them. They were his weapon in a fight; they became his hunting gear when he hunted wild animals. The bow was fashioned from a pliable, hardwood branch, the bow string made from split rattan, and the arrows from a reed fitted with a sharp point of wood or bamboo. Dani men used a second weapon in war when fighting at close range—a long hardwood spear.

Fire is essential to life; it was never lost in the village. Each morning live coals were buried in the ashes. In the afternoon a fire was kindled using those hot coals. Occasionally the coals did go out; however, someone in the village always had a live coal to use in starting a fire.

Making a fire in the forest was something else. This required a fire-making stick, a length of strong vine and some tinder (very dry leaves or moss) all kept together as a kit in the man's shoulder bag. The tinder was placed on the ground. Then the vine was fitted into the groove on the stick, placed over the tinder and held in place with the man's foot. Standing, the man held one end of the vine in each hand and rapidly worked the vine back and forth. In a few seconds a column of smoke appeared and the tinder caught on fire. Now, with care and lots of blowing, a fire could be built—even in the rain.

Everyday Life

The forest around us offered plenty of trees for all of our basic needs, but harvesting the wood was not easy. Our tools were made of wood and stone; we also used fire as a tool.

To fell a tree in the forest, fire was the first tool used. For several days a fire was kept burning around the base of the tree, eating away at the trunk. A stone axe finished the job. Cutting the log into usable lengths again required more hard work using fire first.

Several of the men in our village owned a stone axe. The special greenish black stone [jadeite], hard enough to make an axe, came from one stone quarry many days walk away. The stone had to be broken out at the quarry using fire. Rough pieces of the stone were carried back to the village where each one was smoothed into the useful shape of an axe-head, or perhaps a knife blade, or a chisel. The shaping took many months of rubbing the piece of hard stone on a certain abrasive boulder. Finally a wooden handle was fashioned with a hole just big enough to fit the end of the stone axe. With the stone in the handle it was tied firmly in place with rattan vine.

As a young man, I worked with the village men using fire to fell trees and cut the logs into usable lengths. To split the log into boards a man began by making a small split into the log with a stone axe. Then we worked a wooden wedge into the split and pounded the wedge with a wooden maul. It took lots of hard work and sweat to split off each rough board. Firewood was split in the same way. At the end of a day in the forest I carried a load of split wood down to our village. I soon learned why a man carrying wood descended the mountain in a quick, light jogging step. That wood was heavy!

We needed the split boards to build a fence protecting our garden from pigs or to build a house. Wood for fires in our huts was also essential for life—for cooking our sweet potatoes and for the fire that kept us warm at night. There never seemed to be enough firewood drying on the rack above the fire.

Many years passed in my life—how many was not a matter of consideration because my people did not reckon their lives with measurements of time. Our focus was on survival, using the tools and methods given to us by our ancestors.

Then one night, a visitor in the men's house told us about a wonder he had heard about—an axe-head not made of stone. Some time later I got to see one and touch it. The axe, or what was left of it, was made of metal with a hole to insert a wooden handle. The blade on the axe I saw was very short. It had been worn down, by repeated chopping and sharpening, until only a couple of inches remained. Many Mee tribesmen had used this

Out of the Stone Age

axe to cut down and split the wood from scores of trees. I could well imagine how much back-breaking work this one axe had saved.

Now, what remained of the axe had been carried by traders for two weeks over the trail to the Ilaga. Here they exchanged this stub of an axe for two prize breeding pigs. The axe head was too short to cut or split wood, but it worked wonders in sharpening a wooden digging stick used as a tool in the garden or for sharpening the end of a board to be put in the ground when building a fence or house. No piece of stone could do what this small piece of steel could do.

BIBLE LESSON

So God created man in his own image, in the image of God he created him: male and female he created them. Genesis 1:27 NIV

And he [the Lord God] said to the man, "You listened to your wife and ate the fruit which I told you not to eat. Because of what you have done, the ground will be under a curse. You will have to work hard all your life to make it produce enough food for you."

So the Lord God sent him out of the Garden of Eden and made him cultivate the soil from which he had been formed. Genesis 3:17, 23

The Damals and Danis, like every other human being, were created by God and in His image. Because of sin, man was put out of the Garden of Eden. From then on all people have had to work hard to make a living. The Damals have lived for centuries in a very hostile environment, in complete isolation from the rest of the world.

Scientists suggest from diggings and carbon dating that people have lived in these mountains for hundreds of years. The people, they say, may have come from the Malay Peninsula. Using canoes and rafts they island-hopped across the Indonesian archipelago all the way to New Guinea. No one, neither the scientists nor the people themselves, really knows how they came to live in this mountainous region or how long they have been there.

While the rest of the world developed new technology, the people of New Guinea continued to live in the Stone Age. Living as they did meant life was very hard, yet they learned to adapt to their environment and have survived for centuries. I wonder if any

Everyday Life

Westerners would survive if a group of us were forced to live over a period of time in that same Stone Age environment. I don't think so. These are a remarkable people.

Here they were, living in the Stone Age, until the outside world discovered them in the twentieth century. Having said all of this we must remember these Stone Age Damals and Danis are people, men and women, boys and girls just like us—all created in the image of God.

ISSUES TO CONSIDER

1. Do you believe the statement in the Bible that God created all human beings?
2. The Damals had no metal of any kind. What would be left in your home if everything metal disappeared? After that, what would be left if everything that required metal to make it disappeared?

Chapter 2

Paths of Right and Wrong

Introduction

The Ilaga Valley is about four degrees south of the equator. This makes the hours of daylight and dark almost equal all year around. It also explains why there is no change of season. Without seasons the Stone-Age Damals had no concept of years. They did not measure time at all, not years by the sun, not months by the moon and certainly not weeks. On occasion they did count how many sleeps until something was to happen. Sometimes a man tied knots in a string, one knot for each day until an important event like a pig feast. Each morning the man untied one knot in the string. This was his calendar.

With its location on the equator one might expect the climate of the land to be tropical. It was not. The days are cool and the nights are cold because the valley is so high in the mountains—7,500 feet above sea level.

Black-Water-Son continues his story:

Each day the sun brought light and warmth into our world. At night inside our hut we had a small fire which kept us warm and gave a little light. The men of our village all slept in one men's house. Each wife had her own smaller house. As a boy I slept in my mother's house. In my early teens I moved to the men's house. The nights were still long but the time before we slept was more interesting to me than when I slept with the women. The hours before sleeping were filled with conversation, talk about the day's happenings, about plans for another day, but most intriguing to me were the tales of adventure and the stories and folklore of our people.

As a boy, my parents taught me what things were right and what things were wrong—even as their parents had taught them. "You may be hungry," my mother said, "but don't steal food from someone's garden. And don't ever steal a pig. You might not

Paths of Right and Wrong

get caught in stealing the pig if you take it to the forest and eat it there, but remember you will be punished. Even if the owner never finds out who stole his pig, you will be punished!"

My father told me, "If a man becomes sick, and he has not confessed and made payment for a pig he stole, he will die. If the owner of the stolen pig comes into the house where the thief is lying ill, the sick man will break out in a sweat, take an immediate turn for the worse and die. Do not steal! A person who steals will die."

In the house at night the men instructed me, "Never run off with the wife of another man. The husband of the woman will kill you; and war will follow. And even worse, never have an affair with a relative. This is incest and deeply offends the spirits. Your own family must kill both the man and the woman involved. If they didn't kill them, the spirits would bring great tragedy to the entire village. Perhaps a plague of sickness will break out or we would have no power to withstand our enemies in war. Be sure the breaking of this taboo will be found out and you will die."

My father spoke often of these taboos. He taught me I should not lie. He said, "A person who lies will be found out and trouble will come to him."

"Don't be lazy," my mother admonished. "A lazy man sleeps cold. Always keep plenty of firewood drying on the rack in your house above the fire."

Sometimes my Dani mother would say, "Look at the gardens of the Damal women. They are full of weeds and the sweet potatoes are small. Look at my garden. We Danis work hard and keep our gardens clean from weeds. Our potatoes are big."

As I grew up in the village, I learned the ways of my people. If I worked hard planting gardens and raising pigs of my own, then I might become a *nagawan,* a chief. Part of being a chief was having more than one wife. Because the woman cares for the pigs and tends the garden, having more than one wife means the man has more pigs and more wealth. As the man's wealth increases he might take a third wife. In our village, however, none of the men had more than one wife.

The next step toward importance might be learning the secrets of a *tabu kalok him me,* a practitioner in evil spirit appeasement. People bring a pig to the shaman when someone dear to them is seriously ill. As the shaman kills the pig he offers the spirit of the pig to appease the spirits who are causing the illness. For the price of a small pig the shaman, using magic, will draw the spirit of the illness out of the sick person. After any ceremony the shaman has all the meat of the pig for himself. He need not share this meat with others because it has been given to the spirits.

Out of the Stone Age

In the men's house at various times I heard, "Learn how to dig a garden and make a fence the proper way. A woman does not want a man for her husband who has not learned the ways of Damal living. A son who obeys his father's words will live to have a gray beard."

I learned that the most important virtue of all is to share whatever you have with others. When a stranger comes into your village, welcome him into your house and feed him well. Never eat a piece of meat by yourself; cut off a piece and give it to someone else. A generous man always has many friends.

Let me tell you this story my father told me. "Two men were walking in the forest one day when they came upon a tree which was hanging down from the sky with roots almost touching the earth. The men climbed up, up, up the roots and through a hole in the sky. There they found the place of *hai*."

My father continued, "Many little people lived in this place of *hai* where no one died. The men had many wives, and the wives bore them many children. Sweet potatoes were so plentiful that they rotted for lack of someone to eat them. The pigs were huge and more than the little people could eat. Everyday the little people shared pork with the two earth-men.

"But alas, the earth-men were greedy and decided to steal a pig. They killed the pig, threw it down to earth through the hole in the sky, and climbed down the tree root and back to earth. The little people discovered that these earth-men had stolen a pig, so they cut the roots of the tree. Never again have people from earth been able to climb to the place of *hai*."

Although my father never stated this to me, I once heard an old man speak in veiled language of a hope he had. Someday a being would come and show earth-people the way to *hai*.

BIBLE LESSON

[The 10 Commandments]

Worship no god but me.

Do not make or worship any images.

Do not misuse the name of the Lord your God.

Observe the Sabbath day and keep it holy.

Honor your father and your mother.

Do not commit murder.

Do not commit adultery.

Do not steal.

Do not accuse anyone falsely.

Do not covet.   Condensed from Exodus 20:1-17

Jesus said: You know the commandments: Do not commit murder; do not commit adultery; do not steal; do not accuse anyone falsely; do not cheat; respect your father and your mother. Mark 10:19

For God loved the world so much that he gave his only Son, so that everyone who believes in him may not die but have eternal life. John 3:16

Three basic words were in the spiritual vocabulary of the Damals: *tel,* a chief evil spirit, *tabu,* many lesser evil spirits and *hai,* a Damal paradise. They had a developed system of appeasing Satan and the spirits. Somewhere in the heart of every person was a hope of gaining *hai* or paradise. But the Damals had no concept of God or even a word for "God."

The Damals did have six of the 10 Commandments, albeit some were stated in a slightly different way than they are given in the Bible. The six they had are the ones Jesus lists in Mark 10:19. These moral truths were taught from generation to generation. Where did the Damals get them? The only possible answer is they came from God their Creator.

The Damal fable conveyed the thought that paradise was lost through the sins of greed and stealing. They knew that breaking the moral code brought sadness and death, but that knowledge gave them no power to keep the law. They had no knowledge of John 3:16.

Out of the Stone Age

ISSUES TO CONSIDER

1. Look at the four commandments the Damals did not have. What was lacking in their understanding that kept them from knowing these four commandments?

2. Do you think an American who has never had any teaching from the Bible has in his heart a basic understanding of the moral law? Does he know it is wrong to murder, to steal, to lie and to take another man's wife? If he knows these laws, how do you think he came to understand them?

3. If people all over the world know the basic laws of God and that breaking them is wrong, why do many reject God's offer of salvation when it is presented to them?

Chapter 3
Enter—Missionaries

Introduction

In June of 1954 Don Gibbons and Gordon Larson, Missionaries of the Christian and Missionary Alliance, made an exploration trip to the Ilaga Valley. After two weeks of hiking from their base at the Wissel Lakes they entered the Ilaga at the head of the valley, traveled down river, passed near Black-Water-Son's village, then hiked through the Ilaga River Gorge and eventually came to where the Ilaga joins the Beoga River. From there they traveled up the Beoga Valley returning home by a different route from the one that brought them to the Ilaga. [See story 3 map]

Black-Water-Son continues his story:

One night we heard hooting and calling from one village to the next. Something important was happening. It wasn't an attack from enemies, but what? In the morning rumors were really flying. "Have you heard the news from up-valley?" someone said.

"What is it?" I asked. Everyone had a different twist to the news being passed from village to village.

"Two strange beings have walked into our valley. They might be men, but they are not men like we are. They are traveling with a group of Mee tribesmen who carry their packs."

No one from my village actually saw them. These strange beings stayed up-valley for several days. Then we heard they had gone past our village and on downriver into the Ilaga River Gorge. A large band of armed Dani warriors followed them into the river gorge.

Out of the Stone Age

The Danis returned and we all heard their story as they told it with great pride. The warriors boasted of ambushing the party at the end of the day, shooting one of the carriers in the shoulder and then taking all the loads from the Mee carriers. Each warrior grabbed whatever he wanted and ran with it. [See story 3 map]

Earlier on this same day one of the foreigners [Don Gibbons] was cutting a tree to make a bridge across the Ilaga River so their party could cross. One of the Dani men offered to help him. The Dani took the axe and cut the tree. In an instant, while the foreigner's eyes were glued to the tree as it fell, the Dani ran with the axe and was gone. Of the many things the Danis stole later that day, this steel axe was by far their greatest prize.

Soon after all this excitement, a party of Dani traders came from the Sinak Valley. In a dispute over the bargain being made, a Sinak man shot an Ilaga man. When the man died two days later, everyone from the Ilaga was honor-bound to avenge the death of their clansman and fight all the people who lived in the Sinak. So began the Great War.

A group of Damals in my clan decided to leave the Ilaga to avoid being forced into fighting on the Ilaga side. We moved to the lower Beoga Valley, an area where the people soon became enemies of the Ilaga in the Great War. Some of the Beoga people thought I should have stayed in the Ilaga to fight on that side. So people began calling me Ilaga-Nevi, Ilaga-Deserter, instead of calling me Black-Water-Son. From then on Ilaga-Deserter was my name. [See story 3 map]

The Beoga Valley was now my home. I married a woman from Beoga who also spoke both the Dani and Damal languages. For the bride price my family paid four pigs, and many cowry sea shells. These cowry shells were our currency.

Our first child was born. My wife gave birth to a baby boy and I had a son! But sad to say this was not for long. Very soon our baby boy died.

Because of the war, all travel to the Ilaga had stopped. This meant we got no news from there. No one traveled across the mountains except an occasional party of warriors headed to make an attack in the Ilaga. Some of these men never returned, and those who did brought no news with them.

A long time passed. [Three years] Then, a missionary man [Don Gibbons] crossed over the high mountains from Ilaga to Beoga using the upriver trail. Suddenly he appeared in our valley. He walked part way down the valley and there I saw him. He was giving shots to people who had the skin disease of yaws. People with this disease had growing sores all over their body; some sores had even eaten parts of their body away. The missionary man said, "This injection of long-acting penicillin will heal your sores."

Enter—Missionaries

I had a growing sore of yaws on my ankle and smaller ones on my face and back. The missionary gave me a shot, and in a few days all three sores were gone. A miracle! I was healed!

The missionary spoke a language I understood—Damal. I heard him tell the story of Jesus. Somehow I was drawn to this talk—talk I'd never heard before. I learned Jesus was God's Son. He was born on earth, died for our sins and rose again. That day I believed.

Several months later that same missionary, Damal-Neme [Don] and his wife, Damal-In [Alice] came from the Ilaga to the Beoga crossing the mountains on the trail that enters the valley down-river. The party moved up-valley and camped near my village. On this trip people had just given them Damal names for we no longer thought of them as outsiders. Damal-Neme taught me more about Jesus, the one in whom I had believed. I listened carefully and remembered all he said. [See chapter 6 in Story Two]

The next big event in my life was later when Damal-Neme baptized me. I knew I was God's child and I wanted to follow Him all of my life. After I was baptized, the desire to learn more burned hotter in my heart. But who would teach me?

Time passed. The Great War had ended. However, our friendship ties remained with those who had been our allies during the war. I heard missionaries were conducting a school in the Ilaga to teach people about Jesus but I dared not move back to my birth place. I feared the Ilaga people who were so recently our enemies.

In the Great War the Beoga Damals were allied with the Dani-speaking people of the Sinak Valley. This made Sinak a safe place for me. Four Dani-speaking missionaries now lived in Sinak and had opened a school to teach the Bible. Since I spoke Dani I could attend this school. My wife and I walked the two-day trail to the Sinak. Here the people began calling me by a new nickname: Sinak-Augwe, He-Likes-Sinak. It wasn't that I really liked the Sinak so much, for I felt like an outsider there, but rather I was willing to go anywhere to learn more from the Bible. I wanted to be a *haik kal ham me*, a speaker-of-the-gospel, a preacher. [See story 3 map]

Everyone in the school was learning to read. For me learning to read those marks on a paper was not easy. I had to work very hard to reach my goal of being able to read the Bible. Already the Gospel of Mark was written in Dani and we knew that other books would soon be translated. Zakarias [the man in Story Two] was also in our school. Learning to read for him was a snap because he was so much younger. He wasn't even grown to be a man yet. However, the day came when both my wife and I graduated from the reading class and we each got our own copy of the Book of Mark!

Out of the Stone Age

The Bible classes in the school were perfect for me. Every day the missionary taught us a Bible story and added some "teaching-talk." One by one I memorized the lessons. In the past my people had passed down our tribal teachings, from generation to generation, through memorization. Sitting around the fire at night the older men had taught the younger men, repeating the stories over and over. This made memorization easy for me. Now I followed the pattern of my ancestors. At night in the men's house I repeated the Bible lesson of the day. Before the evening was over others in the house were telling the story themselves.

Here in the Sinak Valley the Danis had not rejected their spirit appeasement to follow the Lord like the Ilaga and Beoga people had done. Some villages forbid us to even enter with our new talk. Others were ready for a preacher to come on Sunday. One village here, and another one there, began turning to Christ. Each Sunday I was assigned along with another school man to go and preach in a village. Then suddenly, the gospel exploded in the Sinak. Many people put away their practice of spirit appeasement and believed on Jesus.

This same turning to Christ in large numbers was also happening in other mountain valleys. Moni tribal people who lived further to the west beyond the Beoga Valley began to turn to the Lord. A missionary family who spoke Moni moved to that area.

A small pocket of Dani people lived in one area of this large Moni population. They were like I had been before I met a missionary; they knew nothing about God. Someone who spoke Dani must go and tell them. The missionaries conferred and asked me to go. Since it was much too far to walk, our family flew there. This was the first time I'd ever been in an airplane, but the flight is not what stands out in my memory. I was going to tell these people the good news of Jesus. [See story 3 map]

That year it seemed I hardly slept. Often I spent the night in one of the men's houses. Always the men kept me up half the night telling stories from the Bible. Men, women and children believed and a church was formed. I taught them about baptism and soon some were saying, "We want to be baptized." The Dani-speaking missionary from Sinak came and together we baptized a group of 20 men and women.

The year was over and I flew with my wife and three children back to the Sinak Valley. What was coming next? I didn't know.

Enter—Missionaries

BIBLE LESSON

    While Paul was waiting in Athens . . . he noticed how full of idols the city was. So he held discussions [he debated] . . . in the public square every day with the people who happened to come by. . . Paul was preaching about Jesus and the resurrection.

    So they took Paul [and] brought him before the city council. Paul stood up . . . and said, "I see that in every way you Athenians are very religious. As I walked through your city . . . I found an altar on which is written, 'To an Unknown God.' That which you worship, then, even though you do not know it, is what I now proclaim to you. God, who made the world and everything in it, is Lord of heaven and earth."

    Paul left the meeting. Some men joined him and believed, among whom was Dionysius, a member of the council; there was also a woman named Damaris, and some other people. Condensed from Acts 17:16-34

    Jesus said, "No one can come to me unless the Father who sent me draws him to me and I will raise him to life on the last day. . . I am telling you the truth: he who believes has eternal life." John 6:44, 47

In Athens the people knew nothing of the true God. The educated men enjoyed a discussion on religious issues, so Paul debated with them speaking in their own language. Because of his speeches in the public square he was called to appear before the town council. There he began his presentation by talking about the inscription on one of their heathen altars, "to an Unknown God." That very day people who heard for the first time believed.

    The missionary in our story began by living among the Damals and learning their language. The Damals accepted this "foreign spirit-man," as they once thought of him, so completely they named him Friend-of-the-Damals. He preached about Jesus, His death and resurrection. Some believed that very day.

    Black-Water-Son already spoke two local languages. His first step was finding a school that could train him in the Bible. From there he began teaching others in the pattern of his forefathers—through memorization and repetition sitting around the fire at night.

Out of the Stone Age

To be a missionary—overseas or at home—we too must know our Bible and then learn the local language, be it a foreign language or a generational language. We must become one with the individuals we are witnessing to. After this, the message we communicate may be received.

People sometimes ask how is it possible that people who have heard so little of what the Bible teaches can truly be born again. The answer is this: no one, anywhere in the world, can be reborn in Christ unless the Holy Spirit draws that person's heart to Him. Jesus tells us this in John 6:44. When the Holy Spirit tugs at the heart of our friend or family member, if he has heard the story of Jesus, he can believe and receive Christ Jesus into his heart. The amazing part of this story is that God, by the Holy Spirit, drew hundreds of people to Himself at the same time. Each came like a little child, as we all must come, and simply believed.

ISSUES TO CONSIDER

1. Did Black-Water-Son become a Christian on the day he was baptized? What did happen when he was baptized?

2. The Lord uses things from every person's pre-Christian background to make him a better witness. In the story in Acts 17 what pre-Christian training did Paul use? What did Black-Water-Son use from his "Stone Age" years? What do you have in your background that God can use?

3. What are two important things an American must do to be an effective missionary in a foreign country?

4. How was it possible that both the Athenian council man and Black-Water-Son came to believe so quickly when they had never heard of Jesus before?

Chapter 4
Faithful in Every Season

Black-Water-Son continues telling his story:

The missionary came back to the Sinak Valley after a year in his own country. He invited me to come for a talk. "Black-Water-Son," he said, "God used you during the year you spent teaching the gospel to that pocket of Dani people who live in Moni country. Now while I was in my country you took my place and preached every Sunday here at the main church."

I nodded. What he was saying was true.

"My brother," he continued, "a missionary is asking if I know of a preacher-family who could come and help him teach his people. These people are a distant branch of Danis. They speak a language you would not understand. And only a very few show any interest in learning about God. Would you go?"

"Where is this place?" I asked.

"It's far away; you've never heard the name of the valley. It's so far to the east that none of your people from the Ilaga have ever walked to that valley. From here the airplane flies an hour to get there."

"I'll go," I said. "I'm ready to tell more people the story of Jesus."

A flight was arranged and I, with my wife and our four children, flew to Tangma. [TONG-meh] When we arrived, we were sent by the Tangma missionary to a side valley a half day's walk away. The people there planted sweet potato gardens like we did and lived in houses not that different from the houses I've always known.

Right away I moved in with the men of the village sleeping in the men's house. However, we couldn't talk to each other because of the difference in languages. I made up my mind to learn this new language; if I could speak it, then I could tell them the way to eternal life. Before long I began to understand what the men were saying. After a couple more months I was speaking well enough to begin telling them of the faith that was hot in my heart.

Out of the Stone Age

At first no one paid any attention to my testimony. Then a few showed some interest. God's Holy Spirit was speaking to their hearts, and I continued to pray. On Sundays I began a preaching service and the number attending grew. In time fifteen men and women, from those who were attending church, cut all ties with spirit appeasement and their past and were publicly baptized.

I decided to follow the pattern used by the missionaries who taught me. Weekday mornings I started a school teaching Bible stories to all who came. The Tangma missionary gave me reading primers in the local language and with local people to help, we began teaching them how to read. From my school five young men stood out in their desire to walk the Jesus path. I laid my hands on them and prayed, dedicating them to be special witnesses in the greater area. During the three years I served in the Tangma area we had two more baptismal services, each larger than the one before.

While at Tangma, I felt my need for more Bible training in order to become a full-fledged pastor. The Dani language Bible School, relatively close to where I was now working, seemed to be the place for me. However, I was ten years older than any of the other men entering this four-year school. My age was an advantage when I shared the story of Jesus in the village, because the older men who were the village leaders listened to me. But when I entered the Dani Bible School, I just couldn't keep up with the reading, writing and tests the school required.

The missionary in Beoga, the one who had baptized me, [Don Gibbons] invited me to enter the Damal Bible School. With my family we flew back to Beoga. In this school the studies were geared more to memorizing and repeating, and less to written work and tests. I spoke Damal just as well as I spoke Dani, so the Damal language used in the school was no problem for me. However, I could not read the Bible in Damal.

All these years I had read my Bible in the Dani language. Now I had to learn to read in Damal. This was very hard. Many of the letters used in Dani stood for a different sound in Damal. Learning to read again took every bit of my determination, for I was getting older—now in my early fifties.

As a young man all my training had been in using tools of wood and stone and growing sweet potatoes. I was schooled in memorization but the idea of reading and writing was completely unknown to my people. Handicapped or not, I did learn. With God's help I learned to read and understand the New Testament written in Damal. In May 1975 I graduated with my class.

My quest, first to hear and learn the words of Jesus and then to teach these words to people who, like me, had never heard, had taken me to many places. Every place I went I was an outsider, not accepted like someone born in the area. Twice the people in these places gave me a new name, a name that had a meaning and spoke of my journey. At birth I was Black-Water-Son. In Beoga it was Ilaga-Deserter. In Sinak my name was He-Likes-Sinak. While I was in Bible school I took a new name for myself, a name from the Bible not used by anyone else. I became Javadi—an obscure name in the Old Testament.

After graduation I returned to the Ilaga Valley where I was born. I had left the Ilaga as an adult Stone Age man, knowing nothing of the God of heaven. Now years later I returned as a passionate preacher of God's Word.

The Ilaga houses and gardens were the same as they had always been, but now most men owned a steel axe which made living many times easier. Travel was no longer restricted because wars had stopped. Trails had been improved and everyone was free to walk wherever he chose to go. Most of the people were Christians and churches were everywhere. All the churches had trained pastors. Two missionaries lived in the valley, one translating the Bible into the Dani language and the other translating it into the Damal language.

Native leaders of the local churches assigned me to serve as pastor at Maki, a village in the lower end of the valley not far from where I was born. On Sunday I preached in Dani because most of the people were Danis. However, since some in my church were Damals, when I talked to them I spoke Damal. In the years that followed I served in three other churches and all of these had a mixed congregation of Danis and Damals.

In 1984 I went to Beoga to attend a five-week renewal seminar for pastors. One of the classes in the course was "Improving Sunday School in Your Church." Damal-In [Alice] taught this class. Each Sunday she assigned us to teach the lesson in a local church, putting into practice what we were learning. Every Friday she called on one man to practice-teach the lesson in our school room. Damal-In writes below about the Friday she called on me to teach:

Black-Water-Son stood in my classroom before his fellow pastors. He was teaching the Sunday school lesson on the death and raising to life of Lazarus. He spoke with intense conviction, "Jesus said, 'I am the resurrection and the life. Whoever believes in me will live, even though he dies.'

"In the past we Damals mourned with no hope for our loved ones because we knew not Jesus. We wailed and cried for days until we were exhausted. We cut off the fingers of our little children and women to show our sorrow and appease the spirits.

Out of the Stone Age

Mourners plastered their bodies with mud and soot, remaining that way for months. Even worse, in anger over the death of an adult man, men cried out, 'Witchcraft! Witchcraft!' Then they killed a woman who was a close relative of the deceased, shouting, 'She is the one who caused his death.'

"Brothers, those old ways of mourning death are gone. True, we are still sad and cry. Jesus Himself cried with Mary and Martha at their brother's death. But now we have Jesus, the hope of eternal life. We believe that Jesus died and rose again, and we too will rise to life on the last day."

Most of Black-Water-Son's "pupils" had graying and balding heads. They too were seasoned pastors. Each had already studied this same lesson in preparation for teaching it in a nearby village on Sunday. Yet as he taught, the banter of side comments ceased and the heads that usually nodded in the midday heat raised to full attention. My husband Don and I also sat enrapt.

Black-Water-Son taught the memory verse and asked the review questions written in the lesson quarterly. The answers came back clearly and with conviction.

When he finished all I could say was, "Praise the Lord." I had planned to ask the class for constructive criticism but there was nothing to say. Black-Water-Son was well-prepared and taught as anointed by the Spirit of God.

BIBLE LESSON

Paul wrote to Timothy:

Preach the Word; be prepared in season and out of season; correct, rebuke and encourage—with great patience and careful instruction.

For the time will come when men will not put up with sound doctrine. Instead, to suit their own desires, they will gather around them a great number of teachers to say what their itching ears want to hear.

They will turn their ears away from the truth and turn aside to myths.

But you, keep your head in all situations, endure hardship, do the work of an evangelist, discharge all the duties of your ministry. 2 Timothy 4:2-5 NIV

During the time that many pastors were gathered for a renewal seminar, another pastor, a classmate of Black-Water-Son, was tempted and fell by the wayside. A war between two clans had broken out where pastor Malachi lived. He listened night after night to the talk of war and revenge; then he succumbed to the pattern of his ancestors. He took up his bow and arrows and led men in fighting with the aim of killing the enemy.

Malachi was drawn away from the truth very gradually. He listened to the repeating voices he had once rejected until he caved in and became one of them. He could have distanced himself from these continual words of temptation, but he did not. Instead he turned his attention from the Word of God to the ways of war.

ISSUES TO CONSIDER

1. Jesus said, "I am the resurrection and the life. Whoever believes in me will live, even though he dies." What words of hope this statement brings to us when we have believed in Jesus.

2. Like Malachi, how might we be drawn away from God's path?

3. Like Black-Water-Son, how can we remain true in season and out of season?

Chapter 5

Always he said, "I'll Go"

Black-Water-Son continues his story:

Time passed. All the missionaries who served in the Ilaga and Sinak valleys had gone. Only one couple remained in the Beoga Valley [Don and Alice Gibbons]. They came to the Ilaga every three months to hold a seminar for the Damal pastors, their wives and other church leaders. Damal-Neme spoke only Damal so the lessons and all the written notes were in Damal. The majority of the pastors in the Ilaga are Danis and do not speak Damal. They said, "We want to have seminars too, but we have no Dani missionary."

That's when Damal-Neme talked to me. "Black-Water-Son," he said, "Will you be on our team and translate for the Danis as I teach?"

My response was, "Yes, I'd like to do that."

After some time, Dani pastors in Sinak who had no missionary heard about the seminars in Ilaga now being translated into Dani. They said, "Sinak people need these lessons too," and every three months a group of pastors walked the two-day trail to attend.

Each time the Damal speakers were given a full set of lessons written in their language. The Danis complained, "The Damals get all the lessons printed out for them. We want the lessons in our language too. We want to teach our people these lessons about the Christian family." On the next visit to the Ilaga the missionaries brought the lessons printed in both languages.

Next came Damal-Neme's question to me, "Black-Water-Son, for the coming rounds of seminars we plan to fly to Sinak and teach there. This way all the Sinak pastors can attend, not just a few who walk to the Ilaga. I need your help to teach directly in Dani. This would be better than translating for me. Will you memorize the lessons and go with us to Sinak?"

Always he said, "I'll Go"

"Yes, I'll go and I'll memorize the lessons."

This assignment combined the skills I'd learned in two different worlds. I began by reading the printed lesson, and the given Bible text that was woven into the lesson. I went over the lesson until it became a living message to me, even adding some details of my own. By this time the skill of memorization, which I'd learned as a youth, kicked in and each lesson was mine. I was very excited about this new ministry. I was going back to Sinak after all these years.

When we got to Sinak, Zakarias [the man in Story Two] was really fired up about the seminars. So were the Danis who came from the 50 churches. Besides the lessons learned and the complete printout of these lessons they received, the three days with the Sinak pastors turned into a social gathering. Everyone enjoyed the company of friends who had traveled a long way to attend. The host church even put on a pit-cooked feed for all the delegates.

Superintendent Zakarias came with an idea, "Our youth need these same lessons. Let's have a three-day seminar just for the youth. Young people from the larger churches can arrange the music—their kind of music. Some groups may even present a drama."

On our next visit the youth turned out by the hundreds. Sitting on the floor 600 young people squeezed into the church building. Their singing *was* different! They added rhythm to the traditional Dani chant-singing and clapped their hands as they sang. On one day they had a special number by a group of 15 young men playing their homemade guitars. Always the youth listened with full attention as I taught the hour-long lesson. On the day I gave an invitation scores stayed behind, each to pray with a pastor-counselor.

As I spoke to the Sinak youth packed in this church building, my mind flashed back 25 years. This was the church where I had preached many years ago while the missionary was on furlough. Back then everyone sat on the ground in the village yard for there was no building. I had preached on Sundays to a much smaller group. Some of them had made their decision to follow the Jesus path and others were still not sure. These young people were their children and grandchildren. Now most of the people in the Sinak Valley were following Jesus.

After the success in Sinak with a three-day youth seminar, the other four church districts added a youth weekend seminar to the midweek seminar for adult church leaders. The government elementary and junior high schools all closed on the seminar weekends. For almost 10 years the seminars were a major event in the life of the church in each church district.

Out of the Stone Age

The seminar ministry came to an end when Damal-Neme and Damal-In announced they were leaving our country. They said, "We came to your country [1953] when we were young; now our hair has turned gray. It is time [1994] for us to return to our country of America. When we came you knew nothing about God and His Word. Now you have the Bible in your own language and everywhere there are churches and trained pastors."

One more round of seminars in the five church districts followed. Each ended with a pig feast of celebration and many speeches, with us Damals and Danis giving our final good-byes.

I continued in my work as pastor even though I too was growing older. As I think back over my life, I'm thankful to God for many things. Before I ever knew there was a God, He had his hand on my life. He kept me from taking two wives. If I had taken this step, I would not have qualified to serve as an evangelist and pastor. If my aim in life had been to become a chief or practitioner of spirit appeasement, I might have been sidetracked from God's best for my life. Even before I took that first step of faith and decided to follow the Jesus path, God had a purpose for all the years of my life. Yes, even before He created the world, He had a plan for my life and it was a good plan.

Two years later a letter came from America. Damal-Neme and Damal-In were coming back for two months and they planned to do another round of seminars. Would I join the team? As always, my answer was a great big "yes!" We thought we'd never see our missionaries again on this earth, but they were coming back!

With these words I, Black-Water-Son, have finished telling my story.

It was on this visit in 1996 that Black-Water-Son told Alice his life's story which she has written here for you.

Eight years later in 2004 the Gibbons planned to return again and hold seminars in each of the five church districts. Again a letter went ahead to Black-Water-Son. Would he join their team and teach? As always, his answer was "Yes." However, when they got there, they were told that Black-Water-Son just didn't have enough strength for the rigors of another round of seminars. He was now 86 years old, a very old age for a Damal.

When the missionaries were in the Ilaga on this trip, Black-Water-Son walked almost an hour from his up-valley village to greet them. He looked good but his step had slowed and he walked with a cane. Yet he remained the same humble, unassuming man, always ready to serve the Lord.

Always he said, "I'll Go"

BIBLE LESSON

    I have done my best in the race, I have run the full distance, and I have kept the faith. And now there is waiting for me the victory prize of being put right with God, which the Lord, the righteous Judge, will give me on that Day—and not only to me, but to all those who wait with love for him to appear. 2 Timothy 4:7-8

    You should think of us as Christ's servants. . . The one thing required of such a servant is that he be faithful to his master. . . Final judgment must wait until the Lord comes; . . . And then everyone will receive from God the praise he deserves. Selected from 1 Corinthians 4:1, 2, 5

    Black-Water-Son's life story may not be as spectacular as some—perhaps because he himself did not focus on the dramatic happenings in his life. At every opportunity given to him he simply did his best to tell others about the Jesus he knew and loved. Our life may seem rather ordinary—quite routine perhaps—but God can use us just as He has made us, and in the place where He put us.

    In his early years before he knew anything of God, God was already directing Black-Water-Son's life, because He had a plan for him. Once Black-Water-Son heard the way of salvation and was given a choice to follow Jesus, he chose the right path. Each time as he learned more, he chose to obey.

    For all of his life Black-Water-Son ran the race of life with a steady pace. He didn't dash about to bring glory to himself; he simply served faithfully using every opportunity given to him. He worked very hard, overcame his handicap of an older age and served the Lord with excellence. "On that Day" when the Lord returns and sits in judgment to reward all Christians, Black-Water-Son will receive his due reward.

    Always he said, "I'll go."

    When my husband Don handed back the text of this story he had just proof-read, he said, "Wow! What a privilege it was to have known and worked with such a man as Black-Water-Son!"

Out of the Stone Age

ISSUES TO CONSIDER

1. What in the life of Black-Water-Son makes him a hero worthy of imitation?

2. Black-Water-Son will receive his reward from Jesus "on that Day." According to the passages in the Bible Lesson, what will his reward be?

Black-Water-Son, man with a cap on right. 2004

Man carrying his stone axe

Woman "crocheting" a net-bag with her fingers

Men discuss payment of cowrie shells sewn on belt (Their currency)

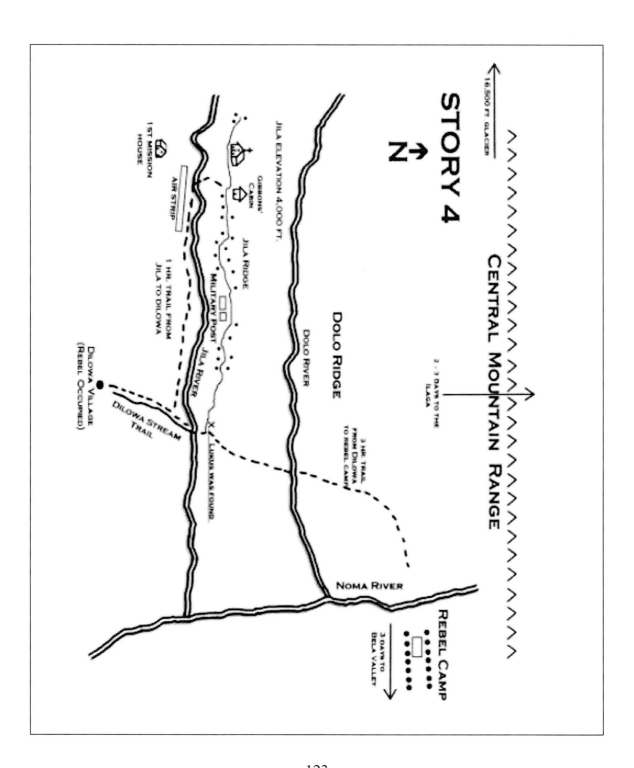

STORY FOUR
LUKAS AND THE REBELS

Introduction

Lukas Dolame was born in the rugged mountain interior of the island of New Guinea—in a region called Bela Valley. It was in this unknown and unimportant place a baby boy came into the world—born to a Damal family. According to our reckoning of time that year was 1961. The people of Bela had no concept of years and months as we count them.

We call Bela a valley, but really, in this mile-high area there is no valley at all, only a steep mountain canyon with the Bela River rushing down, down, down on its mad dash to the Pacific Ocean. The jagged mountains descend from two-mile-high peaks, and are divided by a network of streams flowing into the Bela River. It is here on the steep sides of the mountain that a small group of Damal tribal people had eked out a living since time past. They planted their sweet potato gardens on the sides of a mountain using wooden digging sticks, and they split their firewood with a stone axe.

The father of Lukas, and the generations before him, knew that over the mountains, many days walk away, lived other tribal people who spoke different languages. But to their knowledge all people on earth looked and lived just as they did.

About the time the parents of Lukas were married, reports began to filter back to Bela Valley that some strange white beings had come to the Ilaga, a valley five days walk away. These strangers had a talking box and a flying boat, but most important of all they had steel axes. In time a metal axe found its way back through the trade network to the Bela. It made cutting trees so much easier. The steel axe seemed almost magical to these people who lived *Where the Earth Ends*.

Lukas Dolame came into the author's life around 1980 when he was 20 years old. She and her husband Don made regular trips by plane to Jila where Alice first met Lukas. On these visits the Gibbons stayed in a little cabin Don built on the Jila Ridge. They had fitted the cabin with the basics for living and whenever they came to Jila, they camped for a week in that cabin. Alice looked for someone to help her with chores like chopping wood, building a fire in the cook stove and more importantly, keeping it burning. It was Lukas who agreed to be that helper. After several visits he became more like a son to Alice than just a paid helper. (This same kind of a relationship developed with each helper wherever she went.)

It was years later when Lukas sat in Alice's living room in her home at Beoga and told her his life's story. It's a story of God's grace and deliverance. If your pastor could invite Lukas to give his testimony in your church on a Sunday evening, everyone who heard him would talk about it for weeks. Since that can never happen Lukas will tell you his story here on the pages of this book.

Chapter 1

Born to Live—Not Die

Lukas begins his story:

One day, when I was still a small baby in my mother's arms, my father became very sick—and shortly he died. That night, as my mother was in her hut crying because of his death, a man came to her door. He pulled the rough boards apart that closed the doorway and entered.

"You must run for your life," he said. "I just heard the men making plans to kill you. Your husband's relatives are very angry about his sudden death. They're looking for a woman to blame it on. They've decided you are the witch who caused their brother's death. I don't believe you are that woman. I've come to warn you. If you are here in the morning, they'll kill you. Take your baby and go!"

"Where should I go?" my mother asked. "I've never been away from Bela in all of my life."

"Just go! You must go far away or they'll kill you," he said. "Go west to Jila. "It's three days walk from here."

"Three days walk?" she repeated.

"Yes, three days," he said, thinking as he spoke. "For the first two days of walking, there are no villages or people, only high mountains to climb and descend and several rivers to cross before you climb another mountain. At the end of the second day you will come to a village, but don't stay there. Go on one more day to Jila. I heard a rumor that missionaries have come to Jila."

"Missionaries?" she asked. "Who are they?"

My mother didn't know anything about missionaries or that they had come to Jila, but the rumor was true. Frank and Wilma Ross had hiked over the high mountains from the Ilaga. Frank, with the help of the Damals, had carved out a dirt landing field for the airplane, and also built a cabin where he and his family were living.

"You say I should go west to Jila." my mother said again.

"Yes," he said. "And if you want to live, you'd better go right now!" With those words he stepped through the low doorway and disappeared into the night.

My mother sat beside the glowing embers of the fire and looked down at me nursing at her breast. She knew what the man had said was true. In her lifetime many a woman had been accused of being a witch—the witch who had caused her husband's or her son's death. The accused women had done nothing at all, but she was always killed. My mother knew she too would be killed.

As a girl she had witnessed the killing of a woman who had a nursing baby. The only food for the baby was his mother's milk. Without his mother to nurse him the baby also died.

My mother stared at the fire and thought: *I know nothing about the world beyond my village. I could never go out into that unknown. If they kill me, they kill me. My two other children are older. They will be well taken care of by my husband's relatives. My children will soon call them mother and father. They will lack nothing.*

But you my baby boy, if I die you will die.

Looking down at me again, she spoke in a low voice, "No," and again in a louder voice, "No! They will not kill you, my baby boy. We both will live!"

She placed me in the carrying net-bag that was my cradle by night and a baby backpack by day. Picking up another net-bag full of sweet potatoes she slung both onto her back. She positioned the carrying straps across her forehead, and stepped out into the inky blackness. My brave mother started out into the unknown night to follow a path rarely taken by men and never by a woman alone. Her determination to save my life would lead to a new world for both of us.

This new world at Jila came to include a new father for me, along with a big brother named Simon. Simon's mother had died. In time Simon's father married my mother. This gave me a new father and a big brother.

We boys grew up together. As we grew older we became close friends—almost like David and Jonathan in the Bible. In the future we would have some life-and-death adventures together. I'll tell you more about them later.

Lukas and the Rebels

BIBLE LESSON

David wrote:

> [Lord,] you are all around me on every side; you protect me with your power.
>
> You created every part of me; you put me together in my mother's womb.
>
> When I was growing there in secret, you knew that I was there—you saw me before I was born.
>
> The days allotted to me had all been recorded in your book, before any of them ever began. Psalm 139:5, 13, 15-16

> But Joseph said [to his brothers who had sold him into slavery in Egypt,] "You plotted evil against me, but God turned it into good, in order to preserve many people who are alive today because of what happened." Genesis 50:19-20

Every life is precious in the sight of God—even the life of a newborn or unborn baby. This Damal baby boy was not even old enough to have been given a name when his life was almost snuffed out. David writes in Psalm 139 of God's care of him including the time before he was born. The verses can also be applied to the life of Lukas when he was a newborn. It was God who protected him.

In pre-Christian days the Damals took the lives of innocent women which sometimes included the woman's nursing baby. But they never took the lives of innocent, unborn babies by abortion as is practiced in America today. Life, every life, is precious in the sight of God!

The Bela men, relatives of the father who died, were set on killing the mother of Lukas. No one in Bela had ever heard of God. The Bela people lived in fear of the evil spirits who they felt were all around them and were the cause of all sickness and death. The men feared an imagined curse from a woman who they thought to be a witch, a woman who had "eaten the spirit" of the deceased. They believed this witch caused their brother's death. If they did not kill her, they reasoned, she might kill one of them.

However, God intervened. As in the story of Joseph, God turned what was designed for evil into good for both Lukas and his mother. She chose life for her newborn baby not knowing what the cost might be to her in their journey into the unknown. For them the end result was a good life.

God is able to do the same for an unborn child and his mother who is considering abortion. If the unborn is allowed to live, God will change tragedy into something good.

ISSUES TO CONSIDER

1. Is the question of abortion in the United States today strictly political or is it a moral/biblical issue? With your answer what should your response be?

2. "You plotted evil against me, but God turned it into good," were Joseph's words. Can you recall something very bad in your life that turned out to be a blessing?

Chapter 2
Peeking Through the Crack

Lukas continues his story:

One day when I was still little, my mother said, "I'm going across the river to sell a net-bag of vegetables to the missionary." She put a few sweet potatoes into a net-bag and added several cucumbers and two bundles of greens.

We lived on the Jila ridge, and the missionary lived across the river by the airstrip. My mother carried the net-bag of vegetables on her back with the bag's strap-handle across her forehead. She grabbed me by my arm and swung me up to her shoulders. There I sat ready to watch the world go by. [See story 4 map]

Off we started down the steep, muddy hill to the river. The roar of the water pounding over huge boulders was so loud I could hardly hear her voice. At the river I held on extra tight as she cautiously walked across the poles that served as a bridge. Then we were up the bank on the other side and soon arrived at the missionary's house.

My mother put me down in the yard while she took her vegetables to the door. The first thing I saw was a big, white boy playing in the yard. He was running and shouting. When this huge person came running toward me, I was afraid and ran crying to my mother. This is my first memory of the missionary family.

Months went by. I grew older and braver. I wanted to go back and see these strange, foreign people again. The men of my village had done some work on the airstrip, and they were going across the river to get their pay. My step-dad let me go along riding on his shoulders.

In addition to their pay the men were served a feast of white, fluffy food. They called it *nasi*—rice. I had never seen rice. We Damals ate sweet potatoes, for that is about all that will grow on the steep sides of the mountains where we live. I got to taste some of this foreign food called *nasi*. It seemed like heavenly food to me.

After that day I began crossing the river by myself. I wanted to see all the things that were different from where the missionary lived and the village where I lived. The missionary had a cow, and I ventured up to the fence to watch this monster animal. It just walked around and ate grass—what a strange thing for an animal to eat. We Damals have only two animals, pigs and dogs. They don't eat grass and they aren't big like this cow.

Often I sat in the yard watching to see who might come out of the house. The big boy had gone away in the airplane to attend school so I felt safe. Sometimes his little sister came out to play, and she didn't frighten me. Before long we began to play together.

The missionary house looked so big to me. Our Damal houses were just little huts with a fire in the center. The smoke from the fire found its way up and out through the grass thatch roof. The missionary's house had a shiny, aluminum roof, and smoke from the kitchen fire came out of a stove pipe. The walls in both houses were made from rough-hewn boards. In the big house nails held the boards in place; in our houses the wall boards were tied in place with rattan vine.

On Sundays in our village all the people gathered to sing and listen to a Damal man tell a story from the Bible. I didn't understand everything he said, but I did learn about the Creator and that this God had a son named Jesus.

Across the river again, I wondered what those foreign people did inside their big house. I decided to find out. I sneaked up to the house, and sure enough, there were cracks in the wall. I found a hole just at my eye level, and there I stayed glued for a long time. When the missionary lady came out the door I ran away, but I was back the next day and the next.

One evening I was so intent on watching that I didn't even notice that it was getting dark. The man came out, startling me. He said, "You'd better go home now. It's almost dark. There's no place to sleep on this side of the river." I think he knew I'd been there watching all the time.

He was right; it was getting dark fast. When I got to the river it was black and roaring. I knew I'd drown if I fell in. How glad I felt when I got across the wobbly pole bridge and back to my village.

What did I see inside the missionary house? They spoke a different language, so I couldn't understand what they were saying, but other than that, they seemed like real people. One thing they did was different from anything we Damals ever did. The man or the woman was always doing something with "wide leaves." In our Damal language we call paper "wide-leaves" because the nearest thing we had that looked like paper was a wide, tree leaf. In the missionary house someone was always writing on a wide-leaf or looking at a book of wide-leaves or reading aloud from it. Right then I determined that someday I too would read wide-leaves.

Lukas and the Rebels

Before long I came to understand that God's book, the Bible, was written not only in the language of the missionary, but that another missionary in the Ilaga Valley was writing this same book in my own Damal language. I wanted to read God's book myself. And I also wanted to teach the words of Jesus from that book to my people—to become a *haik kal ham me,* a speaker of God's word. I was only a boy and it was but a small, small voice inside of me, but I knew that someday I would be a preacher.

BIBLE LESSON:

In those days, when the boy Samuel was serving the Lord under the direction of Eli, there were very few messages from the Lord, and visions from him were quite rare. One night Eli, who was now almost blind, was sleeping in his own room; Samuel was sleeping in the sanctuary where the sacred Covenant Box was. Before dawn, while the lamp was still burning, the Lord called Samuel. He answered, "Yes, sir!" and ran to Eli and said, "You called me, and here I am."

But Eli answered, "I didn't call you; go back to bed." So Samuel went back to bed. The Lord called Samuel again. The boy did not know that it was the Lord, because the Lord had never spoken to him before. So he got up, went to Eli, and said, "You called me, and here I am."

But Eli answered, "My son, I didn't call you; go back to bed."

The Lord called Samuel a third time; he got up, went to Eli, and said, "You called me, and here I am."

Then Eli realized that it was the Lord who was calling the boy, so he said to him, "Go back to bed; and if he calls you again, say, 'Speak; your servant is listening.'" 1 Samuel 3:1-10

The small voice that Lukas heard was the voice of God, the Holy Spirit. God speaks to people of all ages. It matters not if you are a young person or an old person or somewhere in-between. It matters everything if you are willing to listen.

Perhaps a person who is young like Samuel or Lukas has an advantage when he first hears the small voice of the Holy Spirit, for he has a fresh clean life to give to the Lord. However, at an older age, when we are quiet enough to hear His voice and respond, it's exciting to know that the path we begin to pursue is one of God's calling.

Samuel answered the Lord, "Speak, your servant is listening."

ISSUES TO CONSIDER

The missionary knew that Lukas was watching through the crack, but he never guessed that God might use this happening to speak to the heart of that Damal boy. Someone might come closer to God by watching your life.

Chapter 3
Reading Wide-Leaves

Lukas continues his story:

I was in my early teens when a man named Jacob came to our village at Jila. Jacob had just graduated from the Beoga Bible School. Now he had come to be the first pastor of our church.

Right away Pastor Jacob said, "I'm going to start a school here at Jila to teach the Bible, and I'm going to teach people to read. You must learn to read so you can read the Bible yourself."

I was so excited, for what I wanted most of all was to learn to read wide-leaves. When I found out that the school was for adults only, I was devastated. Learning to read seemed so close, and then the school was not for me. Who would help me? I did talk to God in prayer about it all, and I asked Him to help me.

I decided to go to the church the morning the adult reading class began. I just sat there with the adults. Pastor Jacob began to teach and he didn't make me leave. After awhile he saw I really wanted to study and gave me a reading primer just like the others. Could it really be happening? It was!

I thought that holding a book of wide-leaves in my hands would be a magic key to reading, but it didn't turn out quite like that.

Pastor Jacob began by showing us how to hold a book. "You must start at the top of the very first page," he said. Pointing to the letter printed there he said, "Every time you see the mark that looks like this *a*, you should say 'ah.' A mark like this always stands for the sound 'ah.'"

I learned that the mark *e* always says "eh," and *o* says "oh." Next came the syllables *ka, ke, ko* and *ma, me, mo*. My teacher said, "Lukas, read these two syllables," pointing to *ko* and *ma*. "Now put them together."

I said, *"Ko-ma, koma,"* which means airplane. *"Koma!"* I said again. I could read a word! On the next page I learned to read *ka* and *ma*. Putting them together I read *kama,* which means "there is none." *Koma kama.* I read it myself—"there is no airplane." *Ka kama*—"there is no firewood." *Me kama*—"there are no people." I was looking at marks on wide-leaves and reading Damal words!

Every morning I went to school and in the afternoon I studied too. Soon I advanced into book two and then books three and four. I learned to say the sounds for *i* and *u*, and the sounds for all 15 consonants. I was reading words—short ones and long ones—each one by saying the syllables separately and then joining them to make a word.

After the primers came four little reading books. The words fit together into sentences and then into short stories. When I had mastered one reader, Pastor Jacob loaned me the next one. Finally the day came when I got my very own book—the Gospel of Mark. I was so excited. I sat down and read a story about Jesus. I even read words that Jesus spoke himself. I was reading the wide-leaves of God's book in my own Damal language!

BIBLE LESSON

Written by Paul to Timothy

> But as for you, continue in the truths that you were taught and firmly believe. You know who your teachers were, and you remember that ever since you were a child, you have known the Holy Scriptures, which are able to give you the wisdom that leads to salvation through faith in Christ Jesus. All Scripture is inspired by God and is useful for teaching and truth, rebuking error, correcting faults, and giving instruction for right living, so that the person who serves God may be fully qualified and equipped to do every kind of good deed. 2 Timothy 3:14-17

Timothy learned as a child the teachings of God's Word which led to his salvation through faith in Christ Jesus. This same Bible was translated into the Damal language by missionaries. Lukas also came to have faith in Christ Jesus, first through hearing the teaching of the Bible and then later being able to read the Word of God for himself. The exact same pattern can be true for us—being taught the truth of the Bible, firmly believing these truths and then reading the Book for ourselves.

How often we take for granted our skill of being able to read. We learned to read as small children. For Lukas and all the tribal people this was not so. However, the Damals have one advantage over those learning to read English. The missionary linguist used phonics when he reduced the language to writing. In Damal every sound is represented by one letter and every letter has only one sound—so much easier than English where one letter can have many sounds!

It's an amazing thing when you stop to think about it. God, the Creator of the whole world—including man made in His own image—chose to reveal to mankind His eternal plan and purpose in written form, the Bible. What a privilege it is to have the Bible translated into our own language from the Hebrew and Greek, so we can read it for ourselves.

ISSUES TO CONSIDER

1. Pastors and Bible teachers encourage every person to have a set time each day to read the Bible. Why is this important?
2. In 2 Timothy 3:16 we read the Bible was written under God's inspiration. What does that mean?

Chapter 4
Lukas Meets Two Pretty Girls

Lukas continues his story:

Every morning we Christians at Jila came together in small groups. We left our breakfast potatoes baking in the ashes of our home fire and gathered in the largest nearby house. The air was still cool and the fire in the center of the hut felt good. One person in the group told a Bible story, one which he had learned in church. Adults and children recited a Bible verse line by line. After each phrase everyone repeated the words in unison. Usually several people prayed. Everything we did in life we did as a village unit and learning God's word was no exception.

Before I learned to read, I often recited a memory verse at morning devotions. Now I told the Bible story, and I wasn't limited to the stories I'd heard the pastor give. The day before, I picked out a story about Jesus in my Book of Mark. I read it over and over until I could tell the story from memory. I was surprised to see how well everyone listened when I really knew what I was going to say. Sometimes I daydreamed about being asked to give the Bible lesson to the whole church on Sunday.

Time passed. The missionaries who lived across the river had moved away. South of the central mountain range, Jila was no longer the only place where Christians gathered on Sundays. Church groups met in valleys to the east and to the west of Jila Ridge. Some of these also had a pastor who had been trained at the Bible School in Beoga.

I decided to go on a trip with a friend walking west to visit two of the distant areas where Damals lived. We set out, and after two days of hiking we came to the first group of villages. Here we found a church much like ours at Jila. In talking to the pastor I told him that I could read, and often told a Bible story during village devotions.

The pastor said to me, "Would you like to speak in church on Sunday?"

Lukas and the Rebels

"Yes, I really would like to," I told him. I chose a Bible story from the Book of Mark and began reviewing it so I could speak. I'd hoped for a chance like this and now I had it.

Something else happened in this village that I wasn't expecting. This pretty girl came up to me and started talking. No one else was around. Suddenly I felt warm inside and drawn to her. In my village no girl had ever spoken to me like this when no one else was around. As we talked I knew it was not proper for a guy and girl to talk alone. I didn't want to hurt her feelings though, so I kept talking. Pretty soon she said, "I like you."

Right then I realized what was happening, and I blurted out, "No! I want to serve God." Saying those words helped me to walk away from her.

Sunday was a good day. This was my first time ever to speak in church. I was very nervous but God helped me. After church my friend and I started out on the trail again. That night we slept in a jungle hut. The next day we hiked on and by evening we reached a valley with several Damal villages.

Here too the people were very friendly and anxious to hear all the news from Jila. The pastor of this church also asked me to speak on Sunday, so my friend and I decided to stay the week before heading home.

All week long I heard talk of plans for a sing-sing to the girls on Saturday night. A sing-sing is an all-night party where young men sing to young women.

The young men sit on one side of the fire in the center of the hut and the young, unmarried women sit on the opposite side. Behind the young people in a larger circle the older adults find their places. In the flickering firelight a man begins to sing and another man joins him singing the harmony part. After each phrase of the song everyone else, both young and old, sings a repetitive response, a response sung without words. The little hut resonates with their voices.

In turn another young man tells a story from his life, composing the song as he sings. He may recount a hunting trip he made looking for a wild pig or perhaps it was to gather jungle nuts. He might tell of his bravery in a fight or the adventure of a long trip. As the evening progresses, his attention is focused on one young woman. He waves his hands across the fire toward her and she returns the gesture toward him, all in time to the singing. Then their hands touch as he gives her a little gift. The singing goes on through the night and emotions increase. Here at the sing-sing the young people are well chaperoned. However, the next day a couple will often meet secretly.

Lukas Meets Two Pretty Girls

All this I knew because, as a child, I had attended sing-sings, sitting in the outside circle with the adults. Now as a young man I realized I should not attend this one, because singing to a young woman all night like this brings strong temptation to sin.

Saturday night the village was crowded with young men and women who had come from distant villages for the sing-sing. They wore their most colorful attire. Some had beautiful bird-of-paradise feathers in their hair. Others had colorful, fragrant leaves tucked in an armband. Everyone had painted attractive designs on their faces with red and black makeup.

One of the girls looked at me and noticed that I wasn't made-up for the occasion. She said, "Aren't you going to the sing-sing, Lukas? Don't be a party pooper. Come on, let's go!"

Suddenly my heart was racing and I was attracted to this girl. Everyone else was going. I wanted to go. A voice inside of me said, *Just go and enjoy the singing. There is nothing wrong with that. Your family is not here. Besides, you can stop before you do anything really wrong.*

Again, I heard the girl say, "Come on, Lukas, let's go!"

I almost went with her. Then I remembered that God had called me to follow Him. "No," I said. "I'm traveling the Jesus path. You go on if you want to." As I walked away, I knew that it was God who helped me make that right choice.

BIBLE LESSON

Paul writes to his son in the faith, Timothy:

> Whoever says that he belongs to the Lord must turn away from wrongdoing.
>
> If anyone makes himself clean from all those evil things, he will be used for special purposes, because he is dedicated and useful to his Master, ready to be used for every good deed.
>
> Avoid the passions of youth, and strive for righteousness, faith, love, and peace, together with those who with a pure heart call out to the Lord for help. 2 Timothy 2:19, 21-22

Lukas and the Rebels

> Son, pay attention to what your father and mother tell you. Their teaching will improve your character as a handsome turban or a necklace improves your appearance.
>
> Son, when sinners tempt you, don't give in. Suppose they say, "Come on; let's find someone to kill! Let's attack some innocent people for the fun of it! We'll find all kinds of riches and fill our houses with loot! Come and join us, and we'll all share what we steal." Son, don't go with people like that. Stay away from them. Proverbs 1:8-11, 13-15

Satan's temptations come to young people all over the world—and they come to not-so-young people in the same way. Each time Lukas was tempted, he made a decision first with his mind. Then he used his own two feet to walk away from the girl who was tempting him. If he had gone to the sing-sing that night, the temptation might have been more than he could withstand. His whole life might have been different. God will forgive any sin if we confess it to him, but once our innocence or purity is lost, it is lost forever. Not even God can restore to us what we have lost.

Defacing or damaging someone else's property, no matter how small it may seem, is vandalism, punishable by law. Whether one gets caught or not, it's wrong. How easy it is for a young person to listen to a friend who says, "Come on, let's have some fun." Before he knows it, he's done something really wrong. To keep out of trouble Proverbs tells all of us—don't hang out with people who do such things.

ISSUES TO CONSIDER

1. What gave Lukas the strength to say "no" to the girls who tempted him?

2. We do not have a sing-sing in our culture, but what similar temptations face us?

3. The words of Paul, "Whoever says that he belongs to the Lord must turn away from wrongdoing," are both powerful and pointed. We dare not overlook them in our present world.

Chapter 5
The Preacher Boy

Introduction

In this chapter you will meet "the rebels." They are a small band of Papua tribal men who are rebelling against the Indonesian government. They seek independence, using any means possible, including violence. Until a few years ago there were no rebels in the mountains, and for that matter there was no Indonesian government either. There were no missionaries; there was no one at all from the outside world. Today whenever the rebels are active in an area and are trying to overthrow the government, all parts of normal life are interrupted.

The goal of the rebel movement is to regain the full freedom and independence they had before the outside world burst in upon them. At the same time they want all the benefits and luxuries they see in the modern world.

In the worldview of the Damal people, as it came to them from their forefathers, they thought that all their possessions and skills had been given to them magically. Supernatural powers had even revealed how to grow sweet potatoes and to make their wooden and stone tools. The possessions of all men came to them in the same way. They believed the foreigners had steel tools and many other things because they knew the supernatural key to obtain them. Now the rebels proclaimed that if the Damals turned the right "magic key," which was removing the Indonesian government they would receive by magic all the marvels of the outside world. These material things would then come directly to them instead of being funneled to the Indonesians.

Lukas continues:

All of us were hearing talk about rebels coming to Jila. This began after the missionaries moved away and the government set up a small civil post on our

Lukas and the Rebels

ridge. The rebel leaders were all tribal people. Some of them were once our own neighbors; we knew them personally. They chose Jila as a place to begin their conquest because the government post there was very small. The Indonesian officials were unarmed—no police or military were stationed on our village ridge.

Word went out from the rebel leaders, almost like a command. "Join with us! Join now! We will fight and overthrow the Indonesian government. As soon as we get rid of these foreigners," they promised, "all the good things they have, like cars and houses, will be ours." To have these marvelous things given to us magically in exchange for ridding our territory of the government sounded like a real prize.

Our church leaders took a stand against the rebel cause. "The Bible teaches we should remain at peace with all men," they said. "We should submit to the government."

Everyone at Jila had to make a decision. Either join the rebels and fight, or remain at peace and support the government. We Damals made this decision, not as individuals, but as a group like we made all decisions.

People living on the upper end of the Jila Ridge chose to follow the Bible and peace. Damals living on the lower end of the ridge joined the rebels. That decision divided our people. With the help of these new recruits the rebels found it easy to overpower the unarmed Indonesian men at the government post. The war of 1977 had begun.

Suddenly, out of the sky came a new kind of flying-boat that did not need an airstrip to land. It was called a helicopter. Soldiers carrying guns came out of the helicopter right in front of the government post. These men, who were dressed in khaki uniforms and spoke only the Indonesian language, had no idea which ones of us were rebel sympathizers and which ones remained loyal to the government. To gain control of the area the soldiers decided to burn every house on the ridge—those below the government post who had joined the rebels and those above who had not. They began going up the ridge—burning houses, one by one, as they went.

We had no time to think. Everyone ran, taking only what they had in their hands at the time. I wanted my three New Testament books. They were in my house and would soon be burned. These books meant more to me than any other thing I had. I decided to risk it. I ran back to the house, grabbed my books and ran on to the forest with the others.

Going back for my Bible books that day was one of the best decisions I ever made in my life, for we spent almost three years hiding out in the forest before we could return to the Jila Ridge.

The Preacher Boy

I ended up in our forest hideout with five families and several men. We built shelters using the vines and trees that grew everywhere. We cleared small pieces of ground in the jungle, planting what we could. Here we were, a little group hidden in the forest. We were alive, God was with us, and I had my three Bible books—the Book of Mark and my new copies of the Gospel of John and Acts.

No one else in our group could read. I thought maybe I could be the church leader, so I asked the older men if they'd like me to lead a church service and speak on Sundays. They agreed. Now I had my chance, but could I do it? I was still a teenager with no training beyond being able to read. I decided to try. From my Gospel of John I picked a story and read it over and over again. I would tell that story in my talk on Sunday morning.

Saturday night before I was to speak the first time, I had a dream. In my dream I saw a person coming toward me. He was tall and dazzling white. Was he a missionary? No, he was an angel. In his hand he carried a gourd, one like we Damals use to carry drinking water. Standing over me with the gourd, he poured something on my head. It was the gospel, the message of the Bible that he poured over me. Then he handed me the gourd and spoke: "Go and pour this gospel, the good news of Jesus, on the heads of many people."

Suddenly I awoke. I knew this was God's voice speaking to me. He would help me tell the Good News to my people. And he did, right there in our jungle camp every Sunday.

BIBLE LESSON

>That night Paul had a vision in which he saw a Macedonian standing and begging him, "Come over to Macedonia and help us!" As soon as Paul had this vision, we got ready to leave for Macedonia, because we decided that God had called us to preach the Good News to the people there. Acts 16:9-10

Paul wrote to Timothy

>In the presence of God and of Christ Jesus, . . . I give you this charge: Preach the Word; be prepared in season and out of season. 2 Timothy 4:1-2 RSV

Lukas and the Rebels

> Set your hearts on spiritual gifts, especially the gift of proclaiming God's message. . . The one who proclaims God's message speaks to people and gives them help, encouragement, and comfort. . . The one who proclaims God's message helps the whole church. Condensed from 1 Corinthians 14:1, 3-4

When Lukas was a boy, he watched the missionary family as he peeked through the cracks in their wall. At that time God put a desire in his heart to someday read the Bible and to tell others about Jesus.

Lukas did not have a complete copy of the New Testament for God to use in calling him to become a preacher. God chose to use an angel in a dream to reassure him of that calling. He confirmed to Lukas that even though he was young and had no formal Bible training, he should teach from the Bible each Sunday like a pastor. In retrospect Lukas might look back and see how God used this extreme period of hardship, almost three years in his life, to propel him toward becoming a full-time pastor.

To guide us, God often uses a Bible story, a verse or sometimes words spoken by a seasoned Christian. Always the Holy Spirit confirms His direction in our hearts. All around the world God continues to call out people to become lifetime pastors or career missionaries.

ISSUES TO CONSIDER

1. Once, God spoke to Paul through a dream. Has He spoken to you through a Scripture passage or a person who gave you direction in your life?
2. A privileged few have felt the gentle urging of the Holy Spirit to make Christian ministry their life's work. This still happens today.

Chapter 6
Manna on a Jungle Vine

Lukas continues his story:

The years that followed were three very hard years for all of us Damals. We Christians were hiding out, way up in the forest. Damals who sided with the rebels and their goal to overthrow the government had fled to the rebel camp area down in the jungle. Those with the rebels always hoped for the riches promised by their leaders, but nothing ever came. All of us knew, whether we were hiding high up in the forest or down in the hot jungle, was that we could not survive much longer if we continued to live as we were.

Finally everyone in both camps, Christians and rebels alike, agreed to live at peace with the government. We all began to move back to Jila Ridge.

While we were in hiding, our gardens were overgrown with weeds and jungle plants. Our staple food, the sweet potato, was wiped out. As long as anyone could remember the sweet potato was about all we Damals ate. We baked the potatoes in the hot ashes under our fire and steamed the leaves of the potato vine in a pit using hot rocks heated in the same fire.

Now the jungle had taken over and all that was left in our gardens were a few potato vines. No potatoes were growing under the ground, yet these vines represented hope for the future. We planted sweet potatoes by cutting off a piece of potato vine and sticking it into the prepared garden soil. The vines still growing in our old gardens were enough to give us a new start but not enough to give us any food.

We had to start from the beginning, first digging the ground, building fences and then planting sweet potatoes. Five months after all this was completed we would dig our first potatoes. What would we live on while we waited?

Several years earlier a traveler brought the first *labu* seeds to Jila. This soft, yellow little vegetable growing on a vine turned out to be, for us, like the manna that God sent to the children of Israel. For forty years God's children ate manna when they were in the desert where there were no gardens. For five months we ate *labu* while our sweet potatoes grew.

When we returned, we found *labu* plants growing everywhere. As each *labu* had lain unpicked, the sun and rain caused it to spoil. The process continued; the *labu* broke open and the rotting squash fertilized the soil. Then the same sun and rain helped the exposed seeds to sprout and many new *labu* plants grew up. This fast-growing little plant, which was really a jungle vine itself, held its own against the advancing tangle of weeds and bushes that covered all the gardens. It had flourished even better than if we had been there to care for the garden ourselves.

Besides eating the *labu*, we also ate the green leaves from the plant. When we steamed them with hot rocks, they tasted something like the greens and spinach we normally ate but not as good. Eating the *labu* itself wasn't as good as eating a sweet potato either. It is a very bland tasting food and didn't fill us up like sweet potatoes do. However, when we were hungry and thought there would be nothing at all to eat, having *labu* and its leaves was very good. As we ate, we thanked God for the *labu* plant He sent to Jila.

The military post was now well established on our ridge. The civil government post was reopened and with it something new came to Jila. The government brought in a teacher who started an Indonesian elementary school. Since this was the first school ever at Jila, the teacher did not limit enrollment in first grade to children only. Anyone who was not married could attend. Now I had a chance to go to a real school. Even though I was fully grown and the oldest student who applied, I wasn't married. I went to school for three years and learned to speak basic Indonesian and also to read and write in that language.

BIBLE LESSON

> The Lord said to Moses, "Now I am going to cause food to rain down from the sky for all of you. The people must go out every day and gather enough for that day. In this way I can test them to find out if they will follow my instructions."
>
> In the morning there was dew all around the camp. When the dew evaporated, there was something thin and flaky on the surface of the desert. It was as delicate as frost. When the Israelites saw it, they didn't know what it was and asked each other, "What is it?"
>
> Moses said to them, "This is the food that the Lord has given you to eat."

Manna on a Jungle Vine

The people of Israel called the food manna. Exodus 16:4, 13b-15, 31a

Jesus said, "This, then, is how you should pray: Our Father in heaven: . . .Give us today the food we need." Matthew 6:9, 13

The Jila Christians trusted God for their needs. God brought peace and reconciliation with the government and with the other Damals. They prayed for food and He gave them the lowly *labu* plant. Who would have imagined that God would use the *labu* to supply the food they needed? It became manna on a vine. God always has a way of taking care of the needs of his children whatever those needs are—food, finances, friends. But have you noticed? He often supplies our needs in a way very different from what we envisioned in our prayer. How exciting it is to trust God!

Only a few of Lukas's peers ever went to school. This was the second time that Lukas took advantage of an opportunity and pressed himself into a school that was not exactly intended for him.

Many a door in life appears closed to us when we first knock. If the venture is important, try knocking on the back door. If that fails try calling to someone through an open window. Not all rules are set in stone. God will open the way, if this is part of His plan for our life.

Lukas didn't know it, but soon everything he had learned in the Indonesian school would become very helpful in his life.

ISSUES TO CONSIDER

1. The Damals didn't enjoy eating *labu* as much as they enjoyed eating sweet potatoes just as the children of Israel didn't enjoy eating nothing but manna for 40 years. Yet in the end, each group was thankful for the food they had been given.

2. Jesus said, "You should pray: Our Father in heaven: . . . Give us today the food we need." The King James Version reads: "Give us this day our daily bread." What exactly do those words mean?

Chapter 7

A Bride for Lukas

Introduction

In Damal culture marriages are arranged by the families. The man's family chooses a young woman and contacts her family. The bride and groom have very little say about whom they will marry. Tribal law says that a marriage is official when the family of the man pays the bride-price to the family of the woman. The men of both families spend weeks, even months, haggling over the price to be paid for the young woman who will be given in marriage. Thus the exchange of payment becomes more important than consideration of the young people.

Lukas continues his story:

Life on the ridge was back to normal. I had finished three years of Indonesian school and wanted to get married. According to our tribal customs my older brother and uncles began bargaining for a wife for me. However, the girl they picked was not a Christian. When I heard about this, I said, "I don't want that girl. I will not marry her. She's not a Christian. How can I serve God with a wife who doesn't have a desire to love and obey the Lord as I do?"

Joanna was the girl I wanted to marry. I liked her and she was a Christian. But my family continued to work on the marriage arrangements for the other girl. I wondered if they would ever listen to me. Months went by. My family was about to make the payments on the girl I did not want. With time running out Joanna and I decided to elope, even though eloping was almost unheard of among the Damals. We ran away and got married without legalizing our union with our families.

When we came home my family was finally convinced that I was not going to marry the girl they had chosen. So they made all the bride-price payments to Joanna's family. This made everything legal and proper for us.

Would you like to hear what my family paid to Joanna's family? All my relatives worked together to gathered the large payment. It was eight big pigs, 100,000 rupiahs [$50] and three *muka* sea shells. The pigs were the biggest part of the payment. The little sea shell is a small, cowry shell, and is what we Damals used for cash until people from the outside world came. In the past we had no contact with the coast and no way for more shells to be brought into the mountains—thus the shells we had were limited in number and became valuable money to us. The *muka* shell is an especially valuable shell, one that has been treasured, polished and traded through many generations of bride-price payments. With this large payment my family was saying they valued me and my marriage to Joanna. Both families affirmed that our marriage was a lasting union until death.

One day, after we had been married for some time, my pastor asked me, "Lukas, do you think you could organize youth meetings? There are 100 students here on Jila Ridge attending the government elementary school. Most attend church but many don't go to Sunday school where they would learn the stories of the Bible. We need something especially for the youth." With this invitation I knew that God had given me another chance to serve Him.

That's how the Jila youth group got started. Young people in the elementary school came from all over the southern mountains because there was no other school, only this one at Jila. Some of the boys had walked two or even three days from their homes to board with a distant relative so they could attend. There were a few girls in the school too, but the families of the girls lived nearby. All youth were welcome to come to the meetings whether or not they attended the Indonesian school. Young married people also joined the group. We began with Sunday afternoon meetings and later added a second meeting on Friday after school.

Everybody loved to sing. We sang the traditional Damal chant tunes with Christian words—the songs we sang in all church services. We also sang choruses with Western music and Indonesian words. The older people didn't like this kind of music but the youth loved it.

Sometimes I taught a Bible lesson. Other times I chose a story from the New Testament and assigned several verses in the story to a different boy or girl who could read Damal. One by one they read their verses and explained them. Then I spoke, putting it all together. They were learning to tell a Bible story just as I had learned. Those who

Lukas and the Rebels

couldn't read in the Damal language soon signed up for the church reading program. They wanted to get in on the action too. After learning to read and getting their Bible the next step for many was to be baptized. For a long time our youth meetings were the biggest thing happening on Jila Ridge.

BIBLE LESSON

>Do not try to work together [be yoked together] as equals with unbelievers, for it cannot be done. How can right and wrong be partners? How can light and darkness live together? How can Christ and the Devil agree? What does a believer have in common with an unbeliever? How can God's temple come to terms with pagan idols? For we are the temple of the living God! 2 Corinthians 6:14-16

>Trust in the Lord with all your heart. Never rely on what you think you know. Remember the Lord in everything you do, and he will show you the right way. Never let yourself think that you are wiser than you are; simply obey the Lord and refuse to do wrong. Proverbs 3:5-7

Choosing the person we will marry is a very important decision, one we should think and pray about long before we have plans to be married. Lukas was very right when he said to his family, "I will not marry the girl you chose because she is not a Christian. How can I serve God with a wife that doesn't love Him as I do?" The Bible clearly says a Christian should not marry a non-Christian.

Joanna was a good choice because she loved the Lord and wanted to go along with Lukas as he became a pastor. However, eloping without his family's approval was not the way to go, since a marriage was not legal without the bride-price payment. He should have prayed and waited to see how God would work it out. Proverbs says, "Simply obey the Lord and refuse to do wrong."

The story of how Lukas eloped reminds me of how Rebecca in the Bible directed her son Jacob to trick his father into giving him the family blessing of the first-born. (Genesis 27) Both Lukas and Jacob desired the best God had planned for them, but they both should have prayed about the problem and let God work it out. Proverbs says, "Trust in the Lord with all your heart. Never rely on what you think you know. . . He will show you the right way."

A Bride for Lukas

It's amazing to see how God used Lukas to develop an excellent youth program even with no formal education. In starting the program Lukas was trusting in the Lord, not himself. God showed him the right way to go.

ISSUES TO CONSIDER

1. Lukas wanted to marry a Christian and he did. Jacob wanted the promised birthright and he got it. Does a good ending make it right when the way you got there was wrong?

2. Most often 2 Corinthians 6:14-16 is applied to marriage. Do other applications come to mind?

Chapter 8

Rebels and the Magic Key

Lukas continues his story:

In 1987 rumors were flying again—rumors about our friends and neighbors. Some of them wanted to rejoin the rebel movement and banish the government from Jila Ridge. Word had it that the big rebel leaders were planning to come from their lowland jungle base and capture the military post at Jila. Everyone said Jila would be an easy post to capture. It was isolated and very far from any other military post. What could a mere 20 soldiers do when scores of rebel men attacked them? The rebel leaders wanted the military guns and were ready to kill anyone to get them.

Over a period of months the rebel leaders moved closer, building a base camp only a day's walk away from Jila. Then a camp was set up three hours away. Finally the village people of Dilowa, [DEE-low-ah] just an hour's walk from Jila in the other direction, joined the rebels. Dilowa village became a rebel base. [See story 4 map]

All this time the rebel leaders were trying to win everyone who lived on Jila Ridge to their side. They began with the same promise they had used ten years before. A magical reward would come to all who joined in the fight to rid the ridge of every Indonesian.

"When we are victors," they boasted, "all the wonders of the outside world will arrive at Jila by magic—roads, cars, foreign houses, everything the foreigners have! All these things will be only for those who join and help in the fight. And this time we won't stop until we've gained our prize." Some of our village men had seen these marvels at the modern American mining town seven days walk to the west. What a prize it would be to have all of this.

When this incentive did not work in getting people to join with them, the rebel leaders came into a village masquerading as friends. Without shooting an arrow, they began treating the villagers like a defeated enemy. They stole their sweet potatoes and pigs, tore up their gardens and molested their women. In time almost all the nearby villages became rebel collaborators. Why not avoid this harassment and at the same time get in on all the wealth that is coming, they reasoned. Two of the three villages on the ridge did not join their cause. Joanna and I lived in one of these villages located up the ridge from the government post. We remained opposed to the rebels and all they were trying to do.

Next the rebels began coming into our village at night. Sometimes they hid in the grass just out of sight along the main path that ran up the ridge. Each day the rebels became bolder in their efforts to win the remaining two villages to join them. With the last two holdout villages on their side the military post would be completely surround by pro-rebel Damals. However, all the people in our two villages remained loyal to the church's Bible teachings. We put God above everything else in life.

One day my brother Simon came to me saying, "The rebels are all around the military post, hiding in the grass. We're going to have to make a decision. Either we join the rebels or we warn the military of what is happening."

Simon and I went to the military post and told them of the danger. The military men began shooting into the grass and the rebels fled. However, the rebels soon returned, even sleeping in the grass at night all around the post, watching for their chance.

One day I met some rebels near my house. I pled with them, "Don't do this thing. Many people will be killed. The church building will be burned. God's work will be crushed—all for nothing."

They paid no attention to me. Instead they said, "Lukas, you are the one who had better change and join our ranks. You are the one who will suffer, not us."

People feared the rebels most because they had three guns. Sometimes they fired them so we knew they had ammunition. They got these guns by killing military men in another area. Their plan was to do the same at Jila.

We never knew from day to day what would happen next. Weeks went by. Then one day we saw scores of warriors quietly gathering on the ridge. All the villages in the area, except our two, had joined the rebels for a major attack on the government post. The men were all armed with bows and arrows and three leaders carried guns.

A rebel carrying a gun came upon a man from my village by surprise. The leader aimed the gun at the Damal man at point blank range and pulled the trigger, but nothing happened. It didn't go off. We knew God was taking care of us. Villagers fled and the war party ran on to the military post.

The soldiers opened fire, not really trying to hit anyone. As they had hoped, the warriors all ran for their lives. Their well planned attack had failed.

Lukas and the Rebels

With this defeat the leaders changed tactics. They left the military post alone and began to target their own people in the two villages loyal to the government. They hoped that we would change sides and join their rebel cause, all the while believing that when we did, they could defeat the military.

"Let the military stay where they are," they said. "We'll hit the Christians."

Living on Jila Ridge were some 200 Damals who remained loyal to the government. Our houses were built along one straight path up this narrow ridge. The church was built near the top, a half-hour walk down the path was the government post, and below that was the village that had sided with the rebels.

The ground on the ridge itself is white clay and no vegetables will grow in the clay. On each side of the ridge is a large rushing river that drains the high mountains to the north. All of our gardens were planted in the better soil found on the steep sides of the ridge. Some gardens were planted even further away, wherever a bit of good ground could be found.

Now the rebels began to rip up our gardens and steal our pigs. Our women did not dare go to the garden to dig sweet potatoes lest they be molested. Food was scarce and we were hungry. How long could we live like this?

BIBLE LESSON

>Like a partridge that hatches eggs it did not lay, is the man who gains riches by unjust means. When his life is half gone, they will desert him, and in the end he will prove to be a fool. Jeremiah 17:11 NIV

>Let no debt remain outstanding, except the continuing debt to love one another. Romans 13:8a NIV

>Save me, Lord, from evil men; keep me safe from violent men. Psalm 140:1

Many of the Jila people went along with the rebels and believed all they had to do to acquire the riches of the outside world was to turn the "magic key"—in this case getting rid of the Indonesian government. To us this sounds ridiculous, doesn't it?

Rebels and the Magic Key

Then I thought how Americans try to gain sudden wealth or get something for nothing. Are there "magic keys" we turn? What about stealing or cheating? What about buying lottery tickets or gambling or buying things with money we don't have by using a credit card? Stealing and cheating are illegal ways to acquire goods. Buying a lottery ticket and gambling are legal ways people use as a "magic key" to try to get rich quick. Borrowing money with a credit card to buy things we can't afford is legal, but is it a good way to live? Is it in God's plan for us? Continued use of a credit card, when we don't have the money to pay it off, leads to financial bondage and worse.

The Jila Christians were involved in more than an earthly fight. They were also fighting a spiritual battle. The Indonesian military had all they could do to protect themselves. They gave no help to the loyal Damals. The Christians were a small band compared to the rebels. For them the choice was clear—either join the rebels or depend on God, and only God, for their survival. They too prayed David's prayer in Psalm 140:1 "Save me, Lord, from evil men; keep me safe from violent men."

ISSUES TO CONSIDER

1. Would you agree that Americans have various kinds of "magic keys?"

2. Consider this statement: For all Damals, Christian or non-Christian, their natural way of thinking was to believe every skill and tool came only by magic. As an example, for Americans today, Christian or non-Christian, the accepted way of living is to use a "magic" credit card. The Damal Christian only breaks his pattern of thinking when he addresses the issue from the teaching of the Bible. Similarly, the American Christian should adjust his credit card use when it does not conform to the standards of the Bible. (Romans 8:13)

Chapter 9

Let's Kill Lukas

Lukas continues his story:

"The rebels stole my pig and I'm not going to let them get away with it!" Simon shouted.

My brother Simon was really angry because the rebels had just shot his one and only big pig—a mother pig who had six little pigs—and carried it back to their base camp at Dilowa village. "They can't get away with this! They'll have to pay me for my pig!" Simon shouted. "Who'll go with me?" [See story 4 map]

"I'm with you, Simon," I said, and three other men also joined us.

It was Wednesday morning. We started out determined to accomplish our mission. Simon kept saying, "What right do these people have to steal my mother pig?"

We were walking up the Dilowa stream bed when all of a sudden rebels, armed with bows and arrows, jumped out in front of us.

Simon shouted, "Why did you steal my pig? You must pay me for it."

"We were waiting for you," they shouted back. "You joined with the government. You are traitors. Now you are coming to our village where we can kill you."

One man tied my hands behind my back and yelled, "Keep going on up the trail." Others tied the hands of my four companions and we were all forced to continue hiking up the stream bed.

Entering the village I spotted the leaders. There were three of them, one carried a gun. I knew all three by name. Before they joined the rebel movement, they had been my neighbors living on Jila Ridge. The one named Jairus was the son of our first Jila pastor—the pastor who taught me how to read. The three wore army uniforms, after a sort.

"Stand out there in the center" they commanded.

All day long we were forced to stand in the village yard while they harassed us. "Why do you continue to support the government? Join us! Together we can soon overthrow these foreigners."

Men kept walking in front of us chewing on a bone of pork from Simon's prize pig. They gave us nothing to eat, not even a sweet potato. When afternoon came, the rebels beat each of us severely. (In our Damal tribe no one ever beat an enemy like this when he was tied and could not fight back.) During the beating three of our group agreed to change sides and join the rebel ranks. These men were released and headed for home. But Simon and I did not budge.

The leaders were in a huddle. Then one stepped forward with a pronouncement. "We will cut off Simon's ear because he won't listen and we'll kill Lukas." The commander gave the word. His subordinate took a dagger and sliced off Simon's ear right down to his skull and threw it in the dirt. "Now go home!" the leader shouted. "Others can see what we do to traitors."

(We Damals mark our pigs for identification by cutting a distinctive notch in their ear. But even in war, we never defaced the body of an enemy.)

It was late afternoon now. The rebel with the gun said to me, "We're going to kill you! We'll do it in our main camp where our big chief can see you first. Come on, let's go." [See story 4 map]

Men grabbed their bows and arrows. Chanting like warriors returning home in victory, the party set out. The men were traveling fast—in high excitement for the kill. Daylight would be gone in a couple of hours.

Down, down the stream bed we went. With my hands tied behind my back I could not dance along as they did, leaping from rock to rock. I kept falling and soon my legs were bruised and bleeding. "Keep going!" my captors called out, and I did. We reached the end of the Dilowa stream where it empties into the Jila River. Crossing the river on a pole bridge we climbed the opposite bank and then crossed the lower end of Jila Ridge. There were no houses this far down on the ridge.

Now we went down again, down the steep trail headed for the Dolo River. This was a long descent. I kept slipping and falling, but I got up again and on we went. The last rays of daylight were almost gone as we came to the river crossing. In a few more minutes it would be dark, and we could not have crossed. Carefully I walked out over the roaring water on the single log pole that spanned most of the river. The log rested on a huge boulder near the far side. From that boulder there was another, smaller, wobbly pole

Lukas and the Rebels

to walk. It was hard to balance with my hands tied behind my back but I made it safely across to the far side of the Dolo River.

Again we climbed up, up—always in single file because the path up the bank was narrow and full of obstacles. It was hard going for me and it seemed we'd never get to the top. Crossing Dolo Ridge was like crossing Jila Ridge, except that Dolo Ridge is much wider and very overgrown with jungle. No people live on this ridge.

It was very dark now. We were going down again into a deep gorge, the Noma River Gorge. I knew we were getting close to the river when I heard the loud roar of the water as it poured over one boulder to be quickly dashed on yet another huge rock a few feet downstream. People who fell in the Jila or Dolo rivers drowned, but the Noma River was much larger. A bridge made of a log balanced on two boulders could not be built here. We came to a swinging bridge made of rattan vines. The bridge was suspended high above the water level and we crossed. Climbing up the gradual ascent I could soon see the many fires of the rebel base camp. My captors increased their gleeful shouting and danced the dance of victory as they entered the camp where the rebel chief waited.

BIBLE LESSON

The Spirit led Jesus into the desert to be tempted by the Devil. After spending 40 days and nights without food, Jesus was hungry. Then the Devil came to him and said, "If you are God's Son, order these stones to turn into bread." But Jesus answered, "The Scripture says, 'Man cannot live on bread alone, but needs every word that God speaks.'"

Then the Devil took Jesus to Jerusalem, the Holy City, set him on the highest point of the Temple, and said to him, "If you are God's Son, throw yourself down." Jesus answered, "But the scripture also says, 'Do not put the Lord your God to the test.'"

Then the Devil took Jesus to a very high mountain and showed him all the kingdoms of the world in all their greatness. "All this I will give you," the Devil said, "if you kneel down and worship me." Then Jesus answered, "Go away, Satan! The scripture says, 'Worship the Lord your God and serve only him!'"

Then the Devil left Jesus; and angels came and helped him. Matthew 4:1-11

> Every test that you have experienced is the kind that normally comes to people. But God keeps his promise, and he will not allow you to be tested beyond your power to remain firm; at the time you are put to the test, he will give you the strength to endure it, and so provide you with a way out. 1 Corinthians 10:13

Three times the Devil presented Jesus with temptations that were very real to him. Each time Jesus answered the Devil by quoting a verse from the Bible. Knowing the Bible—its verses and stories—can help us too when temptations come our way.

Lukas could have ended his ordeal at any time by simply agreeing to change sides. When Satan tempts us, he makes the way look so easy. "Just change sides and enjoy all the goodies," he says. "It's no big deal."

In I Corinthians10:13 God promises he won't give us a harder test than we can withstand. He will give us strength—more than what we naturally have—and make a way so we can get out of range of the temptation. He will help us not to change sides.

ISSUES TO CONSIDER

We are often confronted with situations where we must choose wisely, as Lukas did when he didn't take the easy way out. How might we prepare to meet a test or make the right choice?

Chapter 10

God Sends His Angels

Lukas continues his story:

I was in the main rebel camp. My captors commanded me to stand in the center of the clearing while they greeted their comrades and passed on the news of the day. From the light of the many campfires I saw that everyone was eating. The sweet potato that I'd eaten for breakfast was all the food I had that day. I was literally exhausted from hunger, but they gave me nothing to eat.

Standing there, I could make out the layout of the buildings. This was no ordinary Damal village where the houses are built in a random fashion with no pattern at all. There were three large cook houses, and many sleeping houses built in straight rows. Scores of people lived here.

Then the rebel chief came. His first angry utterance was, "Let's kill Lukas! He's the one who thwarted our plan to kill the military men at Jila." Taking off his belt he began to whip me with it. "You deserve to die" he cried as his anger increased. Then he stopped.

The chief ordered three men to step forward. One had a club, one carried a large rock and the third man held a long jungle knife. Using the Damal word, *tagate,* which means "hit to kill" he commanded them, "Hit him three times, each of you."

I was still standing with my hands tied behind my back. The first man stepped up swinging a club. He cried out, "I've come to kill you. I'm going to kill you now."

Between blows I spoke in broken words. "I'm not afraid of you. You can't kill my soul. You can kill my body and it will rot, but my soul will go to heaven to be with Jesus."

His blows knocked me to the ground. I saw the second man standing over me with a large rock and heard him say, "There is no God. Where is he if he exists? He will not save you. The military men didn't protect you either. I'm going to kill you now."

Then in my spirit I said, "God, I'm dying. Take my spirit to be with you." And I fell unconscious.

God Sends His Angels

What happened next, I learned much later from a man who was in the group watching. After the third man had his turn at killing me, a man took a knife and thrust it into my skull right by my left ear. I'll always have this large scar that marks the spot where the knife went into my head.

Someone said, "He's dead now. Let's throw his body in the river." So they tied my hands and feet to a long carrying-pole, just like we Damals carry a dead pig. Men carried the pole to a high bank overlooking the river.

Still another man took a long jungle knife and slashed my throat and my chest, time after time. Blood flowed everywhere. These scars will always be on my chest. He thought I was already dead, but he still wanted to take his anger out on me.

I was told later that they tied my two hands together, and then they tied my feet. This would keep my body from getting hung up on a rock as it was carried away in the river. From the high river bank they threw me into the raging Noma River. The men shouted, "We'll send his body down the river to the people who live in the lowland swamps." This was their final insult to me. [See map story 4]

The next thing I knew, I was in the cold water bouncing down the river. I caught a glimpse of a tiny moon up in the sky. I prayed in my heart, "God I'm drowning. Take my spirit to be with you."

Then I was vaguely aware of lying on a large rock on the side of the river, the side away from the rebel camp and toward Jila Ridge. I prayed, "God, give me my senses." My hands and my feet were free, so I began to crawl. I crawled up the bank a little ways from the river and passed out.

Again I awoke and prayed, "God, give me my senses so I can get out of here."

There before me, right in the dense jungle, was a wide open path, not at all like any path I'd ever seen. There had been no open path here when I came down the trail a few hours earlier. Slowly I climbed up to the top of Dolo Ridge. I could go no further.

"The rebels can kill me," I thought. "I don't care any more." And I lost consciousness once again.

* * * * *

That same Wednesday night Joanna, my wife, had a very vivid dream. In her dream she saw a man walking on a path. This man must be Lukas, she thought. He was wearing a bright red shirt and singing joyful praises to God. Beside the man she saw

Lukas and the Rebels

birds, beautiful white doves, flying by his side guiding him as he walked along. To Joanna these doves represented angels.

When she awoke, Joanna wondered what this dream meant. Had Lukas been killed and gone to heaven? Or was God protecting him with his angels?

She told the dream to her mother. "Joanna," her mother said, "I believe it means that God is going to deliver Lukas with his angels."

With the first rays of morning light on Thursday I was lying on the ground drifting in and out of consciousness. Where was I? No, I wasn't in heaven. I was lying in the tall grass on Jila Ridge some distance down the hill from the government post. How did I get here? This was the same point I'd crossed the afternoon before, as rebels took me to their camp. Between me and the rebel camp were two rivers, the Dolo and the Noma, and between them was the wide Noma Ridge. How *did* I get here?

BIBLE LESSON

Advisors, who were jealous of Daniel, said to King Darius:

"Your Majesty should issue an order and enforce it strictly. Give orders that for thirty days no one be permitted to request anything from any god or from any man except from Your Majesty. Anyone who violates this order is to be thrown into a pit filled with lions." So King Darius signed the order.

Daniel learned that the order had been signed . . . Just as he had always done, he knelt down at the open windows and prayed to God three times a day. So the king gave orders for Daniel to be taken and thrown into the pit filled with lions. A stone was put over the mouth of the pit, and the king placed his own royal seal on the stone.

At dawn the king got up and hurried to the pit. When he got there, he called out anxiously, "Daniel, servant of the living God! Was the God you serve so loyally able to save you from the lions?"

Daniel answered, "May Your Majesty live forever! God sent his angel to shut the mouths of the lions so that they would not hurt me." Verses from Daniel 6: 7-22

God Sends His Angels

God will put his angels in charge of you to protect you wherever you go.

God says, "I will save those who love me and will protect those who acknowledge me as Lord. Psalm 91:11, 14

What are the angels, then? They are spirits who serve God and are sent by him to help those who are to receive salvation. Hebrews 1:14

Some people consider angels to be almost like God himself, to be prayed to or worshipped. They make pictures and images of angels. They carry them as good luck pieces, or ask them for help. The Bible says this should not be done. The angels, created by God, are not to be worshiped, they are to worship *Him*. (Hebrews 1)

What are angels? They are spirits who serve God. God *sends* his angels to help Christians. We do not call angels to help us.

In the story of Daniel and the Lions' Den, Daniel continued to pray to God and serve him no matter who threatened him. He would not change sides, even to save his life. God sent his angels to shut the mouths of those hungry lions. In the end the heathen king gave credit to the God of Daniel for saving him from the lions.

There was no man who could save Lukas's life. Lukas did not call on angels to save him; he simply gave himself up into the hands of his God. Although Lukas did not see an angel, I believe as Lukas and Joanna do—that God sent his angels to rescue him from a sure death. They carried him across that rugged terrain to his home area when physically he was unable to walk.

ISSUES TO CONSIDER

1. How do you think Lukas got back to Jila Ridge?
2. Who are angels and where do they come from? How does it happen that angels help certain people?
3. Compare this story about Lukas with the story of Daniel and the Lions' Den.

Chapter 11
God's Miracle, Not Man's Magic

Introduction

Early Thursday morning a teenage boy set out to check his traps. The afternoon before, he had set these traps in the jungle area at the very bottom of Jila Ridge. He hurried down the trail—past the military post and past all the houses scattered along the lower end of the ridge. The boy hoped there would be at least one little jungle animal in his traps that morning. As he was about to enter the jungle area, he saw a movement in the tall grass at the side of the trail. There was something there! Going over to see, he found a man stripped of his clothing. The man's chest and back were all covered with blood and he was terribly swollen. As the boy looked closer, he cried, "It's Lukas! It's Lukas!" and ran to get help.

One of the first to hear the news about Lukas was the Damal man who operated the two-way mission radio. This shortwave radio was in the cabin at the top of the ridge that the Gibbons built for their use when they visited Jila. The radio operator regularly called them in Beoga to learn if there were any flight plans for an MAF mission plane to come to Jila. When he got word of a flight he would check the airstrip condition and on the morning of that flight would radio the pilot with a weather report.

As soon as the radio man saw Lukas, he hurried back up the ridge and radioed the Gibbons in Beoga asking them for an emergency flight to take Lukas to the mission hospital. Only a few details could be given by radio. However, the Gibbons realized it might endanger both the pilot and the plane if a landing were made at Jila at this time; the rebels might damage the plane or even attack the pilot, if they were to find a plane on the ground picking up Lukas. (Later when a government plane did make an emergency landing on the Jila airstrip, these same rebels actually destroyed the airplane and took the Indonesian pilot and passengers as hostages, marching them deep into the jungle.) The Gibbons dared not call for a medical emergency plane.

God's Miracle, Not Man's Magic

Lukas continues his story (including details he learned later from others):

Men from the village came and carried me up the ridge to the military post. They put me in a deserted house right across from the military barracks. Word about my condition and where I was found traveled quickly up the ridge. When Joanna got there and saw me, she gasped. "He's covered with blood like the red shirt in my dream, but he's still alive!"

For several days I drifted in and out of consciousness. Once I was vaguely aware of soldiers standing over me and saying, "Let's go kill these rebels who did this to Lukas. So far we've only protected ourselves. We haven't tried to kill any of them. Now we'll go and kill some of them."

I could not speak. My old uncle, a lay pastor who was there, answered for me, "No, wait. Let's not kill them. Lukas would not want you to kill in return."

My friends could hardly believe I was still alive. Everyone on the ridge kept repeating my incredible story. "Just yesterday," they said, "Wednesday morning, Lukas and four other men went to Dilowa village to retrieve Simon's pig. In the afternoon the four men returned home badly beaten-up and Simon was missing his ear. Lukas was forced to go clear across the main valley to the rebel camp. Now this morning, just a day later, he was discovered lying in the tall grass at the bottom of Jila Ridge. In daylight it takes a man in good health almost three hours to make this crossing from the rebel camp to Jila Ridge. No one can cross in the dark. And there Lukas was, back on our ridge more dead than alive."

On Friday a group of rebel warriors came to the Damal Christians at the top of Jila Ridge—to the two villages which had not joined with them. They came dancing and boasting, "We killed one of you. We killed Lukas! Join us now and together we'll wipe out the military!"

They were amazed to learn that I was not dead. "How can this be?" they retorted. "He was dead and we threw his body in the Noma River. Did he use the foreigner's magic?"

My friends answered, "No! He has no foreigner's magic. Since he was a small boy he has served God and only God. It is God and his angels who saved him!"

People told me later that my body had been so swollen, they hardly recognized me.

Every day Joanna came to the military post where I lay and carefully washed the blood away from my many deep gashes. Gradually the bleeding stopped. A military man

Lukas and the Rebels

gave Joanna some sulfa powder which she sprinkled in my open wounds. Beyond this powder there was no medicine.

Each time someone came to see me, they stared in astonishment. The men shook their heads in disbelief to see what the rebels had done to me. The women cried, *"Bau-a, bau-a!* It's amazing he's still alive!"

Everyone said the same thing, "We must get even for what they've done to you, Lukas. The military should go and kill all of them."

I always answered, "No, it was God who took me out of the river. It was God's angels who carried me to Jila Ridge. He saved me. Do not kill in revenge."

Days passed and I was gradually getting better.

The military men had a place for bathing out behind their barracks. When men went out back to bathe, they always took their guns with them. One day as they were bathing, rebels appeared in the tall grass with their three guns. The rebels aimed and pulled the trigger, but no bullets were fired. The military shot back but over their heads, and the rebels fled. Again no one was killed. God kept the rebel guns from firing and He kept the military men from aiming to kill!

BIBLE LESSON

King Nebuchadnezzar had a gold statue made. Then the king gave orders for all his officials to come together to attend the dedication of the statue. A herald announced, "People of all nations, races and languages, bow down and worship the gold statue. Anyone who does not will be immediately thrown into a blazing furnace."

Some Babylonians said, "Your Majesty, there are some Jews who do not bow down and worship the statue you set up." The king flew into a rage and ordered the three men to be brought before him. "Do you think there is any god who can save you?" he said.

Shadrach, Meshach, and Abednego answered, "Your Majesty, if God wills he is able to save us from the blazing furnace. But even if he doesn't, we will not bow down and worship your god or the statue."

So they tied the three men up and threw them into the blazing furnace. Suddenly the king leaped to his feet and cried, "Didn't we tie up three men and throw them into the blazing fire? I see four men walking around—and the fourth one looks like an angel."

The king went to the door of the blazing furnace and called the three men to come out. They were unharmed and didn't even smell like smoke. The king said, "Praise the God of Shadrach, Meshach, and Abednego! He sent his angel and rescued these men who serve and trust him. They risked their lives rather than bow down and worship any god except their own." Condensed from Daniel 3:1-28

As it turned out, God's plan for Lukas did not include the help of a doctor. No human being got any credit for his survival. For the recovery of Lukas God got all the glory!

In giving his testimony to Alice, Lukas compared his experience to that of Shadrach, Meshach, and Abednego. Based on Daniel 3, the comparison is a good one. Both Lukas and the Bible trio were being forced, at the threat of their lives, to compromise a spiritual principle. Each man believed God could save him, but each left it up to God to choose whether he would live or die. Neither Lukas nor the three Bible men tested God by saying, "If you are really God, show your power by saving me." According to the circumstances in both stories the men should have died. Their deliverance was not by human hands. Each gave God all the glory. In both stories men who watched, even unbelievers, acknowledged that it was God who delivered them. Honor was given to the Lord God because of the miracle.

Americans are not likely to face death by taking a stand for their Bible beliefs, but certainly at times they will face coercion to give up their faith. For example one intellectual challenge that demands we deny our faith is evolution.

As Christians we begin with a firm belief that God created the heavens and the earth. With this unshakeable conviction we can, we must, stand firm in what we believe—standing with the same courage Lukas had when challenged to change what he believed.

ISSUES TO CONSIDER

1. It's interesting to note how often passages in the Bible refer to creation. Consider marking them as you read. You'll find references everywhere throughout the Old and New Testaments.

2. Give some thought to the debate between creation and evolution. What do you believe?

Chapter 12

The Rebels' Final Strike

Lukas continues his story:

I awoke suddenly in the middle of the night. My mind was clear. Yes, I was still recuperating in the deserted house across from the military camp but I was all alone. Where were my friends? Where were the military men? Had the rebels taken over? I sensed something was about to happen.

I must get out of there and go up the ridge. Somehow I knew it was not safe to walk on the main path. "God, give me strength," I prayed. In the blackness of night I started up through the underbrush and tangle of vines and eventually met some other village people who were also fleeing. Word had leaked that the rebels were planning a raid to burn houses and kill Damals who had not joined their side. Surely I would be a prime target. With this tip-off every person ran to the jungle to save his own life.

My friends had not warned me when they left for I was in a deep sleep. But God warned me and gave me strength to flee in spite of my wounds.

I spent the rest of the night in the jungle with some of my neighbors. Joanna also fled but I didn't find her until the next morning. No one went very deep into the forest—just far enough to be out of sight of the rebels should they come.

The rebels did come later in the night when the military men were no longer around. They burned my house where my wife had been staying. And they burned other houses of Christians who continued to stand with the government.

If the rebels attacked the post with a large force, the military knew they were in a very dangerous position without the buffer of friendly Damals. They began coaxing us to return. After a short time, we decided to move back to the ridge.

It was so good to be with my brother Simon again. We talked often about how the Lord had taken care of each of us. Many friends visited me, and everyone marveled at how quickly my body was healing. There was only one answer to the question of how this could be. It was God who had delivered me from the hand of my enemies. He also brought healing to my body. I give God all the glory.

One morning exciting news passed up the ridge as fast as wildfire. Simon had captured a rebel gun! During the night he found four rebels asleep in the grass behind the military post. Two had guns and two had bows and arrows. Simon tackled one sleeping man with a rifle and got it away from him. All four of the rebels disappeared into the night. When Simon presented the military with the gun he had captured, they were jubilant. Now the rebels had one less gun.

Although no one knew it at the time, capturing that gun turned out to be the turning point in the war. Because of this, the hard-core rebel leaders withdrew to their distant jungle post taking their two guns with them. Gradually over a period of months the local Damals who had changed sides, came back and made peace with the government. Soon everyone was busy with a garden project. Church groups met on Sunday like they used to meet. Young people enrolled in the literacy program—learning to read so they could read the Bible. In time the missionary made trips by plane to teach and encourage us all.

Life on the ridge became normal again.

BIBLE LESSON

David's song of victory:
> In my trouble I called to the Lord;
>> I called to my God for help.
>
> He flew swiftly on his winged creature;
>> he traveled on the wings of the wind.
>
> He rescued me from my powerful enemies
>> and from all those who hate me.
>
> He helped me out of danger;
>> he saved me because he was pleased with me.
>
> I have obeyed the law of the Lord;
>> I have not turned away from my God.

Lukas and the Rebels

> O Lord, you are faithful to those
>> who are faithful to you.
>
> The Lord lives! Praise my defender!
>> Proclaim the greatness of the God who saves me.
>
> O Lord, you give me victory over my enemies
>> and protect me from violent men.
>
> And so I praise you among the nations;
>> I sing praises to you.
>
>> Selected verses from Psalm 18

God purposely chose what the world considers nonsense in order to shame the wise, and he chose what the world considers weak in order to shame the powerful. 1 Corinthians 1:27

From the time he was a small child Lukas loved the Lord. He continued to listen to God's voice and obey his instructions as a teenager and young adult. All of his life Lukas used the building blocks of faithfulness and obedience—putting one on top of the other. When the gigantic test came, he added one more block and said, "No, I won't change sides no matter what they do to me." And he didn't!

You and I may never face the threat of death while we stand for the right. However, some of the tests that come seem really big. Each trial is about something important in our life making it difficult to stand true. The best way to be ready for the big test is to obey God and do what is right in all the little trials.

Some people quote the saying, "God helps those who help themselves," as if it were a verse from the Bible. Or they say it's a good philosophy for living. This saying is not in the Bible nor is it a good tenet to follow. Psalm 18:25 says, "Lord, you are faithful to those who are faithful to you." God helps those who **depend on Him**—not those who help themselves.

The rebels had most of the local Damals on their side and their leaders were ready to die for their cause. But victory was not theirs. The Indonesian military had men and modern weapons, but they too did not gain victory or resolution in the standoff. God chose Lukas and Simon, the ones the others considered weak, and used them to shame the powerful military and confound the plans of the mighty rebels. (1 Corinthians 1:27)

Peace and stability came to the people of Jila Ridge. Once again they were free to serve the Lord.

ISSUES TO CONSIDER

1. What are your thoughts concerning the saying, "God helps those who help themselves?"

2. Read again the verses from Psalm 18 and consider how the words of David could also be the words of Lukas. How might they apply to your life?

Chapter 13

Forgiving One by One

Lukas concludes his story:

The Damals who had joined the rebels were returning. Each one had to report to the military post and declare that he now wanted to cooperate with the government and live peacefully at Jila.

Their return gave me a chance to tell my story to many of these rebels—the story of how God delivered me out of their hands. The best way to talk to these men, some of whom had actually beaten me, was to invite them to my house to share a meal.

These ex-rebels were hesitant to accept my invitation. Perhaps they feared revenge. They knew that in the Damal way of life no man ever showed love to his enemy. A key part of Damal life and thinking had always been to take revenge. If a man stole your pig, then you and your relatives killed two of his pigs. If your brother was killed in a fight then you and your clan would fight until you had killed more on the other side. The Damal culture provided no police force or court system. Each man personally took revenge for the wrong done to him.

When a man accepted my invitation and came to eat with me, I told him my story. I told him God put a desire in my heart to be like Stephen when he was being stoned. Stephen said, "Lord! Do not remember this sin against them!" and I wanted to do the same. God gave me love for each man who came, and He gave me a desire to see each one of them make his heart right with God.

Marten, who had belonged to our church and later joined the rebels, was one of the men who had beaten me. He accepted my invitation to come and eat with me. Not long after this, Marten prayed confessing his sin to God. Perhaps my testimony helped him turn his life around. Today Marten is serving God. He is back in church, and again takes communion.

One man named Obaiya did not return to Jila Ridge where he had served for some time as our medical worker. He was the man who slashed my throat with a jungle knife just before they threw me in the river. Obaiya was born in the Ilaga. As a young person, he had learned to read Damal and gotten Bible books just like I had. The missionary nurse in the Ilaga trained him to become a medical worker and dispense basic medicines. Obaiya was sent to work in the mission clinic at Jila. His was an honored position in the church and in all the community.

Obaiya did not repent before God or report to the government. Instead he secretly moved to the Ilaga. God himself took vengeance in his life. Not long after arriving in the Ilaga, Obaiya became very sick. The Ilaga medical worker tried to help him but could not, so he was flown to the mission hospital. The doctor diagnosed his illness as cancer of the liver. The doctor said, "There is nothing that I can do. You should be flown back to the Ilaga as soon as possible."

Within a week Obaiya was dead. No man had a hand in his death. The Lord says, "I will take revenge, I will pay back." (Romans 12:19) God did just that.

By myself I could not say, "I don't want to get even with the people who tried to kill me." It was only God who helped me say that. I give all the credit to Him.

Two years later, two of the hardcore rebel leaders turned themselves in to the government. These were the men who made the decision that Simon's ear was to be cut off and I was to be taken to the main rebel camp and killed. The two former rebel leaders are now respectable citizens. One of them named Jairus was in his teens when his dad became our first pastor at Jila. Later, Jairus himself attended the Beoga Bible School for two years. Gradually he put his desire for getting money and becoming a chief ahead of his desire for God. He believed the rebels and their stories of getting rich by magic. Jairus wasted 15 good years of his life serving Satan. Now he has come back to God.

Several years passed. A day came when God again tugged at my heart as He did when I was a little boy peeking through the cracks in the missionary's house. At the earlier time a desire came to my boyhood heart to learn to read God's book and tell His message to others.

I was remembering the vivid dream I had in my late teens after I volunteered to be the preacher to our small group who was hiding way up in the forest. On that Saturday night, before I was to speak the first time, I had a dream. An angel holding a drinking gourd in his hand poured the contents, the good news of Jesus, on my head. Then the angel handed me the gourd and said, "Go and pour the message of the Bible on the heads of many people." The only training I had at that time was my ability to read the Bible. In the years that followed I preached many times.

Lukas and the Rebels

Now I felt the tug of God to go a step further. I decided to go to Bible school. So, with my wife Joanna and our two children, I flew to Beoga to begin four years of training to become a pastor.

I have told you this story through the missionary lady who I call, "Damal-In." While I was in school in Beoga, Damal-In invited me to her house. We sat in her living room and I told her all about my life. I'm glad for this chance to tell you my story. While it is the story of my life, it is really about what God has done in my life.

Thus Lukas finished his story.

Lukas graduated from the Beoga Bible School in May, 1994. He and his family then flew back to Jila.

It was in February 2004 that the Gibbons made a trip back to Papua. They visited all five of the areas where they had lived and worked for more than 40 years. Jila was the fourth airstrip where they landed on the trip. Lukas was at the plane that day to meet them. He now serves as the pastor of a second church on the Jila Ridge—this one built near the government post. Lukas and Joanna continue to serve the Lord faithfully in a very difficult place.

BIBLE LESSON

>Jesus said, "But I tell you who hear me: Love your enemies, do good to those who hate you, bless those who curse you, and pray for those who mistreat you. . . Do for others just what you want them to do for you. . . Love your enemies and do good to them. . .You will then have a great reward, and you will be sons of the Most High God." Luke 6:27, 31, 35

>Jesus said, "This, then, is how you should pray:
>Our Father in heaven: May your holy name be honored. . .
>Forgive us the wrongs we have done,
>   as we forgive the wrongs that others have done to us.

If you forgive others the wrongs they have done to you, your Father in heaven will also forgive you. But if you do not forgive others, then your Father will not forgive the wrongs you have done." Matthew 6:9, 12, 14-15

As I listened to the testimony of Lukas, I was challenged in my own heart. The story of how God delivered Lukas from the rebels was truly miraculous, but an even greater miracle was done in the heart of Lukas when he said, "I will forgive those who tried to kill me. I will love and not hate."

Jesus' teaching about forgiving others is very clear. We even repeat it when we say the Lord's Prayer. Yet it is so easy to forget His words when someone has wronged us. We say to ourselves, "Everyone knows that what the other person did was wrong. He is the one who needs to change his ways. He should ask me to forgive him." Too often we leave it there. Jesus did not leave it there. Instead He told us to pray as follows: "Forgive us the wrongs we have done, as we forgive the wrongs that others have done to us."

When we ask the Lord to forgive our wrongdoing, should we not also ask Him for help to forgive those who have treated us wrongly? This assignment is a difficult one. Only by His enabling power can we hope to fulfill it. Nevertheless, the promised blessing is great!

ISSUES TO CONSIDER

1. Have you ever returned good for hate, blessing for curses or prayed for one who mistreats you? What happened when you did this?
2. As Christians what should our attitude be toward each individual in the groups of the world's people we call our enemies?

Lukas the Pastor 2004

From the co-pilot's seat approaching Jila

Girl crosses Jila River on two poles

On Jila airship: Don, Alice and Lukas – next to Alice in white shirt

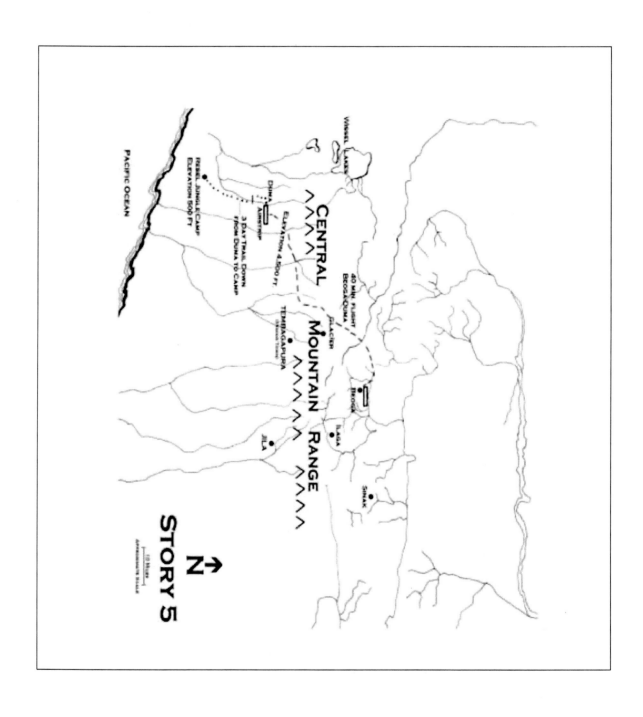

STORY FIVE
THE JULIANA STORY

Introduction

This is the story of Juliana, a Damal girl who was about six years old when our tale begins. She is a real girl, Juliana is her real name and this is a true story. Juliana with her mother and father came to the home of Alice Gibbons to relate this adventure. Actually Alice had a part in putting some of the "props" in place that form the background of the story. She knew about the major events at the time they took place.

Amos, the father, told all this to Alice in a matter-of-fact way. She listened with awe to the tale of how God took care of this little family.

Juliana becomes the storyteller in this adventure of danger and deliverance which takes place—*Where the Earth Ends.*

Chapter 1

To Be a Missionary

Juliana begins her story:

One day when I was about six years old I heard my mother and dad talking. My dad was saying, "I heard they're looking for someone who has medical training to go and work in a Moni valley south of the central mountain range. I'd like to go and be that person. Of course you and Juliana would go too—because we'll stay there a long time."

"Amos, are you sure?" my mother asked. "We'll be far away from our family. Besides we can't walk that far. Juliana can't and I won't!"

"Yes, I'm sure. I feel God wants us to be a missionary family."

I asked my dad, "What does it mean to be a missionary?"

He said, "You know Juliana, here at our home in Beoga all the Damal people have a church in their village. The children can go to Sunday school like you do. But the Moni people who live in the Duma [Doo-meh] Valley have no Sunday school or church. They have no one to tell them about Jesus. You and I and your mother are going to go as missionaries to the Moni people. And Juliana, we're going to get there by flying in an airplane because the Duma Valley is far away, too far to walk." [See story 5 map]

Now in the Beoga wherever I went, I walked on little paths up and down the steep sides of the mountains. But me, fly in an airplane? I'd seen an airplane, for that is how our missionaries came to us. But I never thought I would fly in one.

Finally the day came. We were going! My parents had everything we owned stuffed into two, big net-bags. A large carton held my dad's medical supplies. A third net-bag was full of sweet potatoes. Sweet potatoes are our main food, and my dad said potatoes were hard to get in the Moni village. He was taking enough food with us for a couple of days.

To be a Missionary

The morning we were to leave, the airplane landed on the dirt airstrip in Beoga. My grandparents and my aunts and uncles were all there to say goodbye. Everyone was crying as they watched the pilot load our things into the single-engine Cessna plane.

"Why are they crying?" I asked my mother.

"Because we're going so far away they are afraid they might never see us again," she answered.

The pilot called out, "It's time for you to get in now." My daddy sat up front next to the pilot. My seat was behind him and close beside my mother. The pilot strapped me into my seat and then he climbed in front. There was a very loud, roaring noise. We began to bounce along, down the dirt runway. Suddenly we were up in the air.

I wasn't going to look down, but I couldn't help seeing the mountains that were so close and on both sides. So I peeked a little and there below us was the Beoga River getting smaller and smaller as we climbed higher and higher. After awhile we were flying along, beside the clouds. That was a funny feeling. The plane flew around the edge of a really big white cloud. All the time I could look down and see the ground so far away below us. Then all of a sudden we were very close to a bare mountaintop—flying right over white rock.

Juliana didn't know it, but she had just crossed over the central mountain range of the island, flying at 14,000 feet elevation. She couldn't see it but very close and under clouds to her left was an even higher mountain, 16,500 ft. with a glacier near the top. The glacier is unique because it is located almost on the equator. [See story 5 map]

Juliana continues:

Suddenly, my ears were popping as the airplane went down very fast. Before I knew what was happening we were on the ground, bumping up a dirt airstrip. The engine stopped and we all climbed out. People were crowding all around us. They were all speaking a strange language, the Moni language, and I couldn't understand a word they said.

As the weeks went by, I found a Moni girl to be my friend. As we played together I began to understand what she was saying. Soon I was answering back in Moni. My parents were learning to speak Moni also, but I was learning faster.

The Juliana Story

My special friend had a baby brother. We used to take care of him while her mother went off to the garden. I didn't have a baby brother in my family, but I wished I did.

My friend and I pretended we were grown up. The baby brother was our baby and we carried him around as we played. Each of us had wooden digging sticks just like our mothers used in the garden. We pretended we were planting sweet potatoes. Later we dug the potatoes in our make-believe garden. My friend became like a big sister to me. She filled a special place in my life because I was an only child.

My dad was trained to be a medical worker so every day sick people came to him. He took the temperature of some. To others he gave a few pills. Sometimes to treat a sick baby he gave an injection of penicillin. If someone had a bad sore he put salve on it, or if they had a deep cut he bandaged their arm or leg. Along with giving medicine my dad prayed in Jesus' name for every person who came to him, asking that the person might get better.

Each evening our family of three would sit around the fire in our little hut. The only light was the light from the fire. My parents recited memory verses, and I would repeat after them, line by line. They told me Bible stories and always they prayed. They just talked to God in prayer about our daily needs.

One of the verses I learned quoted the words of Jesus. "Go, then, to all peoples everywhere and make them my disciples. . . and teach them to obey everything I commanded you. And I will be with you always." We said this verse many times.

My dad said, "That verse explains why we've come here. Do you know why we've come, Juliana?"

"Yes, I think so. We've come to tell people about Jesus so they can know and love Him like we do."

"You're right," my dad said. "Something else we know from that verse. God is always with us even though we are far away from our family. That's good to know!"

On Sunday the local people gathered in the village yard. First we had Sunday school and then my dad would tell everyone a Bible Story. He told them they should follow Jesus like our family did.

Sometimes my dad asked for another sweet potato to eat. Often my mother would say, "There are no more, Amos." When I asked for another one my parents would break their potato in half and give it to me. I guess my mommy and daddy loved me very much.

I remember my mother saying, "Amos, the ground around here is so bad that when I dig my potatoes, they are only little nubbins. Let's try making a garden across the valley. The ground is better over there."

My daddy agreed, never dreaming what was ahead.

BIBLE LESSON:

> Jesus drew near and said to them, "I have been given all authority in heaven and on earth. Go, then, to all peoples everywhere and make them my disciples: baptize them in the name of the Father, the Son, and the Holy Spirit, and teach them to obey everything I have commanded you. And I will be with you always, to the end of the age." Matthew 28:18-20

> Moses said to Israel, "Remember this! The Lord—and the Lord alone—is your God. Love the Lord your God with all your heart, with all your soul, and with all your strength. Never forget these commands that I am giving you today. Teach them to your children. Repeat them when you are at home and when you are away, when you are resting and when you are working." Deuteronomy 6:4-7

Missionaries! That's what Juliana and her family really were. The reason for becoming missionaries was the same for Amos and his family as it was for the Gibbons. This first chapter of Juliana's story really fits with the story the five Gibbons girls might tell about their place in a missionary family. Their adventure as the children of missionaries included saying goodbye to their grandparents and flying across the Pacific Ocean. From the coast of the island they flew in a small Cessna airplane, landing on a dirt airstrip. In Beoga they played with the Damal children and learned to speak Damal. Their parents learned the local language too and before long were telling the Damals Bible stories about Jesus. Missionary kids, or M.K.'s as they are sometimes called, enjoy a unique life along with their parents.

Each missionary-trained medical worker in the mountains prayed for every patient before he gave any medicine. The tribal people believed their prayer to God was as important to healing as receiving medication. Years later, when government medical workers were stationed in some areas, the tribal Christians hesitated to receive help from them because the government men were not Christians and did not pray. Perhaps we

The Juliana Story

Christians can learn something from the tribal people—that ultimately, all healing comes to us not from man's efforts but from God's hand.

The words in Deuteronomy 6:4-7 are important instructions to every family with children. Their teaching is very clear. Amos had not heard the exhortation to teach God's commands to his daughter because at that time the Damal Old Testament had not been translated. Nevertheless, he lived out the intent of these verses.

ISSUES TO CONSIDER

1. Today, the term "missionary" is often used rather loosely. Using the Great Commission as given by Jesus in Matthew 28:18-20, how might the term missionary be defined—who he is, where he goes and what he does?

2. Reflect on the differences and similarities between an evening in Juliana's home and one in yours.

3. As the Damals do, might we do well to pray, acknowledging God's part when we seek healing through medication?

Chapter 2

The Roaring River

Juliana continues telling her story:

My parents did decide to make a garden across the valley where the ground was better for growing sweet potatoes. It was about an hour's walk. Halfway to our new garden site there was a mountain river we had to cross. The river water came down the mountain really fast. Men had cut down a tree and put the log in place across the river to serve as a bridge.

The first time I went with my parents to the garden I watched my mother cross on the log. I said to my daddy, "You carry me across on your shoulders. I'm afraid. I might fall off the log." I watched the water turn white as it hit the big rocks in the stream bed. This frightened me. And the noise it made was even scarier.

My daddy answered, "You're too big to be carried, Juliana. Come, I'll walk the log with you and help you keep your balance." That's the way I learned to cross a single pole bridge. It wasn't long until I could cross the log alone.

One morning, after we had been in Duma for about a year, my mother said to me, "Juliana, here is a cooked sweet potato for your lunch. We're going to our garden across the river today. Be sure to put your rain-mat into your net-bag along with your potato. The black clouds look like it may start raining any minute." My mother kept talking, almost to herself. "I guess we'd better go even if it does rain early today. There are no more potatoes ready to dig in the garden near our house."

My rain-mat was still on the sleeping floor of our hut where I'd slept on it. The mat was my bed at night and my rain-cape during the day. My mother had sewn it for me from long palm leaves. Then she folded the mat lengthwise, sewed it across the top, and dried it over the fire. My rain-cape was shorter than the ones my parents used—just the right size for me. When I opened it up and put it on my head, it came down to my knees in back. It was fun to walk in the rain wearing my rain-cape.

This morning it was already raining lightly as our family of three started out for the garden across the river. We each wore our rain-capes. The rain continued all morning

The Juliana Story

as we worked together. My parents dug the sweet potatoes and I helped by putting them in the big net bags. Working with our heads bent down the rain-capes kept us from looking around. No one paid any attention to the dark clouds that were coming lower and lower. In the early afternoon my dad said, "Let's go home! If it has been raining all day higher in the mountains like it has been here, the river will be rising."

Long before we got to the river we could hear its loud, angry roar. When we got to the pole bridge it was partly under water. My dad said, "The water is rising fast. We can't walk across on the pole bridge. Come quickly, Juliana. Get on my shoulders and I'll carry you across." As he stepped into the water, he called over his shoulder to my mother, "Wait here and I'll come back to help you across."

My daddy waded into the river on the up-river side of the pole bridge. The pole was there to help keep him steady. Seated on his shoulders I hunched down and clung with all my might to his head. Wading slowly into the river, the water rose to his waist; it was splashing on my feet. My daddy went very slowly, fighting the terrible force of the water with each step he took. At last he staggered out on the far side and dumped me in a heap on the bank.

My dad turned around and started back across to help my mother. Then I saw that she had already started into the water. She was bent over carrying two large net-bags of potatoes on her back. I heard my parents calling, but neither could understand what the other was saying because of the roar of the water. Both were buffeted by the water's force. Slowly, slowly they inched closer and closer together. Then, just as my dad's hand reached out to touch my mother's hand, I saw her head disappear in the water under the log bridge. I watched as she bobbed in and out of the water, down, down the river and then she was gone.

My dad was still in the river, but he came carefully back to where I was. He ran down the river bank quite a ways. There on the opposite side he could see my mother lying face down at the river's edge.

My dad grabbed me and took me to a nearby Moni hut and left me there. He ran up river a long ways, crossed a bridge built higher above the water and went back to where my mother was. He shook her like a rag doll, and then he saw that she was alive. Her body was cut and bruised from the rocks in the river, but she was alive. He carried her back up stream, across the bridge and to our house.

That night my daddy prayed and prayed. He thanked God we still had a mother and prayed she would not die. He bandaged her larger cuts. I prayed too and thanked God for both my mommy and my daddy.

The Roaring River

For three weeks my mother lay on her sleeping mat on the floor of our hut. I would go in and sit beside her. As she got better, she talked to me. One day I asked her, "Why don't I have any brothers and sisters like my best friend has?"

She answered, "Juliana, you were a miracle baby. Your father and I had been married for eight years. I really wanted a baby; I prayed every day. One day I talked to the missionary nurse. She arranged for me to fly to the hospital where the missionary doctor did a procedure. A year later you were born. You are our miracle baby."

Sitting beside my mommy I thought, *When I grow-up I want to be a mother and have children. I'll love them and take care of them just like my parents take care of me.* Our family was good. We each loved Jesus and we loved one another.

My mother did get well. My dad continued to help people who were sick, giving them medicine and caring for bad sores. We all spoke Moni very well by this time. On Sundays my parents taught Sunday school to the children, and then my dad spoke from the Bible to those who gathered and sat in the village yard. Our Moni neighbors were hearing about Jesus. Some of them had decided to follow Jesus like our family did.

One day some outsiders came into our valley. My parents called them *ema-kop-me,* forest men, rebels. They were tribal people just like we Damals and Monis, but they didn't act like other men we knew. They were very gruff and demanding. These men did not bring wives and children with them. They did not build a house in the village and plant sweet potatoes like others did. They ate sweet potatoes, but they were *ours* not ones they planted. I heard them say they wanted to overthrow the Indonesian government so the tribal people would be in charge, not foreigners. Three of the men carried guns. In the Beoga only policemen carried guns, but there were no policemen around here. Everyone was afraid of the rebels and so was I!

BIBLE LESSON:

> Jesus answered them, "Have faith in God. I tell you: When you pray and ask for something, believe that you have received it, and you will be given whatever you ask for." Mark 11:22, 24

The story of Samuel's mother, Hannah:

> Hannah often cried and was sad because the Lord had kept her childless.
>
> One year at the house of the Lord at Shiloh, Hannah cried bitterly as she prayed to the Lord. "Lord Almighty, look at me, your servant! See my trouble and

The Juliana Story

remember me! Don't forget me! If you give me a son, I promise that I will dedicate him to you for his whole life."

The family went home. The Lord answered her prayer and Hannah became pregnant and gave birth to a son. She named him Samuel, and explained, "I asked the Lord for him."

After she had weaned the child, she took him to Shiloh. Hannah said to Eli, "I asked the Lord for this child, and he gave me what I asked for. So I am dedicating him to the Lord, as long as he lives." Condensed from I Samuel 1:1-28

Juliana's little family of three was far from home, even cut off from any contact with their family members or the missionaries who helped get them to the Duma. No one back in Beoga knew what was happening in their lives. But God knew. He had not forgotten this family. God answered the earnest prayers of Amos. His wife did not drown and she did recover from the severe beating she took from the rocks and boulders in the raging river.

Juliana's mother knew the Bible story of Hannah and how God answered her prayer giving her the baby Samuel. Like Hannah, she also prayed year after year for a child. God made it possible for her to be flown to a mission doctor for treatment and she became pregnant. Juliana's mother had faith in God and He answered her prayer. Later, when the call came for their family of three to move far away from all their relatives and their secure world, she did not hold back.

No doubt, Hannah of the Bible had prayed many times for a child, but this time in the temple her prayer was one of desperation and passion. When God answered this prayer, Hannah did not forget her promise and brought her young son to Eli for the service of God. She gave up her son—for the rest of his life. That day Hannah prayed a beautiful prayer of worship and praise to God. (1 Samuel 2:1-10)

ISSUES TO CONSIDER

1. Prayer and trusting God for His answers were very important in the life of Amos and his wife. We have that same God for both major crises and minor issues in our lives.
2. Is giving a child back to God even harder than giving ourselves to Him?

Chapter 3
Captured by the Rebels

Juliana continues telling her story:

Two years had gone by since we left our home in Beoga to live with the Moni people. All the village people who lived close by, and some who lived further away appreciated my dad's help given to anyone who was sick. On Sundays the group who gathered for church was growing larger. All the village people were our friends, We felt at home with them.

Everything changed the day the rebels appeared in our peaceful village. These men with their three rifles went everywhere demanding food. Even if the people had little to eat themselves, the rebels took as much as they wanted. Their talk was all about recruiting men to join their ranks and fight with them. They were going to take over the government.

My dad was a prime target of the rebels. He was educated and also an important leader in the village. People listened to him as he preached and treated the sick. With every threat the rebels made to my dad he just kept on repeating his message: "Let's all follow the Jesus path."

The rebels continued to pressure my dad, "Join us in fighting the government and tell the people on Sunday they should all support our cause."

My dad always answered, "No, I will not join your ranks. I won't interfere with what you are doing. Just don't bother me."

Again and again they came, sometimes two men, sometimes three different men. Always they spoke with harsh words, demanding food. And always my parents gave them whatever they had.

Another day they came, all the rebels together. I sensed this day was different from the others. They carried their three guns and all their other gear. They shouted at my parents, "You are coming with us. Bring your potatoes with you and carry our gear." When my dad didn't move, they pointed a gun at him and said, "Get going."

The Juliana Story

My dad picked up their heavy gear and said to me in Moni, "Juliana, you stay here with the Moni elder of the church." Then he added in Damal so the rebels couldn't understand, "We'll run away soon and be back to get you."

I cried as I watched my parents leave the village, bent down under their heavy loads. They were walking between two of the rebels as they disappeared behind the trees.

Two days passed and my mom and dad did not come back. Then two of the rebel men returned. One of them carried a gun. Pointing it at a Moni man he demanded, "Where is Amos's big pig? Bring it here." The pig was found, and the rebel man killed it. Looking at the village people who had gathered, he commanded, "Butcher it and cook it for me." They did as they were told.

I watched this entire process. When the meat was cooked the two men grabbed big pieces and began to eat. I wanted to cry out, "You are eating my dad's only pig. Give me a piece," but I said nothing. I wanted a piece of that meat so bad but the men didn't even give me a little bite.

The next morning the remaining cooked meat was loaded into carrying net-bags. One of the rebel men said to me, "You are coming with us," and we started down the trail my parents had left on. I walked all day between these two men. I was so very hungry and tired. Once when we came to a swinging, rattan-vine bridge that I could not cross by myself, one of the men carried me across. On we went. It got dark, but we still kept walking. [See story 5 map]

Finally we came to where the other rebels were camped. I saw my parents were there too. My mommy hugged me and cried and cried. I guess she thought she'd never see her little girl again. We didn't have much to eat, but we were together. That night my daddy cried too and prayed, thanking God for taking care of me. We recited Bible verses like we always did. My parents did not have their Bibles with them, but they knew many verses by heart. They recited them from memory and I learned them too.

The next day we had to walk again. Our steps were always downhill. We passed the last Moni houses in the mountain area. After that there were no more gardens and no more potatoes to commandeer from villagers. All the way the rebels were still feasting on the meat from my dad's prize pig, but we weren't given even a little piece. My mother found some small white berries along the path. I ate these, but that was all I had.

We walked for three long days down, down into the hot jungle, finally arriving at the rebel camp. The plants and trees with large shiny leaves were different from any I'd ever seen. The rain too, was different, almost warm compared to rain in the mountains. No people lived in this jungle and there were no gardens of any kind. Nothing was to be seen except the huge, towering trees and the tangle of jungle vines. Strange flying insects and crawling bugs were everywhere. Mosquitoes kept biting me. Since my dad was trained as a medical worker, he knew mosquitoes could carry malaria. We had no medicine so my parents prayed. In all the time we spent in the jungle none of us ever got sick with malaria.

Sometimes my dad had to work for the rebels cutting down certain trees. They thought evil spirits lived in this one type of tree, and they feared the spirits. We knew no evil spirit could hurt us; we were God's children.

Each day we asked God to help us find something to eat. There were no jungle animals or birds that came near, not even any wild fruits. My parents found a palm tree that had a soft juicy center. Chewing it and sucking the bitter-sweet juice from the palm trunk gave us a little food. When a rebel man tried to eat this palm-heart juice, he got very sick. We kept on eating it and never got sick.

Every day my dad would approach the rebel leader and ask him very politely if we could go into the jungle and hunt the palm tree we used for food. Each day he said we could. For two and a half months we lived like this, leaving the camp, going into the jungle to hunt palm trees and returning before dark. Always the three of us went together. My dad never left me or my mother in camp no matter how hungry or tired we were. Every night I cried myself to sleep because I was so hungry.

One night my parents thought I was asleep, but I heard them talking about me. "Juliana can't live much longer like this. She will die soon if we don't get food for her." The last thing I heard that night was my mother crying.

BIBLE LESSON

My dear friends do not be surprised at the painful test you are suffering, as though something unusual were happening to you. Rather be glad that you are sharing Christ's sufferings, so that you may be full of joy when his glory is revealed. Happy are you if you are insulted because you are Christ's followers; this means that the glorious Spirit, the Spirit of God, is resting on you. If any of you suffers, it must not be because he is a murderer or a thief or a criminal or a meddler in other people's affairs. However, if you suffer because you are a Christian, don't be ashamed of it, but thank God that you bear Christ's name. 1 Peter 4:12-16

The Juliana Story

> Blessed are you when people insult you and persecute you and tell all kinds of evil lies against you because you are my followers. Be happy and glad, for a great reward is kept for you in heaven. Matthew 5:11-12

> The Lord is my protector . . . and with him I am safe. Psalm 18:2

Juliana and her parents may not have known the words of Psalm 18:2. However, they certainly knew and experienced the truth of this verse. They trusted the Lord to be their protector all through this story. "The Lord is my protector . . . and with him I am safe."

Persecution or suffering for our faith in Jesus, like that endured by Juliana's family, seems far removed from those who live in America. We may hold our breath in horror when we hear stories of what takes place in other countries. We think that this could never happen to us where we live. But stop and consider. The conflict with the rebels was a political issue. Even so, Amos was not willing to compromise what he knew to be right even when it brought danger to his wife and daughter.

Not so long ago in our country the biblical definition of right and wrong was believed and honored by everyone. Today the world demands these same moral values be redefined in a politically correct manner. We face a growing world acceptance of abortion, of a non-biblical definition of marriage, of living together with no marriage at all, of evolution taught as truth instead of the theory it is, and the removal, as much as possible, of the mention of God in our public life. You may add other issues you know about. These are more than political issues. They are presented in direct denial of moral truth taught in the Word of God.

To speak for the truth often brings persecution. May God help each of us to stand for God's moral truth whatever the cost may be.

ISSUES TO CONSIDER

1. Should true followers of Jesus expect persecution?
2. Do you know someone in America who has experienced persecution because of his stand as a believer?

Chapter 4
Miraculous Escape

Juliana concludes:

The next day my dad went to the rebel leader just as he did every day. "Please, may we go into the jungle to hunt for palm trees? Also may I borrow an axe?" My dad hoped he would let him use the new steel axe the leader had stolen from him. He did not. But my dad was still thankful to be given a small, worn axe. Then my dad added, "The nearby palm trees have all been cut so we have to go further to find them. It may be dark before we get back."

The three of us started out that morning as we always did, walking down deeper into the jungle in the opposite direction from the mountains. But we were not looking for palm trees. My dad soon led us in a very round-about way to the trail we had come on almost three months before. We were headed toward the mountains and escape from the rebels. Walking in the jungle was not like walking between villages in Beoga. It was hard for me. Every step we took was climbing over a log, walking through deep mud or balancing on slippery tree roots.

My dad was in the lead, I was in the middle and my mother walked behind. After what seemed like a long time to me, I said, "We are going too fast. I want to stop and rest."

My daddy stopped and prayed, "Dear Heavenly Father, you see that Juliana is getting tired. Please give her extra strength and give strength to her mother too." After the "Amen," we started off faster than ever. All that day we found only one palm tree near our path. My dad cut it down, we quickly sucked its juice, and we kept going.

In the afternoon my dad prayed, "Dear God, look at our tracks! If the rebels come after us they can easily catch up with us. Please send a rain to wash our tracks away. We ask this in Jesus name." It wasn't long before it began to rain hard, and for two hours it kept pouring. Our tracks behind us were all washed away.

That night we were too tired to even to build a shelter. We slept on our rain-mats huddled together at the base of a big tree. Before we fell asleep, my daddy prayed, "Dear Heavenly Father, keep the rain away from us tonight." Twice during the night we awoke

The Juliana Story

to hear the sound of rain coming toward us as it pelted down on the jungle trees. But then we could hear it moving away again. No rain fell on us all that night.

As soon as it began to get light, my daddy prayed, "Thank you, dear God, for keeping the rain away from us during the night. Now, please give Juliana strength to keep walking." And we started off on the trail.

By midday we were climbing and it was even harder for me to keep going. I kept stopping and crying because I was so very hungry. My mommy comforted me, and she prayed, "Dear God, give me a sweet potato for my little girl." This was an impossible request in the middle of the jungle, and we just kept on walking. Then, right there on the side of the path, my mother saw something. It was an egg from a large jungle bird. We saw no bird, only this one large egg. We all prayed thanking God for the egg. My parents let me eat most of it. As we walked on, we were climbing and the trail was getting really steep.

In the afternoon we saw the first sweet potato gardens in the distance. God had helped us walk in two days what it took the rebel men three days to walk, and they were going downhill all the way.

Suddenly we met a man. My dad said to him in Moni, "Please, give us some potatoes. We are very hungry. We've been walking two days, running away from the rebels and their jungle camp. My little girl needs food."

The man seemed to be afraid. If the rebels found out that he helped us, he feared for what they might do to him. He said, "If you go to that house over there, you'll find some cooked sweet potatoes. Just take them. Then hurry on across the rattan swinging bridge—and cut the bridge after you get across."

The potatoes were there as the man said. Oh, they tasted so good! All the time we were in the jungle we hadn't had even one potato. We couldn't sit down to eat these. We ate as we walked, even faster, toward the bridge.

We came to the river. At this point the water was so swift and deep no one could wade across. However, the swinging rattan bridge was there, the same one the rebel man had carried me across. This time my daddy carried me across the bridge in the other direction. Then he took that short, worn axe the rebel leader had given him and cut the main rattan vines of the bridge. If the rebels came, they could not cross the river now.

It was dark when we finally came to a Moni village. Here the people were friendly; they knew who we were. My dad had given medicine to some from this village when they were sick. The people gave us all the sweet potatoes we could eat, and we stayed with them just eating and resting for a whole week.

Miraculous Escape

Once I overheard my parents talking. "Amos," my mother said, "It's a miracle that Juliana was able to keep walking when she was so hungry and we had no food. You never could have carried her; she's too big now." After a pause she said, "It's still hard to believe I found that jungle-bird egg right there on the path. I'd just asked God for a sweet potato and there was the egg. And we never saw one bird egg all the months we were in the rebel camp."

"Yes," he said, "And I think it was even a bigger miracle that the rebels didn't come after us." He shrugged, "Maybe they did try to catch us. All I know is that God was good to us, and He helped us to escape."

BIBLE LESSON:

Escape and preservation on the Israelites' journey to Canaan:

[After the tenth plague] the Egyptians urged the people to hurry and leave the country. Exodus 12:33

The Israelites asked the Egyptians for gold and silver jewelry and for clothes. The Lord made the Egyptians respect the people and give them what they asked for. In this way the Israelites carried away the wealth of the Egyptians. Exodus 12:35-36

[Later] The Lord drove the sea back with a strong east wind. . . The water was divided, and the Israelites went through the sea on dry ground. . . The Egyptians pursued them and went after them into the sea with all their horses, chariots and drivers.

The water returned and covered . . . all the Egyptian army. . . But the Israelites walked though the sea on dry ground. Exodus 14:21-23, 28-29

[Later] "You, [Moses,] have brought us out into this desert to starve us all to death."

The Lord said to Moses, "Now I am going to cause food to rain down from the sky for all of you."

The Israelites ate manna for the next forty years, until they reached the land of Canaan. Exodus 16:3-4, 35

When they call to me, I will answer them;

When they are in trouble, I will be with them.

The Juliana Story

> I will rescue them and honor them. Psalm 91:15

It is good to be reminded that God takes care of his people as He promises in Psalm 91:15 whether they are the Israelites in Bible days, or a missionary family of three who were deep in the jungles on the island of New Guinea, or they are people like you and me who love God.

We know the Israelites escape-story from the Book of Exodus, but sometimes we fail to recognize God's deliverance in our lives today. Juliana was close to exhaustion from days of hunger when her mother worded this desperate prayer, "God, give me a sweet potato for my little girl." The request was an impossible one because the closest potato gardens were several hours walk away. But God was watching over this little family. How often God answers our prayer in a way we could never have imagined. Or perhaps we see no answer at all because we never prayed. We thought the request to be impossible. At all times our God hears and answers prayer!

Two verses highlighted in earlier chapters of this story bear repeating. Jesus said, "Go, then, to all peoples . . . And I will be with you always." David's song of victory was, "The Lord is my protector . . . and with him I am safe." Juliana and her family experienced these promises of God.

ISSUES TO CONSIDER

1. Juliana's father prayed about rain twice, once that it would rain and once that it would not rain. God answered his prayer both times. What do you think about praying for rain to come or not to come?

2. Why do we call the events that helped Juliana's family to escape miracles?

3. Have you ever experienced something you might call a miracle in your life?

[THE JULIANA STORY can be told in Sunday school, children's church or Vacation Bible School. Several have used it in this way.]

Juliana, her father Amos, and mother

STORY SIX

ONLY ONE LIFE

Introduction

This is my story, a story I can hardly believe happened. I am an ordinary person who, by the providence of God, was given the extraordinary opportunity of living my life on the island of New Guinea—*Where the Earth Ends*. It all took place on the world's most exotic island with people living in complete isolation from the rest of the world. My husband Don and I served for 42 years with The Christian and Missionary Alliance on the western half of the island. Dutch New Guinea was the name when we went there in 1953. Today it is called Papua, a province of Indonesia. [See map at the beginning of the book.]

The people we found in the rugged mountains were still living in the Stone Age, people who had never imagined there were other human beings—real people—living outside their mountain fortress. They had never heard the name of Jesus and didn't even have a word for God. Yet deep within their hearts they had a God-given longing to learn the way to *hai*, a place defined in their thinking as paradise. When Don arrived in their midst they wondered, could he be the being who would show them the way to *hai*.

Don and I together were privileged to bring them the message of the gospel.

The title above, Only One Life, comes from a couplet on a little plaque my fifth grade Sunday school teacher gave me for Christmas.

> Only one life 'twill soon be past
>
> Only what's done for Christ will last

Those words, hanging on my bedroom wall, greatly influenced my life.

Chapter 1

God's Call to Alice

I was born to Bob and Gladys Rhoads in October, 1930. For my first name my parents chose Alice, a name from our family tree. Alice was my Mother's middle name and also the middle name of my grandmother on my father's side. But what would my middle name be? They could not decide. They thought a nurse in the hospital had a unique and pretty name: Verdelle. So I was named Alice Verdelle.

My parents married in their late teens only months before the Great Depression began. They made their home in Burbank, California. With so many people out of work, jobs were hard to find. It didn't help that my Dad's education had ended with graduation from the eighth grade. He tried his hand at various jobs, working in a butcher shop, driving a candy delivery truck, working in a lumber yard and in a vegetable dehydration plant. No job lasted very long, times were hard.

When I was six my Dad decided to give panning gold in northern California a try. We moved up north and lived in a small cabin with only one city convenience, an electric light bulb hanging from the ceiling of the main room. I attended first grade in a one-room school house and walked to school down the dirt road that ran in front of our cabin. Every Saturday my Dad went to town with the gold collected from his week of hard labor. The $5.00 he got each week just didn't buy enough food for our family, which now included my baby brother. So back to Burbank we went.

Having no money, we moved in with my mother's parents. Still my Dad couldn't find any work. However, my Mother did find a job in a laundry in Hollywood. She was paid according to the number of white shirts she ironed each hour. Since her hands were nimble, our family again had enough money for food and even a bit more.

In 1937 my parents bought a four-room house for $1,900 with $100 down. Payments were $25 a month delivered in cash to the owner. The interesting part about this little house was its location in the San Fernando Valley and what was happening all around us. Across the street was a huge, commercial truck-garden growing root vegetables for the Los Angeles market. Beyond the fields I could see a movie studio and

Only One Life

lights on the set when they filmed at night. Warner Brothers Studio was four miles away and soon Walt Disney built his studio a couple of miles from us in another direction. Lockheed Aircraft was also close by. With rumblings of World War II my Dad got his first steady job. It was at Lockheed, helping to build P-38 fighter planes.

My Mother loved the Lord. She never missed a Sunday taking us children to Sunday school. However, my Dad would have nothing to do with that church. Nothing that is, except when I was in a Sunday school program. For these occasions he coached me in learning my lines and was always there for the performance.

When I was about seven, my Dad attended some evening meetings at church with an evangelist as speaker. There he experienced a life-changing conversion. He stopped smoking and no longer went out on occasion to drink beer with the boys at the local pool hall. He was hungry for solid Bible teaching and began his search for a good church for our family to attend. We ended up in the Christian and Missionary Alliance Church in nearby Glendale. The pastor was an excellent Bible expositor. God had led our family to this church that offered more than good Bible teaching. I grew up in a church with a strong emphasis on foreign missions.

Now in the evenings at home my Dad sat in his big chair, read the newspaper and read and studied his Bible. We had a radio and sometimes tuned in to listen to a Christian speaker. One Saturday night when I was eight, we listened to a radio evangelist who was talking to young people. God got my attention and I listened carefully. No doubt I'd heard before what the preacher was saying, but this time God's Holy Spirit was speaking to me in a very personal way. I understood that going to heaven required a decision on my part. Having Christian parents or attending church wasn't enough. I needed to place my faith in the Savior who died for my sins. The speaker made it clear that to do nothing was actually a decision to reject Jesus and remain on the broad road which leads to eternal separation from God, the road to hell. To choose Christ was to begin life on the narrow road which leads to heaven.

Alone in my bedroom that night, I knelt down beside my bed and asked Jesus to come into my heart. He did just that. He came to live in my heart!

During my Sunday school years I learned all the Bible stories. Contests motivated me to memorize Scripture and read my Bible. Honor was given to those who had perfect attendance. Even with gas rationing during the war years our entire family was always in church and I received a pin each year for perfect attendance.

A childhood ambition of mine was to play the piano. However, my parents had no money for a piano or lessons. When my younger cousin began to take piano lessons, I got

God's Call to Alice

my chance. My aunt, who knew nothing about the piano herself, listened each week as the piano teacher taught her daughter. On Saturdays I went to my Aunt's house. Using a John Thompson's Piano Book she assigned me the same lesson given to her daughter.

Where could I practice? My elementary school had one piano, which was in the auditorium. I got permission to stay after school and practice on that piano. Seeing my ambition my uncle found a big, old piano for $25 which was squeezed into my tiny bedroom. When I advanced beyond what my Aunt could teach me, my parents found enough money to pay for lessons with a lady who was an excellent classical piano teacher. I learned to play music written by the great composers and played their works by memory at my teacher's recitals. In my junior year in high school I changed from piano to organ lessons from our church organist. With no organ at home I walked a long way after school to practice on the church organ. After practice I rode a city bus to a stop near our house and hiked the rest of the way up a steep hill.

Another interest of mine was the logic of mathematics. I enjoyed helping other students understand a difficult math problem. My stated ambition since the eighth grade was to become a high school math teacher.

By the time I was twelve I was ready to work and earn some spending money. However, it took my Mother to speak to the neighbors and get me a job of cleaning house or babysitting. I was just too shy to speak up for myself. When I was almost fifteen, it was my Grandmother, a very outgoing lady, who approached the manager at a Van de Kamp's bakery store asking for a job for me. These were war years when many adults were occupied in defense jobs or in the service. She got me a job sight unseen. The manager, who was Grandmother's age, taught me how to meet the public and work hard in an adult position. I learned to approach each customer with the same question, "How may I serve you?" From behind the counter and wearing the chain's Dutch costume, I felt safe in interacting with all kinds of people. All through high school I worked on Saturdays and full time every summer selling bakery goods, saving money for college.

Even though I grew up in a Christian and Missionary Alliance church and heard lots of missionaries tell their stories and show their pictures, I had no personal interest in missions. I never found enough courage to share my faith with words either at church or at school. When our youth group went door-to-door inviting people to church or giving out tracts, I never accompanied them. I felt I did my part at church by occasionally playing the piano or organ.

Every summer I looked forward to our church family camp, especially going to the nearby beach in the afternoons. The year I was almost fifteen, the morning camp meetings for youth were about going deeper with God, being filled with His Holy Spirit.

Only One Life

The leader taught about setting one's life apart for God and walking in complete obedience to Him. From the age of eight I never doubted my salvation. However, this day I made a decision to fully surrender my life to God. I asked the Holy Spirit to fill my life completely.

The following summer I was back at camp. One evening waiting for the service to begin I sat looking at the posters that decorated the sides of the rustic chapel. These were the same posters they put up every year. Each one pictured a person from a foreign country where Alliance missionaries served. Written under the picture was the name of the country and how many tens of thousands or even millions of people lived in that country who had never once heard the way of salvation. As I sat there in silence, the Spirit of God said to me, "I want YOU to go and tell the story of Jesus to people who have never heard. They are lost and bound for hell. Some will never hear unless YOU go."

My heart's response was, *"Who me, Lord? You don't mean me! I'm going to be a math teacher not a missionary. I can't talk to people. I'm afraid to speak in public. Besides, I've already sent my application to Wheaton College. I'm going to be a math teacher!"*

When I went home from that camp the conviction that I must go and tell people who had never heard did not go away. Instead it grew stronger. Since I was too shy to speak to anyone of this growing conviction, I had no one to talk to, no one to ask for advice. Was this the voice of God calling me or was it my imagination? I felt most unqualified to become a missionary, but on the other hand I knew if it truly were God's voice calling me, I dare not disobey.

From Sunday school I remembered the story of Gideon. (Judges 6) God called Gideon, a wheat farmer's son, to lead Israel in battle against the mighty Midianite army. Gideon heard this call but later wondered, was he really to do this? Surely God wouldn't ask a farm boy to lead Israel's army in battle. Gideon asked God to confirm to him what he should do. He put out a fleece of wool that night and said to God, "If in the morning there is dew only on the fleece and all the ground around is dry, then I will know you will save Israel by my hand." That's exactly what happened. In the morning Gideon squeezed a bowl full of water out of the fleece while the ground around was completely dry.

I decided to put out a fleece like Gideon, so I prayed, "Are you really talking to me, Lord? If you are, please cause Wheaton College to reject my application. If that happens, I'll change my plans and become a missionary."

I had applied to Wheaton two years in advance as the college required. I was an "A" student and was sure I'd be accepted.

Just two weeks after my prayer, a letter came from Wheaton. With a pounding heart I opened the letter. It said I had NOT been accepted. The answer was clear. I told my parents for the first time that I was going to be a missionary.

At the time I was only fifteen going on sixteen and really didn't know what it meant to be a missionary. However, I knew our church sent out missionaries and had a training school, Simpson Bible Institute, in Seattle. In two years, after graduating from high school, I would go to Simpson and prepare to be a missionary.

BIBLE LESSON

> Salvation is found in no one else, for there is no other name under heaven given to men by which we must be saved. Acts 4:12 NIV

> Everyone who calls out to the Lord for help will be saved. But how can they call to him for help if they have not believed? And how can they believe if they have not heard the message? And how can they hear if the message is not proclaimed? Romans 10:13-14

As I write my story, I am amazed again that God called me, just an ordinary girl, to have a part in reaching thousands of stone-age people, who had never heard the Good News. God had chosen these tribal people to be converted before He created the world, just as He chose you and He chose me. How could they hear and believe if no one went to tell them the message?

At fifteen I could not quote or even find the verses written above in the Bible Lesson. But I had learned the basic content of their message in church or perhaps from the missionary speakers. These verses were somewhere in the back of my mind when God's Holy Spirit whispered to me that I was to go to those who had never heard. It was not an emotional experience, but it was very real.

Many times on the field when I was lonely or discouraged, when I felt like giving up or going home, God brought his call back to my mind. He had commissioned me. I was where He wanted me and by his grace I would stay.

Only One Life

As a teenager, I could not have found the story of Gideon in my Bible but I knew it well. An angel told Gideon he was to lead his people in battle against the Midianites. Gideon talked back to the angel explaining he was not qualified for the job. He was from the weakest tribe and he himself was the least important member of his family. Later when he continued to doubt, he asked for a miracle of confirmation. God reassured Gideon. He made the wool wet and the ground dry.

Like Gideon I was not sure if it was God's voice calling me, but God heard my prayer. The fleece that I laid out became a confirmation to me: for my lifetime I was to serve as a foreign missionary.

ISSUES TO CONSIDER

1. Do you think it is important for a person who becomes a missionary to have a "call?" What is a "call" anyway?

2. Why are verses from the Bible important to a person being led to serve in missions?

3. Consider this statement: it is necessary to fully surrender one's life to God before He will reveal His plan for our life. Why is it true?

4. I might say, God called me three times in this chapter. If a call is defined as God getting our attention in a personal way to lead us to make a decision or take a specific action, might a person be called to something other than missions?

Chapter 2
Three More Questions Answered "Yes"

A letter from Simpson Bible Institute confirmed it was time to head for Seattle. I really didn't feel very confident about going, for I was a Southern California girl who had never traveled far from home, but I'd made the commitment and I would go. Somewhere we got an old steamer trunk and into it went my clothes for the colder weather of Seattle, plus all the things for my dorm room. My Dad managed to transport me and that trunk to the Greyhound bus depot in Los Angeles and I set off on a 30-hour bus trip.

In 1948 Simpson Bible Institute was a small school with less than 200 students, even if one counted the off-campus married students. The dorm was perched on a hillside and other buildings were squeezed close by—a chapel, a dining room/kitchen, a Quonset hut building which provided several classrooms, and an old house which offered a snack bar in the basement, library on the main floor and offices upstairs. Simpson became my home for the next three years except for Christmas and summer vacations.

The faculty, dean of women, and my fellow students all had a major part in setting my standards and goals for life. This three-year school didn't even offer a Bachelor of Arts degree. However, every class I took proved to be excellent preparation for the life God had planned for me. Basic classes included everything from speech and English to 30 hours of Bible. My major was missions. After my first summer experience I added classes in Christian education which were very practical courses on how to teach children. Christian education became my minor.

Every student was required to have an evangelistic assignment, a weekly outreach into the local churches using what we were learning. Since I was taking piano lessons, my outreach assignment was to accompany a lady's trio. Again I had avoided an assignment that would require speaking to people.

Chapel services often featured a missionary telling of his ministry and ended with the challenge to come overseas and help that missionary in his work. Suddenly, going overseas seemed much closer. My mind was spinning. How could I, Alice, go to a foreign country? I had a hard time even traveling by myself to the faraway city of Seattle.

Only One Life

Ever since I was a little girl, I had dreamed and planned on being married. What if I never met someone who shared my calling to missions? Was I willing to go as a single woman? To answer "yes" this time was much harder for me than the first time that I told the Lord I would go. My emotions kept bringing up the question again and again. Each time I answered rather weakly, "Yes Lord, with your help, I'll go as a single person."

One day during second semester a notice appeared on the bulletin board: "Summer volunteers needed to teach children in Vacation Bible School." The words jumped out at me: "teach children!" How could I expect to go overseas as a missionary and teach people about the Bible if I'd never spoken a word to anyone in America? I knew I should go and learn how to teach children. Still, back and forth in my mind, I reviewed the three reasons why I was anxious to go home for the summer.

I was homesick. No doubt about it.

This year the family camp where I'd heard God's call was featuring an outstanding missionary speaker, Darlene Diebler Rose. She had been a pioneer missionary on the island of New Guinea before the Second World War and had survived a Japanese concentration camp. I really wanted to hear her.

Most important of all, I needed money to continue at Simpson. No student was allowed to register unless he had cash to pay for the full semester. My summer job at Van de Kamp's bakery was waiting for me.

Yet, in the end, I did answer, "Yes Lord, I'll go and learn how to teach children."

Saying "yes" to the Lord each time did not change my personality. It didn't make me more outgoing or feel adequate for the assignment. God knew this and He provided someone to help in what was, for me, a difficult responsibility, leading a Vacation Bible School. My outgoing roommate, Carmen Aiken Nelson, and I teamed up. Carmen grew up helping in her church's vacation Bible schools. Leading one was no problem for her.

I chose to teach junior age children and the Scripture Press teacher's manual had everything well-laid-out for the two weeks of lessons. The Bible lesson was even written out in full. I discovered with good preparation I *could* teach children! The lessons I taught them were also applied to my own heart. I think I learned more that summer than the kids did.

The second church we were assigned to teach was on Whidby Island near Seattle. On the opening Sunday morning there, Carmen stayed in the main church to sing a solo. I was assigned to speak for twenty minutes in a small branch Sunday school. What could I say that would fill twenty minutes? I had no teacher's manual this time. I remembered the

Three More Questions Answered "Yes"

twelve-minute reading about missions I'd memorized for speech class. To this I added my testimony and call to missions. My audience turned out to be a dozen people, children and adults, including a young man named Don Gibbons. Don was the one who started the Sunday school. He asked for one of us to come and speak and had driven me to the assignment. On the thirty-minute drive back to the main church Don told me he too had received a call to missions.

During the next two weeks Don and I saw each other a lot. The church youth were always doing something and when that didn't happen, Don came calling at the home where I was staying. He even got himself invited to dinner more than once. At the end of our two weeks stay Don volunteered to save the pastor the long drive back to Seattle. He took Carmen and me across the ferry and then into the city to see us off on the bus. Greyhound was on strike so we went to the Trailways bus depot. Don worked his way through a large crowd of people in the waiting room and convinced the ticket agent that Carmen and I had an important schedule to keep. We got on the bus going to California when most of the people didn't. I saw for the first time some of Don's outgoing personality and his ability to get over a mountain that I could never have crossed alone.

Don's letters followed me to our next church and then to my home. My letters to him found their way back to the Island. It didn't take long for my parents to figure out that something more than a casual friendship was growing between Don and me. My Dad wanted to meet this young man who was courting his daughter. So he decided our whole family would drive me back to school. Before school started the family would enjoy a vacation on Whidby Island. For Don and me nothing could have been better.

During my next school year Don continued to live and work on the Island but for some reason he found his way to Simpson quite often. Since I lived in the dorm, this put both of us under the school's social rules. When he came we were allowed to be together on campus for half an hour after a noon or evening meal. Every two weeks we could have a four-hour date off campus.

Don had special plans for the birthday we share, October 29. We saved up our date-time for a month. When Don tells the story of our eight-hour date he says, "This was the day Alice said 'yes,' but it wasn't the first time I'd asked her to marry me."

Before we met, Don had graduated from another Bible school. With credits transferred from that school and classes he took at Simpson during a summer session, he qualified to become a senior. Thus we were both seniors during my third year at Simpson. In the spring we applied to be career missionaries with the Christian and Missionary Alliance and were accepted. At that time one requirement to be an Alliance missionary was to graduate from an Alliance school.

Only One Life

In June we met that requirement and graduated with the class of 1951. We were married that same month—no time wasted! I smile as I write this, for impetuous Don wanted to get married between our junior and senior years while practical Alice wanted to graduate first and be debt free. We "compromised," waiting only three weeks after graduation to be married.

The reason for waiting was really about finances. I said we compromised but actually we came together on a principle that would be ours for life—living debt-free. After we met, Don bought a new car on credit. To get out of debt he sold it and worked very hard to pay off the remaining money he owed. Through the years we've gone without some extras because a missionary's allowance isn't that much, but never have we lacked any essentials. Always we've given to the Lord first. By God's provision all five of our daughters graduated from college debt-free. Now in retirement, still lacking no good thing, we continue to live debt-free.

We did achieve our financial goal before we were married but had no money left over. For our honeymoon Don rented a cabin in Mt. Rainier National Park. Except for a bed, a table and a wood cook-stove the cabin was bare. My part before the wedding was to pack our food, cooking equipment and bedding. At Mt. Rainier we could hike and enjoy the beautiful mountain scenery at no extra cost. Little did we know that how we spent our honeymoon week and the coming two years in rural Oregon would be perfect preparation for our lifetime ahead.

Ten days after the wedding we were on our way to fulfill our final requirement to become Alliance missionaries: two years of Christian service in the States. Don could find no church needing a young missionary candidate on its staff. He did find a position where we could serve with Village Missions, an organization dedicated to opening the long-closed doors of country churches. However, our personal assignment was not to open a closed church but to start one in a large area in eastern Oregon that never had a church. About 300 ranchers and US Forest Service personnel lived there. Paulina, where we lived, had no electricity when we arrived and the nearest piece of pavement was 56 miles away. Our rough cabin had been built for summer sawmill workers. For cooking it had a wood stove, for lighting a borrowed Coleman lantern. There was no plumbing, only a hand pump in the yard for water and a path which led to the rest of what belongs in a bathroom. Sometimes in the winter ice froze on the bucket of water standing in the kitchen. To this place Don took me, his southern California bride.

We learned to live on love and the knowledge that together we were headed for God's calling to be career missionaries. Village Missions gave us $200 a month. In time local people added more. It took $40 a month just for gas and oil to drive our old '37

Three More Questions Answered "Yes"

Plymouth over the dirt roads in our 30 by 60 mile territory. However, we never lacked any good thing, not even the money to pay the doctor and hospital bills when our baby, Kathy, was born a year after we came to Paulina.

Always we had food, although sometimes it was just more of the same food. In the spring we ate eggs three times a day when the ranchers had more eggs than they could use. In the fall when a rancher butchered a steer, he sometimes gave us a piece of meat but more often it was the liver. I still remember the special gift of a side of pork chops which had been cured like ham. I'd never tasted anything so good. We feasted for days.

One winter afternoon with snow on the ground, we were returning from an overnight visit to another community. For a couple of hours we bounced slowly along a Forest Service road fit only for a Jeep or logging truck. Five-month-old Kathy napped in the folding baby buggy in the back seat. Once we got stuck in a mud hole. Don managed to get the car out using small poles he found nearby. Finally we came to the graveled county road. What a wonderful sight it was, chuckholes and all! The hour was getting late by then and we still had 15 miles to go to get home. Suddenly the car bumped to a stop. Don declared, "We broke a steering tie-rod. I can't fix it out here."

We both knew that during the night the temperature would drop well below freezing. On our entire drive we had not seen another vehicle. Waiting for someone to come by wasn't an option. Don said, "We have no choice. A mile or so back there we passed the Miller ranch. We'll walk back to their house. I'm sure they'll put us up for the night." We took a few things from the car and began pushing the baby buggy down the road with Kathy bundled inside. Shivering, we hurried a little faster because it was getting dark. As we walked, we thanked God that the tie-rod, probably damaged on the Forest Service road, had lasted until we got to the county road. Few people ever used that back road. We'd told nobody in Paulina about this trip, so no one would have noticed if we didn't get home.

At the ranch we discovered no one was at home. Don walked around the house until he found a window he could pry open and crawled through. When we were all inside, he built a fire, lit a kerosene lamp and we helped ourselves to some food. About 9:00 o'clock we decided the Millers weren't coming home so we went to bed in the spare bedroom. An hour later we were awakened by their arrival. When they saw the old Plymouth on the road, they knew it was ours and wished they'd been at home. After finding us in their house they were glad we were safe for the night.

When our two years of home service was complete, we left behind a dozen adults and several children meeting each Sunday in our little church. The church building was

Only One Life

an abandoned school house moved to town and given a new coat of white paint. Now, after all these years have passed, those church doors still remain open in Paulina.

BIBLE LESSON

> The Lord God said, "It is not good for the man to live alone. I will make a suitable companion to help him." Genesis 2:18

> The Lord who saves you says: "I am the Lord your God, the one who wants to teach you for your own good and direct you in the way you should go." Isaiah 48:17

> The Lord will make you go through hard times, but he himself will be there to teach you, and you will not have to search for him any more. If you wander off the road to the right or the left, you will hear his voice behind you saying, "Here is the road. Follow it." Isaiah 30:20-21

God asked me if I was willing to go overseas as a single woman, to trust Him for my financial needs for my second year at Simpson, to step out and teach children in Vacation Bible School. In each of these He knew my true inability. He only wanted me to trust Him—and I did. What if I hadn't said "yes" to the Spirit's prompting to go and teach Vacation Bible School? During that summer the only place I gave my testimony and call to missions was in the little branch Sunday school. Don was there! It was God's design that Don should hear me speak for he too had heard God's call to career missions.

I needed someone in life to go ahead of me and break trail as it were. Don needed someone to come along-side and be his companion and helpmate. God brought us together to serve Him in a unique place in the world where according to God's plan thousands would turn to Christ.

Even in 1951, when living was much simpler than today, our mission leaders would have been hard pressed to find an assignment in the US more challenging than ours in Eastern Oregon. This too was in God's plan for us. God filled in all the cracks around the hardships of our assignment with good things, making it a wonderful time in our lives.

Three More Questions Answered "Yes"

ISSUES TO CONSIDER

1. God sometimes asks us to give up someone or something that seems so very good to us, and then He replaces it with something far better. Have you a story to tell about such a happening?

2. In your life is there an opportunity you hesitate to accept because you feel unqualified? How might God equip you so you could fulfill the assignment?

3. Addressing the question of debt in each of our lives is important, though sometimes painful.

Chapter 3
Pushed Out to Fly on My Own

Our Royal Dutch Airlines plane touched down in Biak, Netherlands New Guinea. When we applied to the Christian and Missionary Alliance for missionary service, our application stated we were willing to go wherever they chose to send us. New Guinea was the mission's choice and also God's choice, yet a place we knew almost nothing about. For over a month we had been on our way, traveling first by freighter to cross the Pacific and then by plane from Manila. We had finally arrived. Our excitement ran high. [See map in front of the book]

In his pocket Don carried a letter from the field chairman with instructions about our next flight which would take us from the coast to our final destination in the interior of the island. Each Friday the mission was allowed 200 kilos (440 pounds) on an amphibian plane of the Royal Dutch Navy. The military plane flew from the airfield in Biak to the island's interior where it landed on the largest of the Wissel Lakes. The letter instructed us to find a certain Chinese merchant in Biak who would help us prepare for the flight. He would weigh our bodies and add luggage to fit into the total weight allowance on the military plane.

As it turned out, we were met by a missionary who had just returned from furlough. His sea freight and ours were to arrive in Biak within the week, so he and Don would remain on the coast, each to repack his sea freight making it ready for later plane flights. Only baby Kathy and I would fly to the interior on the Friday flight. I certainly did not want to go without Don, but the ball was rolling and I couldn't stop it.

Kathy and I boarded the Catalina amphibian plane on Friday morning. After 40 minutes of flying the plane slipped through a pass in the mountain range at 10,000 feet and began to descend by circling over the large lake—a lake discovered less than 20 years before by an adventurous Dutch pilot. We landed on the water and taxied toward the shore. Two virtually naked men, with only their private parts covered with a gourd, paddled a boat out from the dock to get us. This was a reality check for me. I was entering a culture still in the Stone Age. As I climbed out of the little boat and on to the dock, I could see the missionaries standing far back on shore. This plane made the weekly government flight; all the personnel and freight were governmental except for the 200 kilos allowed to the mission.

Carrying Kathy, I walked toward the missionaries: two men, five women and two children. Words of welcome were quick. The field chairman, a veteran of many years, said, "It's a steep hill up to the mission houses. Jonah will carry your baby. He's a Bible school student and works in the kitchen of the house where you'll be staying." He motioned to a man dressed in shorts and a t-shirt. In seconds my 14-month-old blond baby girl was sitting astride this black man's shoulders, and we all began climbing up the long, steep hill.

Looking around as we walked I saw lots of tribal people of all ages. None wore Western clothing. On Sunday I wrote a letter to my mother and commented, "Now I don't even think of the fact the native people aren't wearing clothes. . . Kathy is quick to find her way to the kitchen and to the company of local people who work there. . . Fleas live in the woven bamboo floor of this large log cabin and they really enjoy biting us. . . Language study for me is to begin on Tuesday, and I just got here on Friday. . . Don isn't even here yet and won't come for another week."

For the next three months after Don came, we studied the Indonesian language (an easy-to-learn trade-language used by the government). Then our assignment was changed to study the more difficult Mee tribal language spoken by the people with whom we were to spend our lives. The mission required we pass the two-year Mee language proficiency exam in order to remain on the field.

We lived in the large mission house with another missionary couple, their two children and a single man. Every other week it was my responsibility to see to the cooking and serving of the meals for this family of eight. In the house and in the Dutch government community where we lived most of the local people used Indonesian to communicate with us. We heard very little of the Mee language spoken. We were desperate for a better language-learning setting and longed for a home life of our own.

A Mee pastor, now back in Bible school at the main station, offered to let us live in his house across the lake. He built this house for himself, a house without the usual native hearth for an open fire. His only materials for building were poles, rough hand-split boards, jungle vine and for roofing, bark and grass thatch. In his eyes, the house was modeled after the missionary's house. In my eyes, it was really a native shack. However the mission could offer us nothing better. We decided to move across the lake and live not only close to the native people but, as we soon discovered, close to the earth as well. The "floor" had many wide cracks and was only a few inches above the poorly drained ground. In the frequent rains everything turned to mud, even the ground under the house. We realized later the Mee pastor never slept in this house; it was only a house that gave him a feeling of prestige. He slept with a fire in a regular native house built higher from the ground.

Even here, getting practice in speaking the Mee language proved difficult because the local people were not Christians. They had no interest in our learning their language. (Two years later they would join their neighbors in an effort to rid their land of all foreigners. See chapter 5.)

Before long I began to wonder if I were pregnant. I knew for sure when morning sickness set in with a vengeance, the kind that lasts all day long. Food was scarce, even for the local people. The only fresh food they had for sale was sweet potatoes and greens. Thankfully, we had our little wood range set up in this house and I could make bread with flour that was flown from the coast.

I craved meat, for we had only a limited supply of tinned meat. When Don got word of a local man butchering a pig, he went to that village and tried to buy some pork for me. If he got anything, it was usually a piece of liver which would have gone to the women.

During my three years in Bible school liver was served every Friday so on that day I became a vegetarian. Also on Fridays Don got lots of liver to eat as other students didn't like it either. He was known as the guy who "liked liver and loved Alice." At Paulina a rancher often gave us a whole liver. Don enjoyed the liver. I cooked it and he ate it. Now in this village there was nothing else. I needed protein to help build my baby's body so I ate all the liver Don could buy. During that time I learned to enjoy liver, even without onions, for the sake of my unborn baby.

Don started raising rabbits to provide us with a little fresh meat. The Mee people had nothing but pigs for meat and only a few of them. Rabbits were imported by the Dutch in hopes of helping the people increase their meat supply, but raising rabbits was too complicated for them at this time. However, natives came from far and wide to see our amazing animals, our *woda* (jungle rat) as they called them. (A jungle rat is an edible animal for the tribal people.) One day when we were standing around the rabbit pen with a group of local people, I said something to Don in English and called him "bunny." In disgust our two-and-a-half year old Kathy turned to the people and said in very good Mee, "She just called him 'jungle rat.'"

After six months when a missionary family went on furlough, we moved back across the lake to live in a small log cabin of our own. It was here in the bedroom loft that our Joyce Verdelle was born, the first white baby ever to be born in these interior mountains.

BIBLE LESSON

I have learned this secret, so that anywhere, at any time, I am content, whether I am full or hungry, whether I have too much or too little. I have the strength to face all conditions by the power that Christ gives me. Philippians 4:12b-13

And we know that in all things God works for the good of those who love him, who have been called according to his purpose. Romans 8:28 NIV

Near the beginning of my journey to become a missionary the Lord gave me extra support from people when He knew I needed it. Help came from Carmen Nelson in teaching Vacation Bible School. Later, I leaned heavily on Don. Flying to the lakes I was on my own; all the props were taken away.

Living in that native shack, having a full-blown case of morning sickness and all the while trying to put in four hours a day in Mee language study, I knew I'd come "to the ends of the earth." (Acts 1:8) It was a time to remind myself why I was here, and recall Jesus' words of command and promise as I knew them in the King James Version—"Go ye therefore, and teach all nations . . . and lo, I am with you always, even unto the end of the world." (Matthew 28:19-20)

I smile when I remember plans for summer vacation after my first year in Bible School and how I so wanted to hear Darlene Diebler Rose speak. Hearing her was one thing I gave up at that time. Now, five years later, I was the missionary in the exact place where she had lived and worked. I met Darlene, not as the speaker at my church's summer camp, but when she came to a mission conference at the lakes. She stayed with us in our log cabin home. This little story illustrates how God brought about a happy ending to an almost forgotten disappointment. Romans 8:28 is true not only in the big things of life but also in the little things.

Only One Life

ISSUES TO CONSIDER

1. When I needed more protein in my diet, God provided liver. At two earlier periods in my life I'd chosen to go hungry rather than eat liver. This time I thanked God for His provision and learned to enjoy eating it. He changed my taste for liver!

    In your life have you an example of how God supplied a need with something you considered unacceptable or not good, and in the process He changed your thinking so that it became good?

2. If you are a young person reading this book or an older person looking forward to more life ahead, consider keeping a journal. As you read from its pages, you will be amazed to see how God turns things around in your life, things that were not as you wished. He transforms them into something far better.

Chapter 4
Called to the East

Don was often out and about. Sometimes he worked on buildings for the Mee Bible School. Sometimes it was taking the mission boat with outboard motor across the lake to pick up a load of hand-split boards. Once a month he had a different load in the boat. Preparing his cargo, Don packed basic supplies into carrying tins for the six missionaries and four children who lived three-days-walk back in the mountains. These were the same foods we had at the lake: basics like flour, sugar, tinned meat and peanut butter. The supplies, the all-important mail and three or four Mee men to carry the packs were all loaded into the boat. Three hours up the river where the boat could go no further, the carriers took their loads and began hiking on the trail to the east.

On one of these boat trips up-river Don met a missionary, Gordon Larson, who had just walked over the trail from the Moni mission station. He was coming out to the main station on business. The two men hit it off right away. Gordon found an enthusiastic audience in Don as he told story after story about the native traders from the east. These traders came to Moni country in search of salt which they collected from the salt spring near the mission station.

Gordon was a trained linguist and had determined the travelers were from two tribes, each speaking a very different language. These Dani and Damal tribal people lived somewhere to the east, many days walk from the mission station. No outsider knew how many people were in the tribes or where in the mountains they lived. In the boat that day, Gordon shared his dream of taking the gospel to the Dani and Damal people—people untouched by anyone from the outside world.

Gordon, the scholar, was learning the Moni language and wanted to do translation work. However, another Moni missionary, also a Bible translator, would soon be returning from furlough. The Moni station was well manned without Gordon. Don, the outdoorsman, was learning the Mee language but felt the seven missionaries on the station were pretty well covering all the local bases. Thus, the two men bonded together that day with a common vision to reach these two new tribes who lived deep in the unexplored interior of Dutch New Guinea. Before Gordon returned to his station I

Only One Life

embraced the same call that Don had experienced. Our commission was to reach the Damal people with the gospel.

Soon after this meeting, Don set out to the east on a one-month exploration trip. He had with him six Mee carriers and limited supplies. There was no room for a two-way radio for communication. Don was looking for Damals who lived south of the central mountain range. The Moni salt-springs and mission station are located on the north side of this daunting mountain range whose peaks reach 16,500 feet. [See Story 1 map]

Little was known about people who lived on the north side of the range but even less was known about those who lived on the south side where Don was headed. After hiking through two valleys populated with Mee tribes people, and then through two more with Monis, Don came to valleys populated by Damals. He found each southern valley had only a couple hundred people because the rugged terrain could support no more. Another evidence of the rough country on that 30-day trip: Don wore out two new pairs of Australian army boots!

No missionary serving with The Christian and Missionary Alliance ever makes work-related decisions on his own. We serve as a team under our field leadership. We had only been on the field a few months when our first Field Conference convened with all the missionaries gathering on the main station where we lived. A mission leader from headquarters in New York City came to lead the conference. On the second day, conference members began making work appointments for each missionary. Our fellow missionaries listened to our testimony and heard our clear desire to pioneer to the east. However, they appointed us to continue in Mee language study with the view of opening an unreached Mee area far to the west.

I felt devastated; I was sure our call to the east and the Damal tribe was from God! Walking up the hill after the meeting I spoke to the leader who had come from New York. Tears began to flow as I talked. This stoic gentleman hardly knew how to deal with a weeping woman. He said something like, "If this is God's plan for you, He will work it out." Our conference assignment was not changed. We continued our language study and eventually passed our two-year language exam in Mee.

Life on the mission station where we lived was very routine, even monotonous. We needed a break, but there was no place to go and no way to get there. So like the proverbial mailman who went for a walk on his day off, we decided to hike the three days to where the Moni missionaries lived and celebrate Thanksgiving with them.

On the trail our eight-month-old Joyce and three-year-old Kathy were carried like native children—no problem for them. However, hiking for six or seven hours each day turned out to be a challenge for me. Some of those hours we walked in the rain. Always there was another mountain to climb and always another one to go down. At the end of our second day Don had to set up the tent in the continuing rain. While I waited, my muscles ached terribly, I shivered in the rain, and I favored a broken blister on my heel, all the while holding a hungry crying baby who was wet in more ways than one! All this was part of my first trail experience.

Our Thanksgiving table was set with all the elegance our pioneer hostess could muster. One thing we didn't lack on the table was sweet potatoes. For this meal they were candied. Our dessert was pumpkin pie made from sweet potatoes. In place of turkey we had roast rabbit complete with dressing. (Like Don, the Moni missionaries were raising rabbits to provide a break from the staple of canned corned beef or the Dutch version of Spam). It was good to give thanks around a table with new missionary friends.

In the months that followed, the passion of Don and Gordon to reach the tribes to the east continued to burn in their hearts. The men got permission from the mission leader to make their first exploratory trip together. In later years mission leadership required that men on trek take a two-way radio with them. This time there was no radio available.

Don and Gordon were in the Ilaga, two weeks walk from home, when they faced the potentially lethal arrows of Dani warriors. Throughout the day the aggressive Danis had been demanding axes and cowrie shells. Three different times the Danis got away with a carrying tin of supplies. They also blocked passage over a bridge, took a steel axe from Don and frightened some of the carriers into surrendering their personal knives and cowrie shells. Still the party continued to press on.

At one point the trail narrowed as it wound along the Ilaga River. Here Gordon led the march, the twenty carriers followed in close rank and Don brought up the rear. The Danis followed right behind, chanting loudly and flaunting their weapons.

A warrior pushed around Don and grabbed the personal net-bag of a Mee carrier. In the bag were his hard earned cowrie shells, enough to buy a pig. In anger the carrier raised his bow and arrow to shoot. Immediately a cry rang out from the other carriers, "Don't shoot! Keep going! If anyone shoots they'll kill us all." The Mee men all carried bows and arrows and knew how to use their lethal weapons. They also knew if one man shot an arrow, none of them would escape with their lives.

On they went. The chanting and demands of the fifty Dani warriors increased. Don called out to Gordon. "You all keep going. I'll slow down and keep them at bay." The pursuers soon caught on. Arrows flew over Don's head and at his side and he decided to catch up with the others.

Only One Life

Shortly the party came to an open place and were immediately surrounded by the Dani warriors. "Give us all your shells and axes," they demanded.

Don and Gordon hesitated, talking together, "What shall we do?"

Suddenly there was the twang of a bow string and the cry of pain from a Mee carrier. Panic reigned. The carriers threw their packs down and fled. The Danis pounced on the bounty, each man grabbing whatever he found.

The missionaries and the Mee carriers ran for their lives.

The warriors returned to the Ilaga with their loot.

Just as the blackness of night descended, the missionary party reached an overhanging rock—a camp-site used by hundreds of native travelers before them. There they stopped for the night. The carriers soon slept by a fire. The two men talked for awhile and prayed.

"Tomorrow is my third wedding anniversary," Don commented. "All day I kept thinking of what it would mean for Alice if I were killed today." Again they thanked God for His preservation of all their lives. [Read the full story in the prologue of my book, *The People Time Forgot*.]

Walking home the men found all the people in the Beoga Valley were Damals and they were very friendly. The men also discovered a small side canyon where an airstrip could be built. The trip was a success!

Later, the mission plane made a survey flight over the Beoga Valley with Don on board. The weather was clear that day and the pilot gave his okay for building an airstrip on the site Don pointed out.

Months passed. Don and Gordon were again on the ground in Beoga beginning to lay out the airstrip. On a cloudy day the pilot flew over to make a free drop to the men. This time the pilot said, "The area is not acceptable for an airstrip. The high mountains all around are just too close." Discouragement reigned as the men abandoned the project and hiked the two weeks back to the lakes.

During these days of separation and disappointment, my mind flashed back several years to the time when Don and I were nearing the end of our last year in Bible school. We were nervous about the oral exam coming up for us as Alliance missionary candidates. A senior administrator flew from New York for this all-important interview. The oral exam determined whether we would be accepted or rejected as candidates. Since Don and I were only engaged, we understood we would be called in separately. But that's not the way it happened—they ushered us in together. First, the examiner asked Don a long string of questions about Bible doctrine. I sat there wondering what sort of doctrinal questions he would ask me and could I answer them.

He finished with Don and turned to me with these words. "On the mission field will you be willing to be separated from your husband for long periods of time?"

I hesitated, wondering how I could answer that when I wasn't even married. After some thought, I responded, "Yes." He repeated the same question, perhaps perceiving my dependence on Don. Again I answered, "Yes." A third time he asked the identical question and I was becoming rather flustered. What did he want me to say? At this point the school president, who happened to be the brother-in-law of the examiner, interrupted with a bit of his dry humor. Everyone laughed and the examination was over.

Now the time had come for that question to be answered not only with words but in action. I was married and on the mission field. I had joined my husband in this calling to explore and reach the Damal people. During the months when it seemed as if we were getting nowhere, Don always found encouragement by making plans for another trip. "Next time we'll make it!" he said. My role didn't change. It was simply to stay behind, take care of our two little girls—and wait. Times of separation were to become longer and longer. God was merciful in protecting me from knowledge of increasing hard times and dangers lurking in our future.

BIBLE LESSON

David hiding from King Saul at Ziklag:

> When David and his men arrived back at Ziklag, they found that the town had been burned down and that their wives, sons and daughters had been carried away by the Amalekites. David and his men started crying and did not stop until they were completely exhausted. David was now in great trouble and his men were threatening to stone him; but the Lord his God gave him courage.
>
> The Lord answered David and said, "Go after the raiders; you will catch them and rescue the captives."
>
> So David and his six hundred men started out, but two hundred men were too tired and stayed behind.
>
> David got back all his men's sons and daughters, and all the loot the Amalekites had taken.

> Then David went back to the two hundred men who had been too weak and stayed behind.
>
> Some worthless men said, "They didn't go with us, and so we won't give them any of the loot."
>
> David answered, "My brothers, you can't do this with what the Lord has given us! He kept us safe and gave us victory over the raiders. Whoever stays behind with the supplies gets the same share as the one who goes into battle." Condensed from 1 Samuel 30

> And whatever you do, whether in word or deed, do it all in the name of the Lord Jesus, giving thanks to God the Father through him. Colossians 3:17

> This is the message from the one who is holy and true. He has the key that belonged to David, and when he opens a door, no one can close it, and when he closes it, no one can open it. Revelation 3:7

While my husband served as a missionary explorer, I learned in my heart I could fulfill my missionary calling through Don's activities. I remained his backup at home—staying by the stuff. Sometimes my part there in our home seemed routine, even of little value and always lonely. At those times it was good to be reminded from the Scriptures that whatever we are given to do should be done as unto the Lord. God rewards the one serving in a mundane job just as much as the one who is upfront in the spotlight.

Closed doors to the east seemed to be the order of the day. Yet by faith we continued to ask and believe God would open the way into the Damal tribe.

Called to the East

ISSUES TO CONSIDER

1. Would you consider the role of a stay-at-home mom to be similar to the position Alice was in? In what ways?

2. "Whatever you do, whether in word or deed, do it all in the name of the Lord Jesus, giving thanks to God the Father through him." In daily living what a challenge it is to follow the steps outlined in this verse from Colossians 3.

3. When a door is closed or a roadblock appears in our way, it's easy to say, "This hindrance is from Satan." Is this always true? I'm thinking of the story in Numbers 22:21-33 of Balaam and his donkey.

4. Doors opening and closing—where have you observed this happening in your life, in our nation, in the world? Is it not God who is in ultimate control of all of these?

Chapter 5

Disappointments and Danger

It was August 1956. Once again Don and Gordon started out on the trail to the east. This time their goal was permanent residence in the Ilaga Valley. Earlier the goal of the men had been to establish a base in Beoga but the airstrip site had been declared unsatisfactory. The Ilaga was a wide bowl-like valley and from the air our pilot had found a satisfactory site to build an airstrip. To make this entrance to the Ilaga possible the mission executive committee met and changed our work appointment. It had formerly read: "Appointed to continue in Mee language study with the view of opening an unreached Mee area to the west." After the change it read: "Appointed to the Ilaga Valley to work with the Damal tribe." We now had the official blessing and backing of our mission.

The men left with the promise that we wives would soon be able to join them in the Ilaga—just as soon as they got the airstrip built. Instead, a separation of ever-extending months was to follow, months filled with deserting carriers, threats of tribal war, serious illness, increasing requirements about the airstrip before a landing could be made, and only the native food of sweet potatoes and greens to keep the men from serious hunger. Seven months were to pass before I flew with my girls to the Ilaga.

Even though I had a part in this story, I am spellbound when I read again the account of these months as it is written in my book, *The People Time Forgot.* In the book the first 100 pages tell the true story of a Damal man as he was bon and lived in the Stone Age. Next comes the tale of our adventures as we burst into the world of the Damals, followed by the story of God's marvelous working in their lives. Did all this really happen as part of *my* life?

Two months into this time of separation, with Don far away in the Ilaga, it was my turn to be involved in a life-threatening saga. Since our mission had just received a new Cessna airplane we all had hopes of receiving supplies again. Less than a month earlier the mission's first Cessna had been wrecked on its initial landing at the Moni

Disappointments and Danger

station. Once again, all of we missionaries were dependant on the government for a meager 200 kilo (440 pounds) allotment on their weekly flight.

Saturday this mission plane was to land on a new airstrip built across the lake at Obano. [o-BON-o] Onboard would be a mission leader from headquarters. He would lead a dedication service for the new airplane. An air drop of critical supplies to Don and Gordon in Ilaga was also scheduled.

Getting a new airplane was a big deal and everyone wanted to go to Obano— adults and children alike. The five children on the station were so excited. On the way home we planned to stop at the one sandy beach on the lake and enjoy swimming and a picnic lunch. The kids hadn't been to this beach in a very long time. Without an airplane everything was in short supply. No gasoline could be spared for a trip across the lake just for fun.

In the Ilaga Don was sick with infectious hepatitis. The diagnosis had been made by a Dutch doctor talking to Don on the mission's two-way shortwave radio. The doctor's prescribed treatment was bed rest with a high-protein diet. Neither of these was possible for Don in the Ilaga. To make matters even worse, all work on the airstrip had stopped for the men were out of trading items to pay the workers.

Axe, beads and cowry shells were packed to take to Obano for the drop. It was Don's birthday (and mine too for that matter). I added a cake, chocolate fudge, and letters with the other supplies. I felt closer to Don because I would be at the airstrip when the plane took off for the drop.

Saturday morning the usual sunshine was missing. Low clouds and fog hung all around the lake. Rain ponchos were added to everything else. We nine missionaries and six children, counting little Joyce, all loaded into our small boat for the trip to the dedication ceremony. With the 6 HP out-board motor it took two hours to cross the lake.

As we landed on the muddy bank at Obano, I looked for local people to carry my two girls over the mile-long trail to the airstrip. Not one person was in sight. Strange, I thought. Surely they had seen and heard our boat coming. So the one Mee man, who was with us to help with the motor, carried Joyce. Four-year-old Kathy had to slog through the mud herself trying to keep up with the older children and adults.

Nearing the airstrip I could see seven new buildings and another big one not yet finished. These were all part of a new school complex being built by the mission for Mee school children, grades four to six. But there was no plane on the airstrip. Had it turned back due to weather? After a bit we heard the faint drone of the single engine and in five minutes the new Cessna was on the ground. We all got to meet the new mission leader from New York.

Shortly after, the pilot announced, "The weather has closed down. I'll make the drop to the Ilaga on Monday. Just load everything you brought for the drop into the airplane. It will be safe there." Don's birthday cake would have to wait two more days. I felt sorry for Don, lonely and sick, so far away.

Just then we felt the first drops of rain. Our station leader announced "Everyone gather under the wing of the plane for the dedication service. Then we'll eat an early lunch in the school house and head right back across the lake."

At the service all the Mee school children joined us along with an Indonesian school teacher and his wife, two Indonesian students boarding with them, the coastal carpenters building the school and two policemen who had come to guard the plane over the weekend. In the rush we hardly noticed that no local people were out to see this strange new bird come to rest in their valley.

Accompanying us back across the lake were the two men who came in the plane and a Dutch missionary school teacher, a lady who now lived at Obano. She planned to return on Monday for her classes. We squeezed into the boat and shared the ponchos that kept off some of the rain. Joyce slept in my arms. As we passed the sandy beach, the sad eyes of five children peered in silence from beneath their rain gear at the beautiful white sand. They too, like their elders, were learning to accept disappointment.

Saturday's events were good for me, to break the unending routine of life, but Sunday was normal again. After teaching Sunday school for the missionary children and attending a Mee church service, I had a lonely dinner with my two little girls. Then I lay down for a nap with them in our upstairs bedroom.

All of a sudden I realized that something was going on below my bedroom window. I heard the panting voice of a Mee pastor who had run to tell our station leader what he had seen from across the lake. "Mirror signals are flashing and billows of black smoke are rising from Obano," he blurted out. We could not see this from the government village where we lived because a small island near Obano blocked our line-of-sight.

Wasting no time, all the missionary men headed for the lake. On the way down the hill they stopped at the police station and told them of the mirror signals and smoke at Obano. The police loaned the men a 25 HP outboard motor and they were soon speeding across the lake. They got as far as the small island when they met a native dugout canoe loaded with people smeared with mud, the mud of mourning. These people were fleeing from Obano. Coming alongside they told the missionaries, "Everyone is dead at Obano—

Disappointments and Danger

the schoolteachers and the two children boarding with them, the carpenters, the police—everybody was killed. All the mission buildings are burned and the plane is chopped to pieces." With heavy hearts the missionaries turned around and headed home. What could all this mean?

The chief government officer ordered everyone on the mission station to move into the largest of the three mission houses. We were thirteen missionaries and eight children counting the two babies who had not gone across the lake. Everyone came together lugging mattresses and bedding, bringing homemade bread and whatever prepared food they had.

After dark some very shaken-up school boys from the Dutch missionary's class came to our door. From their tale and other eyewitnesses who came later we pieced the story together.

A group of mature Obano men had banded together to rid their land of all foreigners. They wanted to be rid of police control, schools and religious teachings. They saw the young people leaving the influence of their elders to follow these aliens. Obano was fast becoming the foreigner's village like the one across the lake. Now their pigs were dying in large numbers. In their minds this epidemic could have only one source—the outsiders' intrusion on their sacred traditions.

Their plans were to make the initial attack at Obano on Sunday morning when all foreigners who lived at Obano would be gathered together in church. On Saturday as soon as they observed the arrival of the missionaries' boat and then the airplane landing, the word went out. "Come quickly! The foreigners have come and we will kill all of them today."

Indeed we were there, 18 of us, and not one would have been able to escape if the warriors had reached us that morning. In the providence of God this did not happen. He sent an unusual morning rain which slowed the warriors and sent us scurrying for home.

Sunday was a beautiful day at Obano. Everyone was in church. Even the two policemen, there to guard the plane, came to church. According to Mee custom all the local people left their bows and arrows outside the church door and the policemen left their guns there too. The Indonesian school teacher, whose first calling was that of a pastor, preached in the Mee language. He had lived with the Mee people many years and learned their language while serving the tribal people. As the congregation filed out, they were confronted by native warriors who had gathered quietly outside. The warriors began a war dance with drawn bows and arrows and everyone knew what this meant.

Only One Life

The Indonesian teachers with the two school boys ran to their house for cover, but it was no protection. They were quickly shot with arrows and their house was burned. Also killed were a coastal policeman and the carpenters. (One policeman managed to escape to the jungle). All the buildings were burned. The warriors chopped through the thin aluminum covering on the airplane and found to their delight all the axes, trading items and tools that were ready for the drop to the Ilaga.

With the excitement of this accomplishment the warriors sent runners around the lake to every village asking for men to join in the fight to rid their land of the foreigners. A number of areas joined the Obano men. The village next to Obano, where we had lived for six months of language study, was one of the first to join. Across the lake, the village just an hour's walk up the hill from the government community where we all lived also joined the attackers.

Monday morning I started my washing as usual. What else could I do with a pile of clothes and cloth diapers to wash? (In those days there was no such thing as disposable diapers). Before the clothes were all hung on the line, word came that the people from the nearby village were coming to attack. Already they had killed two Catholic teachers in that village and burned the buildings. We were ordered to go immediately to the small government hostel down the hill from our house. Here the few police could more easily stand guard. Thus began a week of alerts filled with confusion and danger—all the while caring for our children, running again to the government post and trying to find food enough for everyone.

We really did not know where we stood with the local Mee people who were everywhere around us. Every man carried his bow and arrows. Word came from Obano that it was the teacher's best friend who shot the first arrow to kill him. We dared not trust the local people, yet we could do nothing else. The black bodies of friend or foe all looked alike. Someone got the idea of giving out strips of old white sheets which had been rolled to use as bandages and mailed to us by Alliance Women in America. Every local man who pledged loyalty to the government wore a band of white around his head day and night. Had these closest village people turned against us, there would have been little hope. Instead they warned us and fought for us. Some were wounded and one died.

Tuesday, we again spent the day sitting in the government hostel and the night sleeping on the cement floor. White-banded watchmen reported that the hills around the post were covered with enemy warriors. That night we might have been an easy prey—but God kept them from attacking.

Wednesday morning we dashed home for a change of clothing and more food. Back in the hostel the cry rang out again, "The enemy is coming." Down the hill they

Disappointments and Danger

came. For two hours they fought with bows and arrows. The friendly Mee warriors shot arrows back while the policemen beside them used their guns very sparingly. Our side won the battle and as victors, they returned to do a victory dance at the government post.

Dutch marines landed on the lake and were sent to Obano to fight with big guns against an enemy who used bows and arrows. Men from both sides hid in the garden ditches. The bullets and mortar shells did little damage to the enemy. Only the arrows arched up and into the ditch, sometimes hitting a marine. When the soldiers moved out to counterattack, the warriors vanished. For the marines it was like trying to catch a large balloon with greased hands; when their hands made contact the balloon bounced away.

At the government village, with the arrival of police reinforcements flown in from the coast we were allowed to return home and sleep in our own houses. The enemy continued to come down the hill right to the edge of the post but they were no match now for the many police guns, coupled with the tribal people who continued to fight on our side.

Two months after the war began, a thousand Mee warriors from a Christian area a day's walk away came over the mountain to Obano. They defeated the attackers fighting with arrow against arrow—something the Dutch marines could not do.

The formal peace was made in Mee style, even as the war had been fought and won according to their rules. A single line of defeated warriors, without their bows and arrows, came running down the hill to the home of the chief government officer. To the accompaniment of their rhythmic hooting they danced in a circle. Then the Mee who fought on the government side came running and waving branches. They too were hooting. All joined in a circle dance and the war was ended.

BIBLE LESSON

    I alone know the plans I have for you, plans to bring you prosperity and not disaster, plans to bring about the future you hope for. Jeremiah 29:11

    He who dwells in the shelter of the Most High

        will rest in the shadow of the Almighty.

    I will say to the Lord, "He is my refuge and my fortress,

Only One Life

> my God, in whom I trust."
>
> He will cover you with his feathers
>
> and under his wings you will find refuge;
>
> his faithfulness will be your shield and rampart.
>
> You will not fear the terror of night,
>
> nor the arrow that flies by day
>
> For he will command his angels concerning you
>
> to guard you in all your ways.
>
> Psalm 91: 1-2, 4-5, 11 NIV

We missionaries mourned the loss of those who died at Obano. The Indonesian school teacher had left his home island to be a missionary to the Mee people. To support himself, he taught school. The two Indonesian children boarding with the teacher were not spared.

On the first Sunday night when we were all gathered in the big mission house, eight-year-old Kenny asked his mother, "Mama, why did they kill my best friend? Will they try to kill us too?" Kenny's friend had moved to Obano two months earlier to attend the class taught by the Dutch teacher. The two boys had seen each other at the plane the day before. Kenny's mother read to her son the verses from Psalm 91 and he understood the picture painted by the psalmist. Kenny had seen a hawk soaring overhead and watched a mother hen clucking to warn her young. Her little chicks ran to her and disappeared under her fluffy feathers. There the hen stayed covering her chicks until the hawk gave up and flew away. The words from Psalm 91 remained a comfort to each of us, for we all had reason to fear and also to give thanks.

Someone has said, "Our disappointments are God's appointments." Often we never know why God allows a disappointment to come into our lives. For those times we have Jeremiah 29:11. This time we soon learned the reason. The bad weather kept us from a fun stop at the sandy beach—a disappointment for everyone. The rain caused us to hurry back to our boat and slowed the warriors in coming after us. Eighteen lives were spared.

I want to relate a disappointment that came to our family many years later. In Bible college one of our daughters had a serious beau. For some reason unknown to her he dropped her suddenly. For a time it seemed her world had fallen apart. Later the man dated and married another young woman. But sadly, that marriage soon ended in divorce because the man was discovered to be living in a very wrong lifestyle. For our daughter it was a disappointment turned to God's appointment because she married another man and now has a happy life in Christian ministry.

ISSUES TO CONSIDER

1. Each of the verses quoted from Psalm 91 paints a word picture of how the Lord protects his children in danger or trouble.

2. Does a disappointment you experienced pop up in your mind? Can you see a reason why God allowed it? Or perhaps you will never know the reason this side of heaven.

3. "I alone know the plans I have for you, plans to bring you prosperity and not disaster, plans to bring about the future you hope for." These words from Jeremiah 29:11 can bring encouragement in many situations—financial disaster, depression and more—good words to mark in our Bible or send to a friend.

Chapter 6
Math, Music and Becoming a Missionary

Plans for my life as a teenager were to become a teacher of mathematics. Beyond math my other special interest was music, especially playing the piano. When I changed my life's course to become a missionary, I gave up both of these dreams. After I'd been in Beoga for ten years, teaching math did come back into my life but in a very different format.

At our earliest Bible training school in Beoga I became the teacher of a class I called math. The Damals called it *madalingam*—counting. Their title was more accurate than mine for it began with learning to count. To say nineteen in their language—a number in real life a Damal had no reason to express—a man had to say *me nagao amengak emek me nagao eya moep,* the fingers of one man's hands, with the fingers of another man's hand and on his other hand, four more. To say nineteen was like describing the nineteen fingers of two men. To convey anything about numbers using the Damal language was next to impossible.

I began by teaching the Damals to count in the Indonesian language, a language which has a counting system similar to that of English. Next the class learned to read and write numbers. In the beginning we had only one Bible book, the Book of Mark, but soon more would be translated. To find a Bible passage they needed to understand the numbers of chapters and verses. My students soon saw how counting and reading numbers would help them in other ways also—to use a calendar, to use Indonesian paper money, rupiahs, and to tell time. In the past, numbers were unimportant to life. Now that their whole way of life was changing, numbers had become very useful.

Music, in the form of singing, added a great deal to the life of the Damal. The men sang in a group as they were digging a garden, walking on the trail, dancing in the courtyard, celebrating a victory in war or at a community feast. This music, a type of rhythmic chanting, was sung without words.

At night in the men's house their singing included words; it was a form of storytelling. One man began by singing a short, wordless refrain and everyone picked it up, singing it over and over. In the rhythm of this refrain the leader began singing short phrases as he told a spontaneous story. A second man joined the first, singing a harmony part with the storyteller. After each phrase everyone present sang the chant-refrain. The deep voices of the men resonated almost like an organ filling their little hut.

When my husband Don arrived in the Ilaga, he often spent the night in the men's house. Even though at first he couldn't understand what they were singing, he soon realized this indigenous music could be used to present the gospel. He gave two men some facts about the basics of Christianity. The men put the words into good music form and added one of their many responses, a chant-tune. Later, with encouragement, these men stood up on Sunday to lead the whole crowd, including the women, in singing this new song. This too was a new development because in the past only men sang like this—and only in their huts at night.

Months later, when I arrived in the valley, no one had made the break to become a Christian. However, on Sunday 500 Damals were singing this new form of Damal music with two men standing and singing the words while the crowd joined with the refrain. This very song later became a part of the Damals' own hymnology. It was most amazing to me that my husband, who couldn't even carry a tune himself, had helped the Damals compose and sing Christian music. (At the end of the chapter there is more about Damal music and the first Christian song.)

Back at the Lakes the missionaries were fitting Christian words from the Mee language into American Sunday school tunes. This became the music of the church. Young people sort-of learned to sing these western tunes but their elders couldn't sing them at all. In the Ilaga everyone sang the new Christian songs with enthusiasm for they were composed in their own music style. In retrospect I see this tribal Christian music as a gift from God.

When the Damals turned to the Lord, they quickly shared their newfound faith with others. Christian music was an integral part of this new faith and life. Native chant-singing of the gospel, along with their testimony of how God had changed their lives, spread through the mountains to all the surrounding tribes. The gospel story and their music was received by other tribes—tens of thousands of people across the mountains. Immediately, the gospel, along with indigenous music, became their own. It was not something from the foreign missionary.

I began to analyze Damal music. I could do this because in high school I took two years of harmony. For second year harmony I was the only student who signed up for this elective class. The second year harmony teacher became my private tutor that year—another piece in the puzzle put together to bring the gospel to the Damals.

Only One Life

In the Ilaga I discovered to my surprise that Damal music is built on a five tone scale. There are no half-tones. They sing only the whole tones—do, re, mi, sol and la. The major, seven-tone (diatonic) scale of our music includes the two half tones fa and ti. These half-tones were the reason tribal people could not sing western tunes; they could not even hear that half-tone interval. And why should they sing foreign music? We had come to bring the Good News of Jesus not to turn them into Western-style Christians. (Later I learned the indigenous music of tribal people around the world uses the same five tone scale.)

As time passed, Damal Christians multiplied as did the number of their Christian songs. Songs were composed to teach many things—the seven days of creation, the Ten Commandments, the birth and death of Jesus, baptism and communion as well as songs of praise and thanks to God. They needed a printed hymnal to standardize and retain their Christian music. With the help of the Damal Bible school students I collected and wrote down the words and chant-refrain to each song. The first Damal hymnal contained more than 50 songs and an index by first lines. I cut the stencils and Don mimeographed the books. Everyone wanted a songbook. Soon the first printing was gone and Don ran more. By the time I edited the third edition of the hymnal it had 160 songs. This edition was printed commercially and has gone through several reprints. The hymnal is precious to every Damal Christian, second only to the Bible.

Leaving America meant for me leaving behind all possibility of playing the piano. However, as my five daughters were born and later went off to boarding school on the coast, I wanted them to have the opportunity to take piano lessons as I had. This was possible at the school. After two years of lessons each girl made her choice—to continue with piano or stop taking lessons. Our youngest daughter, Darlene, showed unusual talent and really wanted to play the piano. Serious study requires year-round practice but when Darlene was home for four months of vacation each year, she had no piano. A piano would not fit into the small Cessna airplane that was our only means of transportation from the coast to our mountain station.

Of the scores of missionary families then living in the mountains not one had a piano. And there were no pianos for sale anywhere on the island. Still, I had a dream for Darlene: a piano at home.

One vacation when Don and I were visiting Darlene at her school on the coast, I discovered a big old, upright piano in the dorm, left behind years before by a Dutch family. The ivory keys were mostly missing and it was way out of tune. Its only use now was for a passing child to play chopsticks. I tried playing it and found the action of the keys was still pretty good—quite amazing for a piano that had endured the climate of the tropics for 50 years.

I had a piano! Next I went to the chief MAF pilot and asked for his help. He had one airplane with a cargo door large enough for the piano, but that plane was licensed only for relief work in an earthquake area over a hundred miles from our home. After some thought, the pilot said, "I'll tell you what. I'll fly the piano to Beoga. Then, on the backload I'll pick up some Dani workers and take them to help in the earthquake area." In another week the old piano was flown to Beoga.

I sent a letter off to my brother who built pipe organs in San Francisco. Four months later a package came with new ivories to be glued on the keys and tools to tune the piano. White ants had eaten holes in the wood of the cabinet. We filled these with putty and refinished the whole cabinet with dark brown antiquing paint. Using a book written for professional piano tuners, I followed the instructions step by step. With patience and God's help I was able to tune our piano.

Darlene practiced many hours on that old piano. I also had the joy of being her piano teacher when she was home from school. During her high school years in Malaysia, Darlene studied under a conservatory trained teacher. As a result she really excelled in her playing. Although Darlene lived *Where the Earth Ends* God made it possible to fulfill her ambition to play the piano.

BIBLE LESSON

Christ's message in all its richness must live in your hearts. Teach and instruct one another with all wisdom. Sing psalms, hymns and sacred songs; sing to God with thanksgiving in your hearts. Colossians 3:16

As the scripture says,

"And so I will praise you among the Gentiles;

I will sing praises to you."

And again,

"Praise the Lord, all Gentiles; praise him, all peoples!" Romans 15: 9b, 11

Only One Life

>The Lord . . . blesses us with kindness and honor. He does not refuse any good thing to those who do what is right. Lord Almighty, how happy are those who trust in you! Psalm 84:11-12

Don did not consider it a handicap that he had no musical training, that he could not compose a song in a musical form he couldn't even mimic, in a language he couldn't speak. He simply had the idea of using Damal music to convey the gospel. God did the rest, using the Damals themselves to set the church music pattern for most of the tribes across the mountain ranges.

I had a dream of having a piano for Darlene in our home in Beoga. Don and I were not alone in "making the sacrifice," as some would call it, of living in isolation from the rest of the world. Darlene made that same sacrifice. She too loved the Damal people and felt a close kinship with them. However, growing up in this remote place God did not deny her a good thing, her desire to play the piano. It seemed impossible—but God.

ISSUES TO CONSIDER

1. Why do the Damals enjoy their own style of Christian music rather than singing western tunes with Damal words?

2. Dare I ask, how might this same thinking be applied to Christian music of both the younger and older generations here in North America?

3. From the verses in Colossians and Romans above what should be included in all of our Christian music?

Math, Music and Becoming a Missionary

The First Damal Christian Song

For those who are interested in Damal music, here is the first Christian song ever composed. The chant-refrain is sung before each line by every person present. The numbers marked over the refrain are my way, as a Westerner, of designating the notes sung by the group. I gave each note in the scale a number. The 5—3 5—3 written over the je—e wo—o of this song represent sol—mi, sol—mi. The Damals know the tune to be sung simply by reading the letters je—e wo—o. Most ignore my numbering system for this is their music. (Every song has its own chant-refrain.)

Two men (or today, sometimes two women) sing the words line by line as a duet, one singing the tune and the other the harmony part. Each line of the text ends with "wa-e" which has no meaning. It simply completes the musical pattern and is sung on the first note of the scale, do. Between each line the same wordless refrain is sung by the group.

There is only one foreign word in this song: the name of Jesus (*Jetut.*) The Damals had a word, *haijogon,* a good place after death. In the song paradise is defined as the biblical heaven.

In the English translation all 20 lines are written. In the Damal text only ten are written here.

```
5   3   5   3
Je—e  wo—o
```

Jetut-i wa-e/ wa-e

Haijogon jotet-e/ wa-e

Ki me kop motet-e/ wa-e

Haik kal-et motet-e/ wa-e

Me-a tagatet-e/ wa-e

Iju jagatet-e/ wa-e

Only One Life

Haijogon nitet-e/ wa-e

Henong bogoinen molek-e/ wa-e

Haijogon nul-o hinem-o/ wa-e

Jetut-et joletum-o/ wa-e

Jesus, we sing of you

You were in heaven

You came to earth

You came with good news

Men killed you

You died

You rose again

You went to heaven

You will come again

You will come for us

We will go to be with you

Having gone we will stay with you

Heaven is a good place

Heaven has no sickness

Heaven has no sores

Heaven has no death

Heaven has no war

No evil deeds are done there

With Jesus we will remain

Jesus, we sing of you

Chapter 7
Teaching Damals to Read a Talking-Leaf

Teaching became my joy and delight—especially if the student was motivated to learn. In whatever I teach I find fulfillment in beginning where the student is in his basic knowledge of the subject and then building step by step until he masters the new lesson.

Our missionary colleague John Ellenberger was translating the New Testament into Damal but what was the value of this unless the people could read? John developed a phonic writing system for the Damal language. Unlike English, every letter has one sound and every sound is represented by one letter. My challenge was to teach a whole valley of people how to read. In later years it was the entire tribe. Teaching people to read became my lifelong passion.

The Damals didn't have the slightest idea that marks on a paper could represent words before we came. In the Ilaga several months before the girls and I arrived, Don began building a cabin using only materials from the forest, except for one thing: nails.

The pole frame was up and Don was putting on slabs of bark for the siding. A Damal man held a large piece of bark in place while Don drove the nails through the bark and into the pole studding. Reaching for another nail he saw his little can was almost empty.

Don found a scrap of paper and penciled a note to his missionary colleague, Gordon Larson, asking for some 2 ½ inch nails. Gordon kept the supply of nails across the valley as his site for building was closer to the airstrip. Handing this paper to his helper Don said, "Take this *ogolal,* this leaf, to Larson and he'll give you something I need." (Since the Damals had never seen paper, the nearest thing to it in appearance was a wide tree leaf. They called paper *ogolal,* a leaf.)

The helper looked at the wide-leaf and frowned, "Tell me what you want. I don't want to go clear across the valley for nothing."

Only One Life

"I want some nails like this one," Don said, showing him a nail. "But don't say anything to Larson. Just give him this talking-leaf and see what he gives you."

In an hour the man was back and very excited. "I didn't say anything. I just gave Larson the talking-leaf and he gave me these nails."

The story of the talking-leaf spread far and wide. With it the concept of reading and writing began to dawn on the Damals.

Adults were my first target as I began teaching people to read. Every new Christian had a strong desire to learn because everyone wanted to read the wide leaves of God's Word themselves. Still the process was slow. The student began by learning to recognize a few syllables like *ka, ke, ko* and *ma, me, mo*. Putting these together they formed words, *koma* (boat or airplane) and *kama* (there are none). After months of work, several sharp men were actually reading.

Next I set these men up as teachers of others. This step was even more difficult. When I taught, I used the non-phonic primers written by another missionary and added flash cards and a large chart of the eleven initial consonants with the five vowels. The Damal teachers couldn't do all this.

Eventually I wrote new primers putting the charts and flash card drills right in the book. Also, I divided the words into syllables, separating them with an apostrophe. If the student knew the individual syllables of a word, then he could put them together, sound the word out and read it. Using these books any person who was literate could teach someone else. In time they did just that!

When the student mastered a primer he came to me with his teacher for testing. If he passed, he exchanged his book for the next one. After four primers and three readers he took his final exam which was reading several verses at random from the Book of Mark. I rang a bell and many in the crowd around the literacy house looked up to see who had just passed his test. The student had come prepared with a few rupiahs to buy his own Scripture portion. As more Bible books were translated his token payment gave him a New Testament, a hymnal and still later the Old Testament. By the end of our first 15 years in the Beoga Valley I'd estimate that well over fifty percent of the adults under 40 years of age had learned to read.

Tuesday was literacy day. People walked for hours, even a day, to take their test and advance toward their goal of being able to read. Tuesday was my big day too. The crowd of people who came was noisy and pushy but that didn't bother me. Sitting on the ground with one person at a time, I was lost in my world of testing, analyzing the student's problem, teaching, helping the teacher and passing the student on to the next book if he was ready.

I remember one literacy day when my girls were home from school and I was outside working with the Damals. My oldest daughter pushed through the crowd and said, "Mommy, what can we have for a snack?"

Without looking up I answered, "Anything you want." And the girls were gone.

Pretty soon all four of my giggling girls were back. They were chanting, "Open your mouth and shut your eyes and I'll give you something to make you wise." Still paying no attention I obeyed, expecting to be given a bite of their snack. Instead they popped a roasted grasshopper into my mouth. Out it came with a cry from me and a roar of laughter from everyone who was watching.

Let me fill in this story for you. Damal children ate roasted grasshoppers. When my girls were small and playing with their friends, they too ate grasshoppers. They knew that I couldn't bear the thought of eating one myself. Some child in the crowd must have shared a grasshopper with one of the girls. So they had their fun with their preoccupied mother.

In my early missionary years my challenge was teaching adults to read. In later years it was inspiring the second and third generation of youth to learn to read in their tribal language. Many youth were learning to read Indonesian in government schools. However, the Bible they could understand was written in their own language, Damal or Dani, and these complex languages are difficult to read.

At this time we were conducting seminars for the Damal and Dani youth in five church districts. We handed out seminar notes to everyone who could read. After attending a seminar many Damal young people who couldn't read entered the literacy program going on to graduate and get their own Bible. The Dani youth were not learning to read like the Damals though, because they had no phonic reading primers.

I wondered how I could produce a set of Dani primers since I didn't speak a word of Dani and there were no Dani missionaries remaining on the field. Once again I brought my "five loaves and two fish" to God and He multiplied them!

Kando was a Dani pastor who spoke Damal fluently and had worked for years translating Damal Sunday school books and seminar lessons into Dani. He produced hundreds of handwritten pages of Dani text. Using my new computer I was able to keyboard the Dani lessons and prepare them for printing even though I didn't understand what I was typing. However, producing reading primers was something else. They could not be translated because the two languages have different alphabets and many different sounds. The languages are as different as night and day. Only the concept of using phonics and drills would be the same.

Only One Life

After Pastor Kando flew to Beoga, we set up his work area in our living room next to my computer. We introduced the Dani letters in the same order I found them in another Dani primer. I guided Kando in using drills, dividing words into syllables and writing short sentences as we introduced more letters. Kando put together the set of four Dani primers which he titled: *Lulu Jogwi.* I called them the "Lulu" books. After doing the page layouts on the computer, we sent them to the coast for printing.

When we took the Lulu books to the next seminar in Ilaga and Sinak, the response of the Dani youth was tremendous. Scores soon signed up for the reading course. Each studied with his or her own Dani teacher, a relative or friend who was already literate. When they finished the fourth Lulu book and passed all the tests, they could read! That very day they bought their own copy of the Dani New Testament. With these students, who could now read, we had proof that Kando's work on the Lulu primers was good.

Our annual mission report written two years before we left the field gives some interesting statistics about literacy. Almost 40,000 Danis and Damals were living in our ministry area. A team of 26 literacy workers visited the churches on Sundays signing up new students, each with a teacher. These same workers tested students as they advanced through the literacy books and in the end recorded the names of graduates and sold each one a Bible. In 1991, 1,113 got their Bible and a year later 830 more passed their final exam. The Lulu books along with the Damal primers were paying off.

In the Ilaga at a weekend seminar, 900 Damal and Dani youth jammed into the church building. When I asked how many had a New Testament seventy-five percent of their hands went up. Praise be to God!

The biggest gain of all was a spiritual one. When each youth made his commitment to enter the literacy program, he was really expressing his desire to get a Bible in his own heart language and to be able to read it. For most of the youth this led to baptism and a determination in life to follow the Lord.

BIBLE LESSON

    Jesus said, "What is impossible for man is possible for God." Luke 18:27

    Remember that ever since you were a child, you have known the Holy Scriptures, which are able to give you the wisdom that leads to salvation through faith in Christ Jesus.

Teaching Damals to Read a Talking-Leaf

>All Scripture is inspired by God and is useful for teaching the truth, rebuking error, correcting faults, and giving instruction for right living. 2 Timothy 3:15-16

On furlough one Sunday evening, just before returning to the field, I remember asking our church to pray that God would help me produce a set of Dani phonic primers in a language I did not know. Explaining there were no Dani missionaries to do this I said, "The youth need such a primer so they can read the Bible." At the time I almost felt apologetic voicing a request that seemed next to impossible. However, God answered prayer! He used two people working together, Kando who knew nothing about the structure of a reading primer, and me who spoke no Dani, to produce a primer that taught hundreds of Danis to read.

Each one of us, like Timothy of old, should begin as a child reading the Bible to gain wisdom that leads to salvation. The inspired word of God teaches the truth, confronts error and corrects our wrongdoings all the while pointing out the right way to live. Wherever we are in life, being able to read and then reading the Bible, is an essential building block for a strong Christian.

ISSUES TO CONSIDER

Reflect on the place the Bible has in God's plan of revealing Himself to mankind. Why was giving us His message in written form, rather than passing it on only by word of mouth, so important?

Only One Life

Samples from the Damal and Dani Primers

From Damal reading primer #2—a chart that was memorized

	m	k	t	n	l	ng
a	ma	ka	ta	na	al	ang
e	me	ke	te	ne	el	eng
o	mo	ko	to	no	ol	ong
i	mi	ki	ti	ni	il	ing
u	mu	ku	tu	nu	ul	ung

List of Damal words to read after mastering this chart

| mit | ming | nal | pat | mong | jup | nim |
| kip | mung | kut | nul | tak | kul | peng |

Sentences from primer #4—the apostrophe divides syllables

Kal kor'e'aga'ma-yo imi ka'mo-ak tib'i'yaga'tet-e.
Me ara bu'aga'tet kal hang'kail'ing'am-o ha'tet-e.
Ung'kang'am Me-a bo-o hang'am kal jol'e'at-e.

From Dani reading primer #1—a chart that was memorized

	k	n	t	w		m
a	aga	ka	na	ta	wa	la	ma
i	igi	ki	ni	ti	wi	li	mi
o	ogo	ko	no	to	wo	lo	mo

Teaching Damals to Read a Talking-Leaf

Dani sentences to read after chart—a hyphen divides syllables

    an to-wat na-gin o.   at a-gom ka-gi o.

    wam mi-li ti wa-ga o. kat la-wi ti na na-ko.

    la-wi i-nom to-wat i-nom ti ki ka-gi o.

Dani sentences from primer #4 from a story about Mary and Joseph. Can you find their names?

  Kwe Ma-ri-ya nogo aap nen kigin wake'lek at tawe.

    Nda-wut ombo-luk Yu-tup nen iyok paga eereege-rak.

    Ala a-put nda-ri-yak op aret o, ye-reege-rak o.

Chapter 8

Five Special Daughters

God brought into our home five special daughters. We had four girls—Kathy, Joyce, Lori and Helen—all born before I had my thirtieth birthday. Eight years after that birthday, when our oldest daughter would soon be returning to the States for college and her sisters were to follow one by one, I felt the heavy hand of loneliness about to descend on me. Right then God answered my prayer and blessed our family with a fifth daughter, Darlene. Isn't God good!

"You have only daughters, no sons?" is a question I've been asked by many an American.

My answer is, "Yes, God gave us five daughters. We get our sons when our daughters marry."

The Damal response to our having no sons was pointed: *In-ak-in,* girls-only-girls! This was the name they gave our fourth daughter, Helen. The truth is that having only girls and being at peace about it, as Don was, became a testimony to the Damals. Their culture once promoted the divorce of a woman who bore her husband no sons. Gradually this attitude changed after the Damals became Christians. A woman now has a new place in their society.

Kathy, our firstborn, was two when she and I went with Don to camp in the woods in Mee country. At the time we were living in the government village at the Wissel Lakes. The mission had only one boat, an aluminum one flown in from the coast. We needed a second boat. A native dugout canoe was unstable and too small for mission use. Don decided he would make a canoe of foreign design using the same kind of tree the Mee people used for their canoes. He hired a crew of men to do the work. Our family set off with the crew to camp in the woods while they worked.

For our boat-building project, Kathy turned out to be our "ticket" for entrance into a somewhat hostile area. Our party was walking single file up the trail into the woods. Don had put the man who was carrying our little girl on his shoulders at the head of the line. Suddenly men with bows and arrows appeared in front of us blocking the path. Kathy, who was always outgoing, greeted them as friends. Here was a child, a little blond girl, of the unwanted foreigners greeting them in their own language. Their hostility softened, allowing our group to go on. After a week of work, the boat was completed. (Two years later the armed men who met us on the trail along with all the other men of that area joined in the Obano uprising, attempting to rid Mee country of all foreigners).

When the girls and I arrived in the Ilaga in the *hol koma*, flying boat, Kathy was four-and-a-half and Joyce was soon to be two. The girls helped build a cultural bridge into the lives of the Damal people by playing with their children and simply being at ease with everyone. Our little girls fascinated the Damals. How could they be so much like their children in what they did and said, and yet be so different on the outside? Kathy's long, straight blond hair fell to her waist. Every morning while I read to her, I braided Kathy's hair into French braids. How different her hair was from the short, kinky black hair of the Damals. To be more like their Damal friends the girls often put on a grass skirt over their clothes. Village people pointed to them and said, "Look! Those little girls are wearing skirts like ours."

Joyce had a doll which she treated like a baby. The Damals wondered how that doll could look so much like a real baby but not be alive. The girls had special friends in the village. When a girlfriend went with her mother to work in a sweet potato garden, Kathy and Joyce went with them. Our girls put on their native skirts and carried their baby dolls in net-bags just like the Damal women. The handle of the bag went across their foreheads and the dolls hung halfway down their backs. The girls even had their own garden tools, wooden digging-sticks. Using these sticks Kathy and Joyce weeded around the potato vines in the garden just like their Damal friends did. All this time the baby dolls slept soundly in the net-bags while their pretend mothers "worked" in the garden.

Kathy's favorite hour of the week was early Sunday morning when I had Sunday school just for her. I used a beginner's Sunday school quarterly. Kathy could retell every Bible story I taught her. Back at the Lakes in a Sunday school class Kathy had expressed her personal faith in Jesus. Now in the Ilaga she understood our motive in coming to the Damals and spoke of her faith to her friends.

Before the Damals could receive our message about Christ, they had to first accept us as flesh-and-blood human beings, *ki me* as the Damals said it, real people. Our faith could not be for them unless they believed we were *ki me* like they were, not spirit beings who did not give birth to children and die like humans. Kathy and Joyce played a large part in helping the Damals understand that we were real people and that our faith could be their faith too.

Only One Life

During their preschool years Kathy and Joyce were sometimes more Damal than American. The first time Joyce went to the States, at three years of age, she spoke only Damal. Kathy had to translate for her when they met their grandparents.

All of our daughters were bilingual and bicultural. They spoke Damal and were at home in their lifestyle. In their early years each one absorbed two lifelong character traits from the Damals: the virtue of generosity, always sharing whatever they had with someone else and the virtue of caring, caring about each person in need who crossed their path regardless of color or social standing. This cross-cultural trait was good. However, they would not always be children living in a Damal world. If they had remained living with the Damals as they grew older, they would have had great difficulty adjusting to American culture when they became teenagers or adults. For our family, who lived so close to the Damals, home schooling was not an option. They needed to absorb culture from their own country along with their education.

The same year that Kathy began first grade our mission opened an American elementary school on the coast for the children of missionaries. Our choices were two: either return to the States as a family or send our children to boarding school. All the parents of our mission and the other mission groups made the same choice. Every MK (missionary kid) on the island went to this mission school. It was easier for us to send our girls to school on the coast because everyone was doing it. No one kept their children at home. When I wrote that last sentence, I first wrote "it was *much* easier" and then deleted the word "*much.*" It was NEVER easy to send my girls away to school! Today the thought is still painful to me. My adult daughters sometimes remind me, "Mom, it was always easier for us to go off to school than it was for you to send us."

Times have changed! Worldwide today, most MK's don't attend boarding school. But for our family—Mom, Dad and each girl—attending boarding school was part of God's best plan in reaching the Damals for Christ. I can only bow my head and say, "Thank you, Lord, for the fact that today, each person in our family loves you and is serving you. The sacrifice we made—both parents and children—does not even compare to the sacrifice you made by giving your Son to die in our place."

Joyce was a college student when she returned to visit us and be again with the people she loved. At the time, I was struggling to get started in writing my book, *The People Time Forgot.* Joyce came up with the idea for the storyline. I picked it up and began to write, working at my Remington manual typewriter for the next 18 months.

For some time before this, Don and I had talked about telling the world the story of the Damal people and what God had done in their lives. We had a unique story but who would write it? The government did not allow journalists into our area. I decided to

Five Special Daughters

go back to college during a furlough year, take training in creative writing and write the story myself.

I enrolled in a creative writing class at a junior college near our furlough home. Taking this same writing class with me were 25 college-age young people and one woman in her fifties. We all began to write the very first week. By the second week volunteers were asked to stand and read what they had written. Two students read their short stories. I was shocked by what I heard that night—stories with details that a sheltered missionary as I was could never have imagined. My story was not ready but I felt compelled to counter what I'd just heard. I stood and read my piece about a Damal man. After class the older lady, Yvonne, came to me and said, "You don't belong in this class! I took a night-school writing class taught by a retired missionary. She has even published a couple of missionary books. You should join that class." And I did.

The teacher took a special interest in helping me. Since I was not working to earn credit, she did not limit my writing assignments to the regular class work. She also used her red pen extensively on my papers and often rewrote the entire sentence. She taught me the craft of creative writing.

Yvonne became my friend. God used her to answer two of my prayers during that furlough year. The first was to learn how to write. My second prayer was that God would use me to bring one American adult to know Him that year. I had a part in the conversion of many native people but had never led one adult person to Christ from my own culture.

Yvonne's husband, a prominent lawyer in the city, was divorcing her for another woman. When I met Yvonne at the college, her husband was about to leave her with no income. She was a woman who had never worked outside of her home.

Don and I accepted an invitation to visit Yvonne. We found her living in a lovely home in an elite, gated community, a home she would soon have to leave. That day Yvonne received the Lord Jesus into her heart and life. Before we returned to the field we saw her attending a good church. Six months later a letter came from the pastor of her church. Yvonne had terminal cancer. And then another letter—she was at home with Jesus.

As the years went by, each daughter graduated from high school and college, was married and then came our grandchildren. Still serving overseas I didn't have the joy of being near my grandchildren during their growing-up years. Now, living in the States, I've just had the privilege of living near three preschool grandchildren. Let me tell you how this happened.

Only One Life

Our youngest daughter Darlene and her husband John were due to come home for furlough. Their plans were to live near us that year in our small town. We ran into two problems: we couldn't find a house to rent near ours and they couldn't afford the going-price to rent a house for a family of five. We prayed and others joined us in praying. I made the need known at church, checked the newspaper listing of houses for rent, talked to realtors, and contacted the owners of three close-by houses that were empty. Nothing turned up.

Then on our walk one Monday morning, I met a neighbor who said, "Did you know that the renter just moved out of the house next door to you and new folk have already moved in?" My heart seemed to stop. How could it be we missed this opportunity? There was no "For Rent" sign. We'd seen no activity of moving as a high board fence separated our house from this one.

Something prompted me to phone the owner anyway. Trying all day Monday I finally made contact in the evening and explained my interest in the house. The landlady said, "The renters moved out unexpectedly. The house was listed in the newspaper over the weekend; a dozen people have responded but a contract is not yet signed. Would you like to see the house tomorrow?"

"Yes!" I said, "And what is the rent?" It was $300 a month less than what other houses around town were asking—just the amount that was available to our children. The house was small, but nice inside, and had a large fenced yard. My daughter had given me two requirements for choosing a house for them: it should be close to our home and have a fenced yard for her children to play outside. This was the house!

On Wednesday the landlady came to our home for me to sign the rental contract. In my hand I had a check, enough for the deposit and the first month's rent. She said to me, "We never rent to a family with more than two children but my husband has agreed to make an exception this time. I have grandchildren of my own." With tears in my eyes I gave her a hug and signed the papers.

We put a gate in the fence and our grandchildren, along with the rest of us, went through that gate all hours of the day and night—for seven happy months.

BIBLE LESSON

Children are a gift from the Lord; they are a real blessing.   Psalm 127:3

Then Peter spoke up, "Look, we have left everything and followed you."

Five Special Daughters

"Yes," Jesus said to them, "and I tell you that anyone who leaves home or brothers or sisters or mother or father or children or fields for me and for the gospel will receive much more in this present age. He will receive a hundred times more houses, brothers, sisters, mothers, children, and fields—and persecutions as well; and in the age to come he will receive eternal life." Mark 10: 28-30

They put their trust in God and prayed to him for help, and God answered their prayers.

I Chronicles 5:20

How true Psalm 127:3 is: our children were given to us by God! They were—and continue to be—a blessing in multiple ways.

Don and I knew God had called us to leave parents, family and country to take the gospel to the Damal people. However, when the time came to send our girls off to boarding school, it was quite another thing.

During the school year our girls were home for five weeks at Christmas and three months in the summer. Also we divided our month of vacation and spent time twice a year at the school. We always packed our times together with many family activities.

At the end of every vacation at home the routine was always the same. We learned from the radio that the plane to take our girls back to school was about to land and we all hurried to the top of the airstrip just in time for the landing. The girls climbed on board, seat belts were fastened, doors shut and the plane took off. I waved, sharing their excitement, then turned as my tears began to flow and walked down the airstrip—alone. Each time we parted, God's grace was sufficient.

According to Mark 10:28-30 families who are separated for the sake of the gospel are promised three things: two positive and one negative. In this life they will receive blessings of earthly things and multiple family members—along with persecution or hardship. In the age to come eternal life will be theirs.

Across the generations our parents, Don and I, and our children could tell many stories illustrating the first two promises here on earth: family blessings and the sadness of separation. And we look forward to the heavenly celebration of eternal life not only with all of our family but with a great number of Damal believers.

Only One Life

One of the earthly blessings God gave our family was the rented house right next door. Through the gate in the fence, three generations of family went back and forth enjoying our closeness both in spirit and in body for seven wonderful months.

A song that's been a favorite of mine since I was a girl puts it this way:

> Trust and obey, for there's no other way
>
> To be happy in Jesus, but to trust and obey.

ISSUES TO CONSIDER

1. Do you think I was correct in applying Jesus words in Mark 10 to our family? Does it apply to others who lay aside family, prosperity and country for the sake of the gospel?
2. What do you think about this statement: To enjoy God's blessings means we have no heartaches or problems?

Chapter 9
Go and Make Disciples

We witnessed the wonder of an explosion of men and women, children and youth all coming to Christ. Almost overnight they were freed from their bondage to the evil spirits they had embraced in animism to serve the living God. Our missionary work that followed was to make them disciples of Jesus. His words in Matthew 28:19 are clear, "Go . . . and make them my disciples."

At one time Don and I were among 18 missionaries working with the Damal and Dani people who lived in the rugged, mountain peak area right in the center of the island. We worked out of five mission stations each with an airstrip. The New Testament was translated into both Dani and Damal. On three of the mission stations Bible schools were established to train pastors; two were taught in the Dani language, one in the Damal language. In time the missionaries who founded these schools turned them over to a teaching staff of tribal men and women. A church served the people in every village center and every church had one or more native pastors who were trained in the Bible schools.

Gradually all of these missionaries moved on to other ministries or retired—all except Don and me. We stayed on for another decade.

The chief vehicle of ministry we used to reach all these people during our latter years was the seminar. We addressed apparent spiritual needs by creating seminar lessons. My part was to write the lessons in English using passages and stories from the Bible to build on the theme. In each lesson the memory verse and other Bible texts were written out in full. Illustrations were little stories put together from the lives of tribal people portraying what things the people were doing or saying and showing how they could change. As the years passed, various topics were covered like "The Christian Family," "Spiritual Warfare" and "Growing Deeper in Christ." Don translated each lesson into Damal from my English text. Pastor Kando, a bilingual speaker, translated them again, this time from Damal to Dani.

Only One Life

I keyboarded the lessons in both languages on the computer and then cut the stencils for mimeographing using my printer. I never could have done this major project using my manual typewriter to cut the stencils as I'd done for so many years. With that old typewriter each miss-typed letter required the use of correction fluid and when the fluid dried, retyping the correct letter. The print head on a dot matrix printer like mine was never designed to cut stencils! People warned me if I used it this way, I'd ruin the machine. However, the printer cut thousands of stencils after I removed the ink supply and fed the stencils one at a time like sheets of paper. And in-between cutting stencils it printed the text of the Damal Shorter Old Testament, my weekly family letters and scores of other documents. Proofreading from a printed copy and making the corrections was so much easier with the computer.

All our new technology made this project possible. Solar panels kept the 12-volt batteries charged that operated the computer. My printer used 120 AC electricity which was generated by our waterwheel. However, the Gestetner mimeograph machine was still operated by manpower. Don hand-cranked the machine—one complete turn for each page—producing thousands of pages for every seminar. The local people just couldn't master turning the crank smoothly in a circular motion and simultaneously re-ink the machine with the other hand whenever the printing grew dim. The Damals did assemble the printed pages and staple them together.

Don could not teach all the seminar lessons alone. I wished I could help but in the tribal culture it was not acceptable for a woman to speak to large crowds that included men. Then God gave me an idea. I would train a man and he would speak in my place. Barnabas, the man who had worked in our kitchen for many years, became my voice. He was used to receiving instructions from me in doing household chores so he was willing to learn from a woman. Working from the printed lesson I tutored him until he could deliver the lesson from memory.

Later I trained two pastors who spoke both Damal and Dani: Kando, who wrote the Dani translation of all the material we produced in Damal, and Black-Water-Son, who tells his story in Out of the Stone Age, Story Three. When these men preached their assigned lessons the people really understood the message.

The youth seminars drew young people by the hundreds. These young people added their own style of music and often presented special musical numbers or a drama. They sat on the church floor packed in so tightly no one could walk from the back of the church to the front without stepping on someone. They listened quietly and many responded when an invitation was given.

Go and Make Disciples

Our preparations for travel and living quarters at each seminar site reminded me of our honeymoon at Mt. Rainer. The cabin there was bare except for a bed and table, a woodstove and one electric light bulb. Packed in our car for our honeymoon I brought our bedding, food and kitchen things. With a few alterations this is how we lived on these seminar trips. In Papua there were no roads so we flew in a Cessna 206 airplane and then hiked for 40 minutes over a muddy trail to get to the house.

The mission house had a woodstove, a bed and table. We had set up each place with bedding, kitchen equipment, and a kerosene lamp. Leaving things at each house was necessary because everything that went on the flight had to fit into our weight allowance of 900 pounds. Each time we flew, we needed to calculate body weights, ours and the two pastors, and everyone's personal things. At the station the pastors would be guests of the local people. For us, I added fresh baked bread and cinnamon rolls, tinned meat, oatmeal and powdered milk. We counted on buying vegetables locally. Always we saved some weight for the mimeographed seminar lessons and a couple of cartons with medical supplies for the clinic.

At each station Don worked with the medical workers who had been trained by missionary nurses. He gave them their wages, paid by the government, and restocked the clinic's medicine shelves.

Don also worked with several pastors who were appointed to promote the Sunday school program. The four-year course of lessons I wrote covered all the stories of the Bible. Teacher's manuals in both Damal and Dani were available to every person who taught a Sunday school class.

My special project was overseeing the literacy workers. These were twenty-four men and two women I had trained. Each served faithfully on a close-knit team in their home area and worked many hours every month. Together we tested students and sold Bibles, inspired the discouraged and challenged new recruits. Once a person learned to read, he had the ability to read the Bible for the rest of his life.

Kilek, a seasoned Dani pastor, added a surprise drama to the program at one of the youth seminars in Sinak. I remember it well. It was Sunday afternoon and 700 youth had just listened with rapt attention to the final lesson about temptations that come on our journey to heaven. Kilek stood and told the crowd of youth they were all about to take part in a drama.

Each person was to cross a small bridge near the church, read the sign posted between two paths and then follow one of the paths. One led to heaven and one to hell, but the youth were not told which path was which.

Only One Life

In single file they crossed the bridge in complete silence. The sign instructed them to choose one path either to the right or to the left. The path to the right was wide and led up stairs cut in the hillside. It disappeared over the hilltop. Everyone knew it led past the mission house and on to the airstrip. The path to the left was less traveled. It led over a hill and down to the river. I, as the missionary, was instructed to be the last person to cross the bridge so that I would not influence the teenagers with my decision.

I chose the less-used path to the left and soon came to another sign that pointed the way over a fence and through a pig yard. Then I had to climb over another fence and wade through mud. The path wound its way through brush, more mud, over another fence and finally through tall grass onto the airstrip. By this time I was really muddy and scratched up.

I spotted a Dani man dressed in red shorts with his black body painted white with clay. To this he added red and black stripes. Over his head he wore a small cardboard carton in which eye holes were cut; it too was painted with designs. In his hand he carried a real war-spear. He was fearsome as he pranced and flexed his muscles. He represented Satan and he beckoned the youth to leave the narrow path and follow him.

A preacher was also there. He urged the youth to stay on the narrow way. As I came over the brow of the final hill I saw on the right a group seated compactly in "heaven." Across the airstrip and confined in another small space were those who had taken the wide, easy path and were now in "hell." Around hell danced nine devils and one little imp. Each was made up to look like Satan and carried a spear. They worked to keep the youth in hell from escaping.

As these devils flexed their muscles and threatened the young people with their spears, they danced in rhythm to guitar music played by three men in hell. The guitar players had given themselves to worldly music and the haunts that go with it. Also in hell was a man preaching from a book. He represented a false teacher. My attention was riveted on this scene, so packed with emotion.

"Look!" someone cried, and pointed to a table set in front of heaven. A man dressed in white stood there representing Jesus. On the table was the Lord's Supper, with broken sweet potatoes which the Danis serve for communion. At one point helpers passed out the sweet potato pieces to those in heaven. At other times people in heaven broke out in singing praise-chants to God.

From time to time while the various scenes were being enacted Kilek, the evangelist who directed the entire drama, stood and explained the scene and exhorted the crowd.

Then in the area behind heaven five young men appeared. Four were dressed in jeans and western clothes, cowboy hats, boots and all. The fifth was attired in the paint and feathers of full native war-dress and carried his bow and arrows ready to fight. These five men lit up cigarettes as if they were going to smoke. Then they started to play cards and gamble. All this was done with intense drama.

Next, three girls came out. (Actually they were men dressed as women wearing long grass skirts.) They were swinging their hips and throwing themselves at the five men. The men grabbed one of the girls and carried her off. Eventually, the group of eight went dancing and carousing over to hell. Near the entrance of hell, a preacher stood exhorting them to stop but they ignored him. Still dancing, they were sucked into hell.

Once some people from hell called over to their relatives in heaven, "Come over and help us!" they begged. Several of their relatives ran part of the way to hell but were turned back by the dancing devils.

A number of the youth who had chosen the broad path were in their early teens. By this time some were actually crying because their confinement to hell seemed so real and final. They did not want to be in hell even in a drama—they wanted to be in heaven.

In the end the devils left and Kilek asked everyone to sit in one group. "This was only a drama," he said, "but heaven and hell are real places. When you die you will be in one place or the other—forever! Now is the time for you to come to Jesus and obey him, attend Sunday school and read your Bible. Make your decision for Jesus today."

BIBLE LESSON

Go, then, to all peoples everywhere and make them my disciples: baptize them in the name of the Father, the Son, and the Holy Spirit, and teach them to obey everything I have commanded you. Matthew 28:19-20

Happy are those who wash their robes clean and so have the right to eat the fruit from the tree of life and to go through the gates into the city. Revelation 22:14

The Son of Man will send out his angels to gather up out of his Kingdom all those who cause people to sin and all others who do evil things, and they will throw them into the fiery furnace, where they will cry and gnash their teeth. Then

Only One Life

God's people will shine like the sun in their Father's Kingdom. Listen, then, if you have ears! Matthew 13:41-43

Bible teaching is very clear concerning the reality of heaven and hell. For someone to say, "I believe that all roads lead to heaven," or to say "I don't believe in a literal hell after death," doesn't change the reality of God's plan. Read again the verses written above.

The Good News is that God in His love made a way for all to escape eternal separation from God. He sent His Son Jesus to die in our place—a free gift to all who believe.

How wonderful it is for you and for me if our sins have been washed away and our names are written in the Book of Life. Then we know that heaven will be ours when we die.

"Go . . . make them my disciples . . . and teach them to obey everything I have commanded you." These are the words of Jesus, his last words spoken to the disciples. Most of Don's and my years were spent discipling and teaching the Damals—the new converts, their children and finally their grandchildren.

In North America who should we disciple for Christ? Those who come to know Jesus in a personal way through our influence and witness or that of others—a family member or friend, a classmate or neighbor, our child or grandchild—these are the ones we should disciple for Christ. Our responsibility does not end with their confessing Jesus as their Savior. We should involve them in Bible study and teach them the mannerisms of Christ from the Bible. With coaching they should go on to live and obey the commands of Jesus.

ISSUES TO CONSIDER

1. Why is it important to disciple and teach a newborn Christian?
2. Have you ever considered coaching a new believer?
3. Do you believe that after death there is a real heaven to be gained or a real hell to be avoided?
4. What are the rules set up by God for a person to enter heaven or be left behind for hell?

Chapter 10

The First and the Last

It was a Sunday morning just eight days before we were to leave our home in Beoga for the very last time. We decided to make a surprise visit to a church an hour's walk from where we lived. I pulled on my hobnail boots once more. The trail we planned to take up-valley was a good one, nothing like it was in the early days, but there were sure to be two or three mud holes we'd have to go through. We picked up our bamboo walking sticks, a water bottle, our hats and we were off.

As we arrived, Sunday school was still in session. Classes with six to ten people were seated on the ground in the church yard. After Sunday school more people gathered. One hundred twenty-five people filed into the church, almost everyone who lived in the community. They sang and prayed together, then listened to the preaching of God's Word.

A Sunday school teachers' meeting convened after church. The new Sunday school year was to begin the following Sunday and I had forgotten all about it. Each teacher turned in his or her old lesson manual. The books were to be stored in the church and used again in another four years. Then the pastor gave each teacher a new manual which had 52 lessons. They would follow the calendar-schedule for the current year printed in the back of the book. Since no one knew we were coming, I was thrilled to see the Sunday school in this church proceeding exactly as I'd set it up.

On our way home a Damal lady named Johanna walked with us. She could not understand a word of the non-stop conversation in English between Don and me. We talked about the baptism of our daughter Kathy at this church when she was eight years old. A little stream of water had been dammed up to make a small baptismal pool. Kathy and a dozen Damals from the church were baptized. Then our conversation jumped back and forth between things we must do before we left and things we looked forward to doing when we got back to the States.

Only One Life

We were halfway home when Johanna got up her courage and interrupted our lively conversation. Like all the other thousands of Damals and Danis whom we served, she felt our leaving very deeply.

"If you had not come," Johanna blurted out, "I would not have heard of Jesus. And because you came and lived with us, I have a Damal Bible and can read it myself." As we talked she went on to tell us how she was born just after we came to Beoga. She understood the way of salvation as a small girl and has followed the Lord all of her life. Now she is teaching each one of her children to read so they too can read the Bible.

The scene I've just described took place after I had been in this land for more than 40 years. Many times during those years the way seemed so hard. Could I go on? Each time I remembered the night I heard God's call and why I had come to this place. Rough time or not I determined I would continue to serve the Lord in this place where He had put me.

I'd like to share with you the story of another trip we took not long before we left Papua. This account is from my weekly Sunday letter to our daughters. Later that month, I edited it for better understanding and sent this same letter to friends who supported us. (Oh, the marvels of having a computer!)

December 19, 1993

We left the house this morning before 7:00 AM to attend church down-valley. It was seven hours before we got home. Partway there we made a side-trip to inspect the progress of a steel cable bridge being built over the main Beoga River.

> (Building steel cable bridges was one of several community development projects Don initiated and managed. He was the "engineer" using cable donated by the copper mining company that operates just over the mountain. Their helicopter delivered the cable to Beoga.)

The trail for our side-trip was like all the trails when we first came, following the line of least resistance between two points. It descended almost 1000 feet to the river. A dozen boys bounced along around us shouting and enjoying the party. A couple of them cut stout poles and dug steps here and there to help in my descent. When we were almost to the river we came to a large sidestream. The "crew" collected driftwood carried down in flash floods and built four little bridges for me so I never got my feet wet. I mused, these were the grandchildren of the people who first welcomed us to Beoga, people who built trails and bridges so the gospel could more easily be carried throughout the valley.

The First and the Last

The bridge site on the Beoga River is at a point where the water flows between two banks of solid rock only 20 feet apart. Here the water is dark and smooth and very deep. Both up and down-river from this point the water is turbulent and white as it pours over huge boulders. Downstream, maybe 3000 feet, is the place where 35 years ago I crossed the river on a temporary bridge on my first hiking trip through the valley. [See story 2, chapter 6]

In preparation for the new bridge Pastor Hilo had drilled holes to insert anchor posts in the solid rock walls. These anchor posts would hold the steel cable in place. Don decided they should drill three more holes at a slightly different angle for the cable bolts. From the river we hiked for almost an hour up, up, up to Tingil Village. Without the hand of a husky man helping me I never would have made it. When we got there people were waiting to begin the church service.

The building is a beautiful wooden church made of hand-sawed boards, six glass windows and an aluminum roof. Inside it had a board floor. The ceiling and walls were lined with more sawed boards. This church is nicer than our house. I counted 90 women, almost all dressed in western clothing, and 80 men all in native attire. When I asked how many had a Bible, sixty-five percent of the hands went up.

As I sat in the church, I remembered it was December 1958—exactly 35 years ago—that I sat on this same ground for the first service ever in Tingil Village. After the sermon today, Pastor Hilo, who was there on our first visit, stood and spoke. He addressed us as "ni-et nerek," mother and father. Hilo said, "You came here leaving your people in America and you have grown gray living among us. You came as young people with only two small children. Now, all the other missionaries have gone. Soon you are leaving us and there are no others to come after you.

"Today, Damal-Neme, you came to help us with a steel cable bridge. However, more than help like that, you brought the good news of Jesus Christ to us, which changed our lives. Now you are leaving. I express my love to you, amolo."

Then speaking to the congregation Hilo said, "The fact that our missionaries came is not a big thing. What is big is the wonderful message they brought to us. We will soon be killing pigs for a big feast and telling them how much we love them. But that's no big thing either. The real way to express our love to them is by all of us following the Lord after they are gone."

Only One Life

Now the time had come for one last visit to each of the five stations to hold our final seminar. At every point we turned over all of our work to the leader of each program: literacy, Bible and book sales, Sunday schools, airstrip maintenance and the medical clinics. Years before, the oversight of the churches and the operation of the three Bible schools had been given to the nationals. From the very beginning we worked alongside the people. We did nothing by ourselves. In every project as we worked together with the Damals, we taught them. Now we were stepping out, and they were on their own.

At each station a big pig feast in our honor was scheduled. Crowds of people came and scores of pigs were killed. Rocks were heated on long racks of firewood in anticipation of the pit-cooking. While the pork steamed in the pits, men gave speeches. After an hour the pits were opened and the meat was served to everyone. The events of this pig-feast day fell into place quite like every celebration in the past. Many things had changed but not the traditional pig feast with its deep roots in Damal culture.

On the final morning at each station before we headed for the airstrip, we turned the keys of the mission house over to the district superintendent. It would be his house and he would move in that very day.

In planning our departure one very hard part for me was to leave our home in Beoga—forever. Our five daughters grew up in this house—we all lived, worked and played together there. It was our home! But as I struggled, God reminded me that our mission had been accomplished. What better ending could there be than to give the keys of our house to the man who was the over-shepherd of the 30 some churches in the Beoga District? God gave me peace.

Jila was one of the stations we visited on our final rounds. Here the people are few in number, just hanging on to life in these most rugged of mountains. On one late afternoon after working all day with the noisy crowds of people, we took a walk down the Jila ridge. We passed a score of Damal houses as we walked. [See story 4 map]

From one of the huts we had just passed I heard a voice calling out. At first I didn't see anyone, for the Damal houses have no light inside and only one door. Then an old man stepped through the low doorway. His sharp black eyes peered at us from beneath his wrinkled skin and straggly gray beard. He wore only the traditional dress of a Damal man, quite like every other man had worn in centuries past.

"Damal-Neme, Damal-In a-e," he called to us using our native names. He knew this was our very last visit to Jila. "If you had not come I would not know the way to heaven and eternal life. But you did come and I have received the gospel and eternal life in Jesus. I want to say thank you for coming."

The First and the Last

This old man was not a church elder or leader in the church—he was just an ordinary village man. He will be in heaven one day joining the saints of all ages in praising God.

BIBLE LESSON

God appoints Ezekiel as a watchman:

> "Son of man, I have made you a watchman for the house of Israel; so hear the word I speak and give them warning from me. When I say to the wicked, 'O wicked man, you will surely die,' and you do not speak out to dissuade him from his ways, that wicked man will die for his sin, and I will hold you accountable for his blood. But if you do warn the wicked man to turn from his ways and he does not do so, he will die for his sin, but you will have saved yourself." Ezekiel 33:7-9 NIV

> Sing to the Lord, all the world! Proclaim every day the good news that he has saved us.
>
> Proclaim his glory to the nations, his mighty deeds to all peoples.
>
> Praise the Lord, all people on earth, praise his glory and might. I Chronicles 16: 23-24, 28

During my first year in Bible College, God spoke to my heart from the passage of Scripture in which He commissioned Ezekiel to be a watchman. When I applied the verses quoted above to myself, I knew I was required to go and tell people, one by one, of the way to the cross and forgiveness of sins. Even if every person chose to reject the true Way, I still would have fulfilled my commission.

In the sovereignty of God quite the opposite took place. Verses in 1 Chronicles 16 reflect what happened. "Sing to the Lord, all the world! Proclaim every day the good news that he has saved us. Proclaim his glory to the nations, his mighty deeds to all peoples. Praise the Lord, all people on earth."

Why was it that God allowed me, with my husband Don, to have a part in this spectacular movement, this turning to God of a large unit of people? Why were our lives

Only One Life

preserved though threatened by native people? Why did we survive several close calls in an airplane? Why were we not disabled through sickness or risks taken in hiking over the rugged mountains?

I can only say, God called us to this work. All that took place was in His perfect plan. To God be all the glory!

ISSUES TO CONSIDER

1. In the Ezekiel passage quoted in the Bible Lesson, Ezekiel was commissioned to warn the house of Israel to turn from their sinful ways lest they die in their sins. The application to my heart was I must warn those across the sea who have never heard the story of Jesus to repent and follow Him lest they die in their sins. What other application is appropriate from this passage?

2. Why is it that some missionaries, though equally as devoted to their work, see far less response than we did?

Chapter 11

Epilogue

Paul speaks of his life on earth as being in a race with the ultimate goal as heaven.

> "I have done my best in the race, I have run the full distance, and I have kept the faith. And now there is waiting for me the victory prize of being put right with God." 2 Timothy 4:7-8

I began my journey on the road to heaven when I was eight, the night I asked Jesus to come into my heart. We might think of running the race of life in several segments. A corner was turned when I finished junior high school, another when I graduated from high school and left home for Bible College. Graduation from college catapulted me into marriage and adulthood. At 22 I began my life's work—the largest part of my life. In each of these phases there was a new beginning, a clean slate with multiple decisions and challenges to be faced and victories to be won.

To my younger readers I would say: perhaps you are in school, in one of these earlier seasons of life. The years of training are the prelude to all you will do in adult life. At the same time they are an important part of the complete race. You have begun well. But take heed! Many runners, who begin well fall to the wayside and do not end well.

In the Old Testament a number of notable characters began well but sadly did not end their years in the same way. Consider Samson, Saul and Solomon. Each of us must strive to run the full course, keep the faith and do our best to the very end. To these the crown of righteousness will be given. (2 Timothy 4:8 NIV)

When I left Papua for the last time, the largest portion of my journey to heaven was complete. Now my only link back to the people we left behind is through letters and prayer. The temptation at this point is to push back from the table, kick off my shoes and relax. However, "the full distance" of this race is not yet finished. As I grow older my days may include health challenges, a decreasing area of outreach in ministry and perhaps grief. My desire remains to continue my walk as I began it—simply trusting and obeying my Lord and Savior.

Only One Life

My mind flashes back 58 years ago to the country church where I went to teach Vacation Bible School where I met Don. The pastor of that little church, Pastor Dave, has served in a number of churches through the years. Five years ago he moved to the town where Don and I now live. Pastor Dave is 89. He has undergone several major operations and health crises. Yet he continues to teach a weekly Bible study, visit the sick and pray for others.

Recently Pastor Dave filled the pulpit at our church when our pastor of seniors was away. With the help of a strong man's arm and a cane, Pastor Dave got to the pulpit. In his opening remarks he gave God praise for regaining more vision after an eye surgery. Then he began to preach speaking with the power and enthusiasm of a young man. A remark he made near the end continues to challenge me:

"These years right now are the best years of my life."

"Best years?" I wondered. How could that be? I know this 89-year-old man is plagued with physical problems, and more keep popping up. So I phoned Pastor Dave. I learned he views life and whatever it brings through the positive window of praise to God. With daily study of the Word, he seeks to know his Savior in a deeper way. And I observe he finds many opportunities to serve others.

I who am a dozen years his junior want to finish this final segment of my journey with the same joy and positive attitude that I see in my friend, Pastor Dave.

>Only one life 'twill soon be past
>
>Only what's done for Christ will last.

Gibbons family (back lft to rt) Joyce, Alice, Don
Lori, Helen, Kathy holding baby Darlene

Don and Alice in front of Beoga home

Alice gives New Testament to a man who just passed literacy text 2004

Four dancing Danis made up as devils, Chapter 9

Kando holding the "Lulu" books – four Dani primers, Chapter 7

Alice teaching a Damal reading class

INFORMATION ON ORDERING THE TWO BOOKS
BY ALICE GIBBONS

Where the Earth Ends is a print-on-demand, self-published book by Xulon Press.

The author has a website, http://www.donandalicegibbons.com When the website is completed you may order *Where the Earth Ends* there.

It may be ordered through most Christian book stores by giving the title and the ISBN number found on the Copyright page.

It may be ordered through Amazon.com by giving the author's name and then searching for the title.

After reading *Where the Earth Ends,* you may have many questions about the Damal people. What is their history? How did they live in time past? How did they come to hear and receive the gospel? How has this changed their lives? Alice Gibbons has written another book, *The People Time Forgot,* originally published by Moody Press. These questions and many more are answered in this 350 page book about the Damal people. *The People Time Forgot* reads like a novel because the author follows the account given by one tribal man, as she writes this almost unbelievable true story.

The People Time Forgot is out of print. However, the author has a good supply of new copies which will also be available at the website, http://www.donandalicegibbons.com

You may contact Don and Alice Gibbons at P.O. Box 1373, Ripon, CA 95366